THIS IS YOUR **PASSBOOK**® FOR ...

ASSOCIATE EDUCATION ANALYST

NATIONAL LEARNING CORPORATION®
passbooks.com

PASSBOOK® SERIES

THE *PASSBOOK® SERIES* has been created to prepare applicants and candidates for the ultimate academic battlefield – the examination room.

At some time in our lives, each and every one of us may be required to take an examination – for validation, matriculation, admission, qualification, registration, certification, or licensure.

Based on the assumption that every applicant or candidate has met the basic formal educational standards, has taken the required number of courses, and read the necessary texts, the *PASSBOOK® SERIES* furnishes the one special preparation which may assure passing with confidence, instead of failing with insecurity. Examination questions – together with answers – are furnished as the basic vehicle for study so that the mysteries of the examination and its compounding difficulties may be eliminated or diminished by a sure method.

This book is meant to help you pass your examination provided that you qualify and are serious in your objective.

The entire field is reviewed through the huge store of content information which is succinctly presented through a provocative and challenging approach – the question-and-answer method.

A climate of success is established by furnishing the correct answers at the end of each test.

You soon learn to recognize types of questions, forms of questions, and patterns of questioning. You may even begin to anticipate expected outcomes.

You perceive that many questions are repeated or adapted so that you can gain acute insights, which may enable you to score many sure points.

You learn how to confront new questions, or types of questions, and to attack them confidently and work out the correct answers.

You note objectives and emphases, and recognize pitfalls and dangers, so that you may make positive educational adjustments.

Moreover, you are kept fully informed in relation to new concepts, methods, practices, and directions in the field.

You discover that you arre actually taking the examination all the time: you are preparing for the examination by "taking" an examination, not by reading extraneous and/or supererogatory textbooks.

In short, this PASSBOOK®, used directedly, should be an important factor in helping you to pass your test.

ASSOCIATE EDUCATION ANALYST

DUTIES AND RESPONSIBILITIES

Under general supervision, performs difficult and responsible professional work in one or more of the following areas of education administration: personnel, budgeting, labor relations, systems development or policy planning; performs related work.

EXAMPLES OF TYPICAL TASKS

Supervises or coordinates a wide variety of school personnel related administration functions covering supervisory and nonsupervisory pedagogical personnel, Para-professional personnel, and support personnel, performing school-related activities, including budgeting; responsible for the distribution of funds (including monies disbursed under the Elementary and Secondary Education Act and federal and state education laws) based on school needs in the areas of instructional services, continuing education, special education, district/central headquarters school administration as well as in accordance with legal mandates for the utilization of education monies; renders highly professional, technical assistance in the conduct of school labor relations activities pertaining to and impacted by the execution of pedagogical collective bargaining agreements, contractual negotiations, union grievances, and related functions within the purview of the school district; conducts educationally oriented management and policy studies of importance to the board of education in areas of school management, budgeting, or education planning and policy development; may serve as a principal assistant to a high-level central headquarters or community school district administrator in performance of liaison fiscal coordination and compliance and planning activities. In any of the above tasks, may prepare, detailed reports or studies with appropriate recommendations for improved efficiency of educational operations or functions where appropriate.

TEST INFORMATION

The multiple-choice test may include questions concerning the analysis of problems in personnel administration, labor relations, budgeting and management analysis in an education environment as illustrated above in the examples of typical tasks statements for this title, including methodology research, and data collection techniques, program planning and evaluation in an education environment, comprehension and interpretation of complex pertinent written materials including technical data; and other areas related to the duties of the position.

In addition, the multiple-choice test will include a series of questions designed to show in-depth professional knowledge of one of four areas of responsibility included under the duties and responsibilities of Associate Education Analyst; personnel, budgeting, labor relations in an education setting, and management analysis, including quantitative analysis techniques and computer utilization. Candidates will choose one of the four areas on which they will be competitively rated and may take anyone or all of the other areas for purposes of selective certification.

HOW TO TAKE A TEST

I. YOU MUST PASS AN EXAMINATION

A. WHAT EVERY CANDIDATE SHOULD KNOW

Examination applicants often ask us for help in preparing for the written test. What can I study in advance? What kinds of questions will be asked? How will the test be given? How will the papers be graded?

As an applicant for a civil service examination, you may be wondering about some of these things. Our purpose here is to suggest effective methods of advance study and to describe civil service examinations.

Your chances for success on this examination can be increased if you know how to prepare. Those "pre-examination jitters" can be reduced if you know what to expect. You can even experience an adventure in good citizenship if you know why civil service exams are given.

B. WHY ARE CIVIL SERVICE EXAMINATIONS GIVEN?

Civil service examinations are important to you in two ways. As a citizen, you want public jobs filled by employees who know how to do their work. As a job seeker, you want a fair chance to compete for that job on an equal footing with other candidates. The best-known means of accomplishing this two-fold goal is the competitive examination.

Exams are widely publicized throughout the nation. They may be administered for jobs in federal, state, city, municipal, town or village governments or agencies.

Any citizen may apply, with some limitations, such as the age or residence of applicants. Your experience and education may be reviewed to see whether you meet the requirements for the particular examination. When these requirements exist, they are reasonable and applied consistently to all applicants. Thus, a competitive examination may cause you some uneasiness now, but it is your privilege and safeguard.

C. HOW ARE CIVIL SERVICE EXAMS DEVELOPED?

Examinations are carefully written by trained technicians who are specialists in the field known as "psychological measurement," in consultation with recognized authorities in the field of work that the test will cover. These experts recommend the subject matter areas or skills to be tested; only those knowledges or skills important to your success on the job are included. The most reliable books and source materials available are used as references. Together, the experts and technicians judge the difficulty level of the questions.

Test technicians know how to phrase questions so that the problem is clearly stated. Their ethics do not permit "trick" or "catch" questions. Questions may have been tried out on sample groups, or subjected to statistical analysis, to determine their usefulness.

Written tests are often used in combination with performance tests, ratings of training and experience, and oral interviews. All of these measures combine to form the best-known means of finding the right person for the right job.

II. HOW TO PASS THE WRITTEN TEST

A. *NATURE OF THE EXAMINATION*

To prepare intelligently for civil service examinations, you should know how they differ from school examinations you have taken. In school you were assigned certain definite pages to read or subjects to cover. The examination questions were quite detailed and usually emphasized memory. Civil service exams, on the other hand, try to discover your present ability to perform the duties of a position, plus your potentiality to learn these duties. In other words, a civil service exam attempts to predict how successful you will be. Questions cover such a broad area that they cannot be as minute and detailed as school exam questions.

In the public service similar kinds of work, or positions, are grouped together in one "class." This process is known as *position-classification.* All the positions in a class are paid according to the salary range for that class. One class title covers all of these positions, and they are all tested by the same examination.

B. *FOUR BASIC STEPS*

1) Study the announcement

How, then, can you know what subjects to study? Our best answer is: "Learn as much as possible about the class of positions for which you've applied." The exam will test the knowledge, skills and abilities needed to do the work.

Your most valuable source of information about the position you want is the official exam announcement. This announcement lists the training and experience qualifications. Check these standards and apply only if you come reasonably close to meeting them.

The brief description of the position in the examination announcement offers some clues to the subjects which will be tested. Think about the job itself. Review the duties in your mind. Can you perform them, or are there some in which you are rusty? Fill in the blank spots in your preparation.

Many jurisdictions preview the written test in the exam announcement by including a section called "Knowledge and Abilities Required," "Scope of the Examination," or some similar heading. Here you will find out specifically what fields will be tested.

2) Review your own background

Once you learn in general what the position is all about, and what you need to know to do the work, ask yourself which subjects you already know fairly well and which need improvement. You may wonder whether to concentrate on improving your strong areas or on building some background in your fields of weakness. When the announcement has specified "some knowledge" or "considerable knowledge," or has used adjectives like "beginning principles of…" or "advanced … methods," you can get a clue as to the number and difficulty of questions to be asked in any given field. More questions, and hence broader coverage, would be included for those subjects which are more important in the work. Now weigh your strengths and weaknesses against the job requirements and prepare accordingly.

3) Determine the level of the position

Another way to tell how intensively you should prepare is to understand the level of the job for which you are applying. Is it the entering level? In other words, is this the position in which beginners in a field of work are hired? Or is it an intermediate or advanced level? Sometimes this is indicated by such words as "Junior" or "Senior" in the class title. Other jurisdictions use Roman numerals to designate the level – Clerk I, Clerk II, for example. The word "Supervisor" sometimes appears in the title. If the level is not indicated by the title, check the description of duties. Will you be working under very close supervision, or will you have responsibility for independent decisions in this work?

4) Choose appropriate study materials

Now that you know the subjects to be examined and the relative amount of each subject to be covered, you can choose suitable study materials. For beginning level jobs, or even advanced ones, if you have a pronounced weakness in some aspect of your training, read a modern, standard textbook in that field. Be sure it is up to date and has general coverage. Such books are normally available at your library, and the librarian will be glad to help you locate one. For entry-level positions, questions of appropriate difficulty are chosen – neither highly advanced questions, nor those too simple. Such questions require careful thought but not advanced training.

If the position for which you are applying is technical or advanced, you will read more advanced, specialized material. If you are already familiar with the basic principles of your field, elementary textbooks would waste your time. Concentrate on advanced textbooks and technical periodicals. Think through the concepts and review difficult problems in your field.

These are all general sources. You can get more ideas on your own initiative, following these leads. For example, training manuals and publications of the government agency which employs workers in your field can be useful, particularly for technical and professional positions. A letter or visit to the government department involved may result in more specific study suggestions, and certainly will provide you with a more definite idea of the exact nature of the position you are seeking.

III. KINDS OF TESTS

Tests are used for purposes other than measuring knowledge and ability to perform specified duties. For some positions, it is equally important to test ability to make adjustments to new situations or to profit from training. In others, basic mental abilities not dependent on information are essential. Questions which test these things may not appear as pertinent to the duties of the position as those which test for knowledge and information. Yet they are often highly important parts of a fair examination. For very general questions, it is almost impossible to help you direct your study efforts. What we can do is to point out some of the more common of these general abilities needed in public service positions and describe some typical questions.

1) General information

Broad, general information has been found useful for predicting job success in some kinds of work. This is tested in a variety of ways, from vocabulary lists to questions about current events. Basic background in some field of work, such as sociology or economics, may be sampled in a group of questions. Often these are principles which have become familiar to most persons through exposure rather than through formal training. It is difficult to advise you how to study for these questions; being alert to the world around you is our best suggestion.

2) Verbal ability

An example of an ability needed in many positions is verbal or language ability. Verbal ability is, in brief, the ability to use and understand words. Vocabulary and grammar tests are typical measures of this ability. Reading comprehension or paragraph interpretation questions are common in many kinds of civil service tests. You are given a paragraph of written material and asked to find its central meaning.

3) Numerical ability

Number skills can be tested by the familiar arithmetic problem, by checking paired lists of numbers to see which are alike and which are different, or by interpreting charts and graphs. In the latter test, a graph may be printed in the test booklet which you are asked to use as the basis for answering questions.

4) Observation

A popular test for law-enforcement positions is the observation test. A picture is shown to you for several minutes, then taken away. Questions about the picture test your ability to observe both details and larger elements.

5) Following directions

In many positions in the public service, the employee must be able to carry out written instructions dependably and accurately. You may be given a chart with several columns, each column listing a variety of information. The questions require you to carry out directions involving the information given in the chart.

6) Skills and aptitudes

Performance tests effectively measure some manual skills and aptitudes. When the skill is one in which you are trained, such as typing or shorthand, you can practice. These tests are often very much like those given in business school or high school courses. For many of the other skills and aptitudes, however, no short-time preparation can be made. Skills and abilities natural to you or that you have developed throughout your lifetime are being tested.

Many of the general questions just described provide all the data needed to answer the questions and ask you to use your reasoning ability to find the answers. Your best preparation for these tests, as well as for tests of facts and ideas, is to be at your physical and mental best. You, no doubt, have your own methods of getting into an exam-taking mood and keeping "in shape." The next section lists some ideas on this subject.

IV. KINDS OF QUESTIONS

Only rarely is the "essay" question, which you answer in narrative form, used in civil service tests. Civil service tests are usually of the short-answer type. Full instructions for answering these questions will be given to you at the examination. But in case this is your first experience with short-answer questions and separate answer sheets, here is what you need to know:

1) Multiple-choice Questions

Most popular of the short-answer questions is the "multiple choice" or "best answer" question. It can be used, for example, to test for factual knowledge, ability to solve problems or judgment in meeting situations found at work.

A multiple-choice question is normally one of three types—

- It can begin with an incomplete statement followed by several possible endings. You are to find the one ending which *best* completes the statement, although some of the others may not be entirely wrong.
- It can also be a complete statement in the form of a question which is answered by choosing one of the statements listed.
- It can be in the form of a problem – again you select the best answer.

Here is an example of a multiple-choice question with a discussion which should give you some clues as to the method for choosing the right answer:

When an employee has a complaint about his assignment, the action which will *best* help him overcome his difficulty is to
   A. discuss his difficulty with his coworkers
   B. take the problem to the head of the organization
   C. take the problem to the person who gave him the assignment
   D. say nothing to anyone about his complaint

In answering this question, you should study each of the choices to find which is best. Consider choice "A" – Certainly an employee may discuss his complaint with fellow employees, but no change or improvement can result, and the complaint remains unresolved. Choice "B" is a poor choice since the head of the organization probably does not know what assignment you have been given, and taking your problem to him is known as "going over the head" of the supervisor. The supervisor, or person who made the assignment, is the person who can clarify it or correct any injustice. Choice "C" is, therefore, correct. To say nothing, as in choice "D," is unwise. Supervisors have and interest in knowing the problems employees are facing, and the employee is seeking a solution to his problem.

2) True/False Questions

The "true/false" or "right/wrong" form of question is sometimes used. Here a complete statement is given. Your job is to decide whether the statement is right or wrong.

SAMPLE: A roaming cell-phone call to a nearby city costs less than a non-roaming call to a distant city.

This statement is wrong, or false, since roaming calls are more expensive.

This is not a complete list of all possible question forms, although most of the others are variations of these common types. You will always get complete directions for answering questions. Be sure you understand *how* to mark your answers – ask questions until you do.

V. RECORDING YOUR ANSWERS

Computer terminals are used more and more today for many different kinds of exams.

For an examination with very few applicants, you may be told to record your answers in the test booklet itself. Separate answer sheets are much more common. If this separate answer sheet is to be scored by machine – and this is often the case – it is highly important that you mark your answers correctly in order to get credit.

An electronic scoring machine is often used in civil service offices because of the speed with which papers can be scored. Machine-scored answer sheets must be marked with a pencil, which will be given to you. This pencil has a high graphite content which responds to the electronic scoring machine. As a matter of fact, stray dots may register as answers, so do not let your pencil rest on the answer sheet while you are pondering the correct answer. Also, if your pencil lead breaks or is otherwise defective, ask for another.

Since the answer sheet will be dropped in a slot in the scoring machine, be careful not to bend the corners or get the paper crumpled.

The answer sheet normally has five vertical columns of numbers, with 30 numbers to a column. These numbers correspond to the question numbers in your test booklet. After each number, going across the page are four or five pairs of dotted lines. These short dotted lines have small letters or numbers above them. The first two pairs may also have a "T" or "F" above the letters. This indicates that the first two pairs only are to be used if the questions are of the true-false type. If the questions are multiple choice, disregard the "T" and "F" and pay attention only to the small letters or numbers.

Answer your questions in the manner of the sample that follows:

32. The largest city in the United States is
     A. Washington, D.C.
     B. New York City
     C. Chicago
     D. Detroit
     E. San Francisco

1) Choose the answer you think is best. (New York City is the largest, so "B" is correct.)
2) Find the row of dotted lines numbered the same as the question you are answering. (Find row number 32)
3) Find the pair of dotted lines corresponding to the answer. (Find the pair of lines under the mark "B.")
4) Make a solid black mark between the dotted lines.

VI. BEFORE THE TEST

Common sense will help you find procedures to follow to get ready for an examination. Too many of us, however, overlook these sensible measures. Indeed, nervousness and fatigue have been found to be the most serious reasons why applicants fail to do their best on civil service tests. Here is a list of reminders:

- Begin your preparation early – Don't wait until the last minute to go scurrying around for books and materials or to find out what the position is all about.
- Prepare continuously – An hour a night for a week is better than an all-night cram session. This has been definitely established. What is more, a night a week for a month will return better dividends than crowding your study into a shorter period of time.
- Locate the place of the exam – You have been sent a notice telling you when and where to report for the examination. If the location is in a different town or otherwise unfamiliar to you, it would be well to inquire the best route and learn something about the building.
- Relax the night before the test – Allow your mind to rest. Do not study at all that night. Plan some mild recreation or diversion; then go to bed early and get a good night's sleep.
- Get up early enough to make a leisurely trip to the place for the test – This way unforeseen events, traffic snarls, unfamiliar buildings, etc. will not upset you.
- Dress comfortably – A written test is not a fashion show. You will be known by number and not by name, so wear something comfortable.
- Leave excess paraphernalia at home – Shopping bags and odd bundles will get in your way. You need bring only the items mentioned in the official notice you received; usually everything you need is provided. Do not bring reference books to the exam. They will only confuse those last minutes and be taken away from you when in the test room.
- Arrive somewhat ahead of time – If because of transportation schedules you must get there very early, bring a newspaper or magazine to take your mind off yourself while waiting.
- Locate the examination room – When you have found the proper room, you will be directed to the seat or part of the room where you will sit. Sometimes you are given a sheet of instructions to read while you are waiting. Do not fill out any forms until you are told to do so; just read them and be prepared.
- Relax and prepare to listen to the instructions
- If you have any physical problem that may keep you from doing your best, be sure to tell the test administrator. If you are sick or in poor health, you really cannot do your best on the exam. You can come back and take the test some other time.

VII. AT THE TEST

The day of the test is here and you have the test booklet in your hand. The temptation to get going is very strong. Caution! There is more to success than knowing the right answers. You must know how to identify your papers and understand variations in the type of short-answer question used in this particular examination. Follow these suggestions for maximum results from your efforts:

1) Cooperate with the monitor

The test administrator has a duty to create a situation in which you can be as much at ease as possible. He will give instructions, tell you when to begin, check to see that you are marking your answer sheet correctly, and so on. He is not there to guard you, although he will see that your competitors do not take unfair advantage. He wants to help you do your best.

2) Listen to all instructions

Don't jump the gun! Wait until you understand all directions. In most civil service tests you get more time than you need to answer the questions. So don't be in a hurry. Read each word of instructions until you clearly understand the meaning. Study the examples, listen to all announcements and follow directions. Ask questions if you do not understand what to do.

3) Identify your papers

Civil service exams are usually identified by number only. You will be assigned a number; you must not put your name on your test papers. Be sure to copy your number correctly. Since more than one exam may be given, copy your exact examination title.

4) Plan your time

Unless you are told that a test is a "speed" or "rate of work" test, speed itself is usually not important. Time enough to answer all the questions will be provided, but this does not mean that you have all day. An overall time limit has been set. Divide the total time (in minutes) by the number of questions to determine the approximate time you have for each question.

5) Do not linger over difficult questions

If you come across a difficult question, mark it with a paper clip (useful to have along) and come back to it when you have been through the booklet. One caution if you do this – be sure to skip a number on your answer sheet as well. Check often to be sure that you have not lost your place and that you are marking in the row numbered the same as the question you are answering.

6) Read the questions

Be sure you know what the question asks! Many capable people are unsuccessful because they failed to *read* the questions correctly.

7) Answer all questions

Unless you have been instructed that a penalty will be deducted for incorrect answers, it is better to guess than to omit a question.

8) Speed tests

It is often better NOT to guess on speed tests. It has been found that on timed tests people are tempted to spend the last few seconds before time is called in marking answers at random – without even reading them – in the hope of picking up a few extra points. To discourage this practice, the instructions may warn you that your score will be "corrected" for guessing. That is, a penalty will be applied. The incorrect answers will be deducted from the correct ones, or some other penalty formula will be used.

9) Review your answers

If you finish before time is called, go back to the questions you guessed or omitted to give them further thought. Review other answers if you have time.

10) Return your test materials

If you are ready to leave before others have finished or time is called, take ALL your materials to the monitor and leave quietly. Never take any test material with you. The monitor can discover whose papers are not complete, and taking a test booklet may be grounds for disqualification.

VIII. EXAMINATION TECHNIQUES

1) Read the general instructions carefully. These are usually printed on the first page of the exam booklet. As a rule, these instructions refer to the timing of the examination; the fact that you should not start work until the signal and must stop work at a signal, etc. If there are any *special* instructions, such as a choice of questions to be answered, make sure that you note this instruction carefully.

2) When you are ready to start work on the examination, that is as soon as the signal has been given, read the instructions to each question booklet, underline any key words or phrases, such as *least, best, outline, describe* and the like. In this way you will tend to answer as requested rather than discover on reviewing your paper that you *listed without describing*, that you selected the *worst* choice rather than the *best* choice, etc.

3) If the examination is of the objective or multiple-choice type – that is, each question will also give a series of possible answers: A, B, C or D, and you are called upon to select the best answer and write the letter next to that answer on your answer paper – it is advisable to start answering each question in turn. There may be anywhere from 50 to 100 such questions in the three or four hours allotted and you can see how much time would be taken if you read through all the questions before beginning to answer any. Furthermore, if you come across a question or group of questions which you know would be difficult to answer, it would undoubtedly affect your handling of all the other questions.

4) If the examination is of the essay type and contains but a few questions, it is a moot point as to whether you should read all the questions before starting to answer any one. Of course, if you are given a choice – say five out of seven and the like – then it is essential to read all the questions so you can eliminate the two that are most difficult. If, however, you are asked to answer all the questions, there may be danger in trying to answer the easiest one first because you may find that you will spend too much time on it. The best technique is to answer the first question, then proceed to the second, etc.

5) Time your answers. Before the exam begins, write down the time it started, then add the time allowed for the examination and write down the time it must be completed, then divide the time available somewhat as follows:

- If 3-1/2 hours are allowed, that would be 210 minutes. If you have 80 objective-type questions, that would be an average of 2-1/2 minutes per question. Allow yourself no more than 2 minutes per question, or a total of 160 minutes, which will permit about 50 minutes to review.
- If for the time allotment of 210 minutes there are 7 essay questions to answer, that would average about 30 minutes a question. Give yourself only 25 minutes per question so that you have about 35 minutes to review.

6) The most important instruction is to *read each question* and make sure you know what is wanted. The second most important instruction is to *time yourself properly* so that you answer every question. The third most important instruction is to *answer every question*. Guess if you have to but include something for each question. Remember that you will receive no credit for a blank and will probably receive some credit if you write something in answer to an essay question. If you guess a letter – say "B" for a multiple-choice question – you may have guessed right. If you leave a blank as an answer to a multiple-choice question, the examiners may respect your feelings but it will not add a point to your score. Some exams may penalize you for wrong answers, so in such cases *only*, you may not want to guess unless you have some basis for your answer.

7) Suggestions
   a. Objective-type questions
      1. Examine the question booklet for proper sequence of pages and questions
      2. Read all instructions carefully
      3. Skip any question which seems too difficult; return to it after all other questions have been answered
      4. Apportion your time properly; do not spend too much time on any single question or group of questions
      5. Note and underline key words – *all, most, fewest, least, best, worst, same, opposite,* etc.
      6. Pay particular attention to negatives
      7. Note unusual option, e.g., unduly long, short, complex, different or similar in content to the body of the question
      8. Observe the use of "hedging" words – *probably, may, most likely,* etc.
      9. Make sure that your answer is put next to the same number as the question
      10. Do not second-guess unless you have good reason to believe the second answer is definitely more correct
      11. Cross out original answer if you decide another answer is more accurate; do not erase until you are ready to hand your paper in
      12. Answer all questions; guess unless instructed otherwise
      13. Leave time for review

   b. Essay questions
      1. Read each question carefully
      2. Determine exactly what is wanted. Underline key words or phrases.
      3. Decide on outline or paragraph answer

4. Include many different points and elements unless asked to develop any one or two points or elements
5. Show impartiality by giving pros and cons unless directed to select one side only
6. Make and write down any assumptions you find necessary to answer the questions
7. Watch your English, grammar, punctuation and choice of words
8. Time your answers; don't crowd material

8) Answering the essay question

Most essay questions can be answered by framing the specific response around several key words or ideas. Here are a few such key words or ideas:

M's: manpower, materials, methods, money, management
P's: purpose, program, policy, plan, procedure, practice, problems, pitfalls, personnel, public relations
    a. Six basic steps in handling problems:
        1. Preliminary plan and background development
        2. Collect information, data and facts
        3. Analyze and interpret information, data and facts
        4. Analyze and develop solutions as well as make recommendations
        5. Prepare report and sell recommendations
        6. Install recommendations and follow up effectiveness

    b. Pitfalls to avoid
        1. *Taking things for granted* – A statement of the situation does not necessarily imply that each of the elements is necessarily true; for example, a complaint may be invalid and biased so that all that can be taken for granted is that a complaint has been registered
        2. *Considering only one side of a situation* – Wherever possible, indicate several alternatives and then point out the reasons you selected the best one
        3. *Failing to indicate follow up* – Whenever your answer indicates action on your part, make certain that you will take proper follow-up action to see how successful your recommendations, procedures or actions turn out to be
        4. *Taking too long in answering any single question* – Remember to time your answers properly

IX. AFTER THE TEST

Scoring procedures differ in detail among civil service jurisdictions although the general principles are the same. Whether the papers are hand-scored or graded by machine we have described, they are nearly always graded by number. That is, the person who marks the paper knows only the number – never the name – of the applicant. Not until all the papers have been graded will they be matched with names. If other tests, such as training and experience or oral interview ratings have been given, scores will be combined. Different parts of the examination usually have different weights. For example, the written test might count 60 percent of the final grade, and a rating of training and experience 40 percent. In many jurisdictions, veterans will have a certain number of points added to their grades.

After the final grade has been determined, the names are placed in grade order and an eligible list is established. There are various methods for resolving ties between those who get the same final grade – probably the most common is to place first the name of the person whose application was received first. Job offers are made from the eligible list in the order the names appear on it. You will be notified of your grade and your rank as soon as all these computations have been made. This will be done as rapidly as possible.

People who are found to meet the requirements in the announcement are called "eligibles." Their names are put on a list of eligible candidates. An eligible's chances of getting a job depend on how high he stands on this list and how fast agencies are filling jobs from the list.

When a job is to be filled from a list of eligibles, the agency asks for the names of people on the list of eligibles for that job. When the civil service commission receives this request, it sends to the agency the names of the three people highest on this list. Or, if the job to be filled has specialized requirements, the office sends the agency the names of the top three persons who meet these requirements from the general list.

The appointing officer makes a choice from among the three people whose names were sent to him. If the selected person accepts the appointment, the names of the others are put back on the list to be considered for future openings.

That is the rule in hiring from all kinds of eligible lists, whether they are for typist, carpenter, chemist, or something else. For every vacancy, the appointing officer has his choice of any one of the top three eligibles on the list. This explains why the person whose name is on top of the list sometimes does not get an appointment when some of the persons lower on the list do. If the appointing officer chooses the second or third eligible, the No. 1 eligible does not get a job at once, but stays on the list until he is appointed or the list is terminated.

X. HOW TO PASS THE INTERVIEW TEST

The examination for which you applied requires an oral interview test. You have already taken the written test and you are now being called for the interview test – the final part of the formal examination.

You may think that it is not possible to prepare for an interview test and that there are no procedures to follow during an interview. Our purpose is to point out some things you can do in advance that will help you and some good rules to follow and pitfalls to avoid while you are being interviewed.

What is an interview supposed to test?
The written examination is designed to test the technical knowledge and competence of the candidate; the oral is designed to evaluate intangible qualities, not readily measured otherwise, and to establish a list showing the relative fitness of each candidate – as measured against his competitors – for the position sought. Scoring is not on the basis of "right" and "wrong," but on a sliding scale of values ranging from "not passable" to "outstanding." As a matter of fact, it is possible to achieve a relatively low score without a single "incorrect" answer because of evident weakness in the qualities being measured.

Occasionally, an examination may consist entirely of an oral test – either an individual or a group oral. In such cases, information is sought concerning the technical knowledges and abilities of the candidate, since there has been no written examination for this purpose. More commonly, however, an oral test is used to supplement a written examination.

Who conducts interviews?

The composition of oral boards varies among different jurisdictions. In nearly all, a representative of the personnel department serves as chairman. One of the members of the board may be a representative of the department in which the candidate would work. In some cases, "outside experts" are used, and, frequently, a businessman or some other representative of the general public is asked to serve. Labor and management or other special groups may be represented. The aim is to secure the services of experts in the appropriate field.

However the board is composed, it is a good idea (and not at all improper or unethical) to ascertain in advance of the interview who the members are and what groups they represent. When you are introduced to them, you will have some idea of their backgrounds and interests, and at least you will not stutter and stammer over their names.

What should be done before the interview?

While knowledge about the board members is useful and takes some of the surprise element out of the interview, there is other preparation which is more substantive. It *is* possible to prepare for an oral interview – in several ways:

1) Keep a copy of your application and review it carefully before the interview

This may be the only document before the oral board, and the starting point of the interview. Know what education and experience you have listed there, and the sequence and dates of all of it. Sometimes the board will ask you to review the highlights of your experience for them; you should not have to hem and haw doing it.

2) Study the class specification and the examination announcement

Usually, the oral board has one or both of these to guide them. The qualities, characteristics or knowledges required by the position sought are stated in these documents. They offer valuable clues as to the nature of the oral interview. For example, if the job involves supervisory responsibilities, the announcement will usually indicate that knowledge of modern supervisory methods and the qualifications of the candidate as a supervisor will be tested. If so, you can expect such questions, frequently in the form of a hypothetical situation which you are expected to solve. NEVER go into an oral without knowledge of the duties and responsibilities of the job you seek.

3) Think through each qualification required

Try to visualize the kind of questions you would ask if you were a board member. How well could you answer them? Try especially to appraise your own knowledge and background in each area, *measured against the job sought*, and identify any areas in which you are weak. Be critical and realistic – do not flatter yourself.

4) Do some general reading in areas in which you feel you may be weak

For example, if the job involves supervision and your past experience has NOT, some general reading in supervisory methods and practices, particularly in the field of human relations, might be useful. Do NOT study agency procedures or detailed manuals. The oral board will be testing your understanding and capacity, not your memory.

5) Get a good night's sleep and watch your general health and mental attitude

You will want a clear head at the interview. Take care of a cold or any other minor ailment, and of course, no hangovers.

What should be done on the day of the interview?

Now comes the day of the interview itself. Give yourself plenty of time to get there. Plan to arrive somewhat ahead of the scheduled time, particularly if your appointment is in the fore part of the day. If a previous candidate fails to appear, the board might be ready for you a bit early. By early afternoon an oral board is almost invariably behind schedule if there are many candidates, and you may have to wait. Take along a book or magazine to read, or your application to review, but leave any extraneous material in the waiting room when you go in for your interview. In any event, relax and compose yourself.

The matter of dress is important. The board is forming impressions about you – from your experience, your manners, your attitude, and your appearance. Give your personal appearance careful attention. Dress your best, but not your flashiest. Choose conservative, appropriate clothing, and be sure it is immaculate. This is a business interview, and your appearance should indicate that you regard it as such. Besides, being well groomed and properly dressed will help boost your confidence.

Sooner or later, someone will call your name and escort you into the interview room. *This is it.* From here on you are on your own. It is too late for any more preparation. But remember, you asked for this opportunity to prove your fitness, and you are here because your request was granted.

What happens when you go in?

The usual sequence of events will be as follows: The clerk (who is often the board stenographer) will introduce you to the chairman of the oral board, who will introduce you to the other members of the board. Acknowledge the introductions before you sit down. Do not be surprised if you find a microphone facing you or a stenotypist sitting by. Oral interviews are usually recorded in the event of an appeal or other review.

Usually the chairman of the board will open the interview by reviewing the highlights of your education and work experience from your application – primarily for the benefit of the other members of the board, as well as to get the material into the record. Do not interrupt or comment unless there is an error or significant misinterpretation; if that is the case, do not hesitate. But do not quibble about insignificant matters. Also, he will usually ask you some question about your education, experience or your present job – partly to get you to start talking and to establish the interviewing "rapport." He may start the actual questioning, or turn it over to one of the other members. Frequently, each member undertakes the questioning on a particular area, one in which he is perhaps most competent, so you can expect each member to participate in the examination. Because time is limited, you may also expect some rather abrupt switches in the direction the questioning takes, so do not be upset by it. Normally, a board member will not pursue a single line of questioning unless he discovers a particular strength or weakness.

After each member has participated, the chairman will usually ask whether any member has any further questions, then will ask you if you have anything you wish to add. Unless you are expecting this question, it may floor you. Worse, it may start you off on an extended, extemporaneous speech. The board is not usually seeking more information. The question is principally to offer you a last opportunity to present further qualifications or to indicate that you have nothing to add. So, if you feel that a significant qualification or characteristic has been overlooked, it is proper to point it out in a sentence or so. Do not compliment the board on the thoroughness of their examination – they have been sketchy, and you know it. If you wish, merely say, "No thank you, I have nothing further to add." This is a point where you can "talk yourself out" of a good impression or fail to present an important bit of information. Remember, *you close the interview yourself.*

The chairman will then say, "That is all, Mr. _____, thank you." Do not be startled; the interview is over, and quicker than you think. Thank him, gather your belongings and take your leave. Save your sigh of relief for the other side of the door.

How to put your best foot forward

Throughout this entire process, you may feel that the board individually and collectively is trying to pierce your defenses, seek out your hidden weaknesses and embarrass and confuse you. Actually, this is not true. They are obliged to make an appraisal of your qualifications for the job you are seeking, and they want to see you in your best light. Remember, they must interview all candidates and a non-cooperative candidate may become a failure in spite of their best efforts to bring out his qualifications. Here are 15 suggestions that will help you:

1) Be natural – Keep your attitude confident, not cocky

If you are not confident that you can do the job, do not expect the board to be. Do not apologize for your weaknesses, try to bring out your strong points. The board is interested in a positive, not negative, presentation. Cockiness will antagonize any board member and make him wonder if you are covering up a weakness by a false show of strength.

2) Get comfortable, but don't lounge or sprawl

Sit erectly but not stiffly. A careless posture may lead the board to conclude that you are careless in other things, or at least that you are not impressed by the importance of the occasion. Either conclusion is natural, even if incorrect. Do not fuss with your clothing, a pencil or an ashtray. Your hands may occasionally be useful to emphasize a point; do not let them become a point of distraction.

3) Do not wisecrack or make small talk

This is a serious situation, and your attitude should show that you consider it as such. Further, the time of the board is limited – they do not want to waste it, and neither should you.

4) Do not exaggerate your experience or abilities

In the first place, from information in the application or other interviews and sources, the board may know more about you than you think. Secondly, you probably will not get away with it. An experienced board is rather adept at spotting such a situation, so do not take the chance.

5) If you know a board member, do not make a point of it, yet do not hide it

Certainly you are not fooling him, and probably not the other members of the board. Do not try to take advantage of your acquaintanceship – it will probably do you little good.

6) Do not dominate the interview

Let the board do that. They will give you the clues – do not assume that you have to do all the talking. Realize that the board has a number of questions to ask you, and do not try to take up all the interview time by showing off your extensive knowledge of the answer to the first one.

7) Be attentive

You only have 20 minutes or so, and you should keep your attention at its sharpest throughout. When a member is addressing a problem or question to you, give him your undivided attention. Address your reply principally to him, but do not exclude the other board members.

8) Do not interrupt

A board member may be stating a problem for you to analyze. He will ask you a question when the time comes. Let him state the problem, and wait for the question.

9) Make sure you understand the question

Do not try to answer until you are sure what the question is. If it is not clear, restate it in your own words or ask the board member to clarify it for you. However, do not haggle about minor elements.

10) Reply promptly but not hastily

A common entry on oral board rating sheets is "candidate responded readily," or "candidate hesitated in replies." Respond as promptly and quickly as you can, but do not jump to a hasty, ill-considered answer.

11) Do not be peremptory in your answers

A brief answer is proper – but do not fire your answer back. That is a losing game from your point of view. The board member can probably ask questions much faster than you can answer them.

12) Do not try to create the answer you think the board member wants

He is interested in what kind of mind you have and how it works – not in playing games. Furthermore, he can usually spot this practice and will actually grade you down on it.

13) Do not switch sides in your reply merely to agree with a board member

Frequently, a member will take a contrary position merely to draw you out and to see if you are willing and able to defend your point of view. Do not start a debate, yet do not surrender a good position. If a position is worth taking, it is worth defending.

14) Do not be afraid to admit an error in judgment if you are shown to be wrong

The board knows that you are forced to reply without any opportunity for careful consideration. Your answer may be demonstrably wrong. If so, admit it and get on with the interview.

15) Do not dwell at length on your present job

The opening question may relate to your present assignment. Answer the question but do not go into an extended discussion. You are being examined for a *new* job, not your present one. As a matter of fact, try to phrase ALL your answers in terms of the job for which you are being examined.

Basis of Rating

Probably you will forget most of these "do's" and "don'ts" when you walk into the oral interview room. Even remembering them all will not ensure you a passing grade. Perhaps you did not have the qualifications in the first place. But remembering them will help you to put your best foot forward, without treading on the toes of the board members.

Rumor and popular opinion to the contrary notwithstanding, an oral board wants you to make the best appearance possible. They know you are under pressure – but they also want to see how you respond to it as a guide to what your reaction would be under the pressures of the job you seek. They will be influenced by the degree of poise you display, the personal traits you show and the manner in which you respond.

ABOUT THIS BOOK

This book contains tests divided into Examination Sections. Go through each test, answering every question in the margin. At the end of each test look at the answer key and check your answers. On the ones you got wrong, look at the right answer choice and learn. Do not fill in the answers first. Do not memorize the questions and answers, but understand the answer and principles involved. On your test, the questions will likely be different from the samples. Questions are changed and new ones added. If you understand these past questions you should have success with any changes that arise. Tests may consist of several types of questions. We have additional books on each subject should more study be advisable or necessary for you. Finally, the more you study, the better prepared you will be. This book is intended to be the last thing you study before you walk into the examination room. Prior study of relevant texts is also recommended. NLC publishes some of these in our Fundamental Series. Knowledge and good sense are important factors in passing your exam. Good luck also helps. So now study this Passbook, absorb the material contained within and take that knowledge into the examination. Then do your best to pass that exam.

———

EXAMINATION SECTION

EXAMINATION SECTION
TEST 1

DIRECTIONS: Each question or incomplete statement is followed by several suggested answers or completions. Select the one that BEST answers the question or completes the statement. *PRINT THE LETTER OF THE CORRECT ANSWER IN THE SPACE AT THE RIGHT.*

1. The prime essential of all good management is the elimination of waste. In school, the GREATEST wastes, as well as the greatest values, are in   1._____

    A. matters of organization
    B. mechanization of routine
    C. teaching and study
    D. care of textbooks and school equipment and efficient use of the school plant

2. The CHIEF purpose of supervision is generally recognized to be to   2._A___

    A. assist teachers to improve their methods of teaching
    B. evaluate the efficiency of instruction
    C. maintain high standards by inspecting the processes and products of teaching
    D. take care of all disciplinary and school administration problems so that teachers may work under the most favorable conditions

3. Principals are required to notify the guardian of a pupil absent for an unknown cause   3._C___

    A. on the day on which such absence occurs
    B. on the third day of absence
    C. promptly
    D. not later than the third day of absence

4. In the absence of the principal, that assistant principal shall take responsible charge of the school who   4._C___

    A. is the senior in length of service in the position
    B. is the senior in length of service in the school
    C. has been so designated by the superintendent of schools
    D. has been so designated by the principal with the approval of the district superintendent

5. All accidents occurring to pupils, teachers, and others on or about the school premises are to be reported by the principal to the superintendent of schools   5._B___

    A. during the following day
    B. without unnecessary delay
    C. within twenty-four hours
    D. within one week

6. Supervisors are directed to give *special attention* to   6._D___

    A. teachers of superior ability whose work might be utilized for raising the standards in the school
    B. teachers of great promise
    C. those teachers of average ability who constitute the majority of the corps
    D. substitutes, inexperienced teachers, or teachers whose work has been recorded as unsatisfactory

7. Assistant principals are required to keep official records of   7._____

    A. attendance, punctuality, and ratings of their pupils
    B. the nature and amount of all kinds of supervisory service they render
    C. all class inspections, examinations, and conferences with teachers under their supervision
    D. notices, directions, assignments, programs, suggestions given, and recommendations made in connection with their duties

8. One of the FIRST books discussing supervision in the elementary schools from a modern viewpoint is THE SUPERVISION OF INSTRUCTION by   8._____

    A. G.A. Mirick   B. H.W. Nutt
    C. W.C. Bagley   D. W.H. Burton

9. The CHIEF purpose of giving an *exploratory test* in any subject is to   9._____

    A. find a beginning average for the class
    B. give the pupils a rapid survey of the new material to be taught
    C. determine the experiential background of each pupil and his needs as related to the learning product
    D. show the pupils how little they know about a new subject

10. In making up the promotion list, a teacher has under consideration several doubtful cases.   10._____
In deciding each case, she should be guided PRIMARILY by one of the following principles:

    A. Promote the pupil because there is a possibility that he will maintain himself in the higher grade
    B. Keep a misbehaving pupil back because his promotion would set a bad example to the other children
    C. Promote the pupil because his repeating the grade will not improve him
    D. Keep him back so that he may master satisfactorily the work in the grade

11. Supervision must grow out of a knowledge of the work of the teacher.   11._____
This implies observing the teacher and the pupils and, CHIEFLY, the

    A. direct observation of the physical and hygienic conditions under which learning takes place
    B. appraisal of the results of instruction
    C. systematic, planned, purposeful observation, and constructive criticism, of teaching
    D. evaluation of the efficiency of instruction by standard tests and other objective measures of quality of learning

12. Actual investigations show that the problems which teachers should like to present MOST often to their supervisors for assistance are those relating to the   12._____

    A. control of disciplinary cases
    B. demonstration of improved methods of teaching

C. adequate furnishing of the best materials of instruction (plans, text and reference books, apparatus, illustrative material, etc.)
D. educational and vocational guidance of pupils so as to make them worthy members of society

13. The one of the following plans preferred for individualizing instruction and for setting definite and different goals for the groups of superior, normal, and slow children is the _____ Plan.

    A. Dalton   B. Gary
    C. Winnetka   D. Batavia

13.____

14. In reducing activities (such as collecting and distributing wraps) dealing with constant factors to a routine,

    A. the initiative of the pupil is lessened
    B. the pupil's moral responsibility is weakened
    C. all class activities tend to become mechanical
    D. the attention and energy of the teacher may be devoted to the problems of teaching

14.____

15. The writing-out of the plan of a lesson serves MAINLY

    A. to clarify the teacher's own ideas
    B. as evidence of preparation for teaching
    C. as a guide to a substitute in the teacher's absence
    D. to keep uniform the progress of the various classes in the same grade

15.____

16. A teacher graphs the standing and progress of her class in the tool subjects. To measure ability in arithmetic, she might use the

    A. Hillegas Scale   B. Stone Reasoning Test
    C. Dearborn Group Test   D. Hahn-Lackey Scale

16.____

17. The MOST essential factor in successful questioning is

    A. maintaining a balance among the types of questions asked
    B. making adequate preparation for each lesson
    C. avoiding leading questions
    D. obtaining speedy responses

17.____

18. A comparison of the scores attained by pupils on intelligence tests given at moderately lengthy intervals indicates that the

    A. I.Q. rating is absolutely constant
    B. I.Q. rating is not absolutely constant
    C. average variation is plus or minus fifteen points
    D. reclassification of all pupils is essential as a result of each testing

18.____

19. School discipline should

    A. be based upon unquestioning behavior
    B. be based upon the personality of the teacher rather than upon authority
    C. aim at automatic and immediate efficiency
    D. appeal to the highest motives to which the pupil can effectively respond

19.____

20. School discipline may BEST be defined as

    A. social control within the school group
    B. individual good order
    C. the automatic desirable responses of individuals and groups
    D. orderliness and good behavior throughout the school because of the influence and control exercised by the principal

20.____

21. The LEAST desirable end to be achieved through the administration of punishment is

    A. reforming the offender
    B. deterring others
    C. expressing society's disapproval of wrong
    D. retribution

21.____

22. A pupil has committed an offense. The offender is known to have been tempted to commit the wrong by others.
The teacher should _____ the offender _____ the others.

    A. punish; and excuse
    C. punish; as well as
    B. excuse; and punish
    D. excuse; as well as

22.____

23. When conducting a fire drill, the teacher should GENERALLY

    A. leave the room last to see that no child remains behind
    B. leave at the head of the class
    C. take a position at the middle of the line
    D. go ahead of the class to see that the exit is not blocked

23.____

24. The one specific and constant problem of the supervisor is

    A. inspection
    B. development and maintenance of morale or esprit de corps
    C. the general improvement of teachers in service
    D. the direct improvement of classroom teaching

24.____

25. One of the first steps in minimizing the number of disciplinary cases is to

    A. insist that the rules of the school be consistently enforced
    B. reduce opportunities for misbehavior
    C. install a system of pupil self-government
    D. install a system of rewards and punishments

25.____

KEY (CORRECT ANSWERS)

1.	C		11.	C
2.	A		12.	B
3.	A		13.	A
4.	D		14.	D
5.	C		15.	A
6.	D		16.	B
7.	C		17.	B
8.	B		18.	B
9.	C		19.	D
10.	A		20.	A

21.	D
22.	C
23.	B
24.	D
25.	B

TEST 2

DIRECTIONS: Each question or incomplete statement is followed by several suggested answers or completions. Select the one that BEST answers the question or completes the statement. *PRINT THE LETTER OF THE CORRECT ANSWER IN THE SPACE AT THE RIGHT.*

1. Schools differ widely as to pupil-principal relationship. Which is MOST desirable? The principal who

    A. by his presence and manner secures the awed respect of all the pupils
    B. encourages individuality and complete self-expression
    C. respects the personality of children and develops cooperation
    D. keeps himself in the background and generally strives to impress his personality on the children only indirectly through the teachers

1.____

2. Demonstration lessons should ALWAYS be

    A. model lessons which all teachers may profitably imitate
    B. subjected to criticism by the observing teachers
    C. examples of advanced forms of teaching procedure
    D. given only for the benefit of those teachers unable to profit by counsel

2.____

3. It is DESIRABLE that an individual conference of teacher and principal follow

    A. every lesson observed
    B. if the lesson observed needs improvement
    C. if the lesson observed is very good
    D. if the teacher asks for the conference

3.____

4. The ideal distribution of the principal's school day should be:

4.____

	Supervision	Administration	Clerical and Other Duties
A.	24 percent	56 percent	20 percent
B.	75 percent	20 percent	5 percent
C.	51 percent	25 percent	24 percent
D.	20 percent	70 percent	10 percent

5. Studies of the leaving back of pupils show BETTER work in repeating the grade in _____ percent of the repeaters.

    A. 5-12   B. 28-35   C. 60-67   D. 85-92

5.____

6. With reference to the special teacher of music, sewing, etc., and the class teachers, which procedure of the principal may be regarded as merely administrative?

    A. Distributing outlines and suggestions to the teachers when received
    B. Talking over conditions with the special teacher after her visit to the school
    C. Suggesting to a teacher a new reference book or two to meet special needs in the subject
    D. Encouraging teachers to cooperate in the activity

6.____

7. The two PRINCIPAL sources of unreliability in essay-type examinations are: 7.____

   A. Time required and difficulty of evaluation
   B. Need for excluding personal opinions and whims of teachers
   C. Variation in teacher rating and influence of teacher temperaments
   D. Subjectivity and limited sampling

8. The CHIEF disadvantage of a horizontal assignment of a block of grades for supervision 8.____
   by one of the assistant principals is that it

   A. has a narrowing effect upon the supervisor
   B. creates gaps between the various blocks
   C. limits the authoritative status and the prestige of the said supervisor
   D. puts too heavy a burden upon the supervisor

9. An angry parent calls to see the principal. 9.____
   Which of the following procedures is to be PREFERRED?
   The principal

   A. endeavors at the outset to explain the school rules to the complainant
   B. immediately recommends that the parent visit the teacher concerned in order to
      get all the facts
   C. permits the aggrieved person to talk himself out
   D. refers all such cases to the assistant principal for careful, sympathetic but firm con-
      sideration

10. The CHIEF advantage of a teacher self-rating plan is that it 10.____

    A. is a democratic step toward teacher cooperation
    B. is time-saving as an administrative device for a principal
    C. is most apt to induce self-criticism, the first step in self-improvement
    D. will benefit the pupils through more efficient instruction

11. Follow-up conferences with teachers to be MOST effective should 11.____

    A. be held as soon as possible after the visit to the teacher
    B. follow a well-thought-out program for the improvement of teaching
    C. be conducted on a sympathetic plane to lessen the nervous tension of the teacher
    D. deal with the attitudes, habits, and skills of the pupils

12. The BEST textbooks of this generation present 12.____

    A. a proper regard for the vocabulary abilities of the children
    B. a union of proper knowledge of the subject and a proper knowledge of the mind of
       the child
    C. opportunities for directed study by the child
    D. a close adherence to the course of study

13. The supervisor's function in relation to the teacher is 13.____

    A. encouragement   B. guidance
    C. administration   D. criticism

14. In judging the work of the early childhood classes, which of these phases of work is regarded as MOST important?

    A. How much interest the children show in the work
    B. How well they read
    C. How well they answer questions
    D. How well they participate in class enterprises

14._____

15. The GREATEST need for successfully measuring teaching efficiency involves

    A. the development of technics for adequately sampling teaching itself
    B. observing pupil growth
    C. the training of teachers in the technic of educational research
    D. the establishment of standards or criteria of teaching success

15._____

16. School groupings should be

    A. fluid   B. heterogeneous
    C. strictly homogeneous   D. avoided

16._____

17. After a visit to the classroom, the principal helps the teacher MOST by

    A. evaluating the lesson and sending a report to the teacher in writing
    B. using the lesson as a basis for a general conference
    C. raising for discussion an intelligent question concerning the lesson
    D. answering the teacher's questions on the lesson

17._____

18. Investigations of the relationship between class register and attainment indicate that the effect of class size upon class progress is

    A. most decided   B. marked
    C. considerable   D. very slight

18._____

19. In the first three years of elementary school,

    A. no home study from books or written homework should be required
    B. home study from books may be required but no written homework
    C. home study should be limited to one hour daily
    D. home study should be limited to thirty minutes daily

19._____

20. The BEST method to be pursued by a principal in improving the teaching in his school is to

    A. conduct frequest tests and to graph the progress of classes
    B. rate teachers on class progress
    C. give demonstration lessons
    D. hold conferences, individual and grade

20._____

21. The CHIEF purpose of supervision is to

    A. check on methods throughout the school
    B. appraise the work of the teachers justly
    C. help the teachers
    D. see that the curriculum is being fully presented

21._____

22. The MAJOR part of the principal's time should be spent in 22._____

    A. room visitation and individual conference
    B. conference with visitors and pupils
    C. perfecting school organization
    D. testing and grading his school

23. When we give an intelligence test, we measure DIRECTLY 23._____

    A. inborn intelligence   B. school accomplishment
    C. acquired intelligence   D. environmental influence

24. School discipline bears the SAME relation to moral education that acquiring knowledge 24._____
bears to the development of

    A. emotions   B. will
    C. intelligence   D. character

25. The MAIN objective in school discipline should be 25._____

    A. obedience to authority
    B. self-control and self-direction
    C. good order so that school work may be done effectively
    D. school spirit

KEY (CORRECT ANSWERS)

1.	C		11.	B
2.	B		12.	C
3.	A		13.	B
4.	C		14.	D
5.	D		15.	D
6.	A		16.	A
7.	D		17.	B
8.	B		18.	D
9.	C		19.	A
10.	C		20.	D

21.	C
22.	A
23.	C
24.	C
25.	B

EDUCATIONAL ADMINISTRATION AND SUPERVISION

EXAMINATION SECTION

TEST 1

DIRECTIONS: Each question or incomplete statement is followed by several suggested answers or completions. Select the one that BEST answers the question or completes the statement. *PRINT THE LETTER OF THE CORRECT ANSWER IN THE SPACE AT THE RIGHT.*

1. Although local, regional, and national efforts are in progress to elevate the status of the teacher to that of a fully-recognized profession, membership in the ranks is not being replenished with an adequate number of high caliber, competent recruits to meet the needs.
   Of the following obstacles to effective recruitment, the LEAST likely to be surmounted through the efforts of educators in the immediate future is
   A. ability of youth to select more remunerative careers whose requirements are lower in terms of time and money spent for preparation
   B. inadequate school buildings and equipment
   C. inadequacy and ineffectiveness of counseling and recruiting programs to attract promising young men and women into teacher preparation programs
   D. belief shared by a large proportion of those enrolled in secondary schools and colleges that teaching is unattractive as a career
   E. undemocratic administrative practices and procedures to which some teachers are subjected

1.____

2. The MOST effective of the following suggestions that educators might use for attracting young people to teaching as a career is:
   A. Arrange for a high school senior day on a teachers college campus where the emotional satisfactions to be gained from following teaching as a career are stressed.
   B. Arrange for as many high school students as possible to obtain such teaching experiences as are provided in playground and camp work
   C. Have outstanding professional educators speak on the importance of the educational system at school assemblies
   D. Plan a semi-annual school career day during which special emphasis will be placed on teaching
   E. Sponsor college scholarships for capable young people who have chosen teaching as their lifework

2.____

3. Of the following contributing causes for the inability of school systems to recruit an adequate number of well-qualified teachers, the MAJOR one is:
   A. Antiquated and biased state certification regulations
   B. Ineffective and meager recruitment programs
   C. Little opportunity for promotion and recognition of merit
   D. Low standards of selective admission to teacher education institutions
   E. Poor working conditions

3.____

4. The one of the following groups of factors which should be MOST important in the selection of educational personnel is:
   A. Educational point of view, health, relations with others, understanding of leaders, social viewpoint
   B. Age, health, speech, knowledge of facts in instruction area, appearance
   C. Knowledge of facts used in instruction, knowledge of instructional material, speech, knowledge of human growth and development, health
   D. Age, high school record, college record, teaching experience, intellectual ability
   E. Understanding of learners, background and experience, health, knowledge of instructional material, knowledge of facts in instructional area

4.____

5. Of the following, the GREATEST limitation of the interview as a means of selecting educational personnel is that
   A. the interview is time-consuming and costly
   B. adaptation of the interview to allow for differences among candidates is sometimes not possible
   C. the interview has been discredited as a selection method
   D. answers obtained are usually superficial because candidates have not sufficient time to think through the full implication of the questions put to them
   E. the procedures involved are essentially subjective

5.____

6. The school administrator has many administrative tools available to solve the problems with which he is faced. One of the most important of these is the conference.
   When compared to other administrative tools, the GREATEST value of the conference is to solve problems which
   A. are familiar and rather simple
   B. are new and difficult
   C. do not require a solution in the foreseeable future
   D. are not amenable to solution
   E. do not involve any research or analysis

6.____

7. You have been asked to answer a letter from the dean of a nearby school of education requesting certain information. After giving the request careful consideration, you find that it cannot be granted.
   Of the following ways of beginning your answering letter, the BEST is to begin by
   A. discussing the problem of releasing confidential information
   B. explaining in detail why the request cannot be granted
   C. indicating, if possible, that the information may be available from other sources
   D. quoting the laws which prohibit the dissemination of information of the type requested
   E. saying that you are sorry that the request cannot be granted

7.____

8. The furtherance of mental hygiene in the schools is desirable PRIMARILY because   8.____
    A. it keeps the disturbing problems of the pupil-teacher relationship at a minimum
    B. optimum conditions for the personal-social development of individual pupils are thus provided
    C. pupils learn essential subject matter better in a favorable emotional atmosphere
    D. serious future problems of maladjustment can be prevented by dealing with maladjustments in their early stages
    E. children should be as happy as possible while in school

9. Education for democracy is BEST formulated when it   9.____
    A. is based on a uniform interpretation of the term "democracy"
    B. recognizes that democracy calls for cooperation founded on self-sacrifice to make it function
    C. holds that a new social order must be built before current economic and social problems can be solved
    D. is based on the thesis that the state has its origin in a social contract
    E. recognizes that social values are subject to constant change

10. The present trend is to extend the period of pre-service preparation for teachers at all levels of instruction. Leaders in the field are advocating that the additional time available be employed in   10.____
    A. additional training in the subject of specialization
    B. course instruction in materials dealing with the psychological bases of pupil behavior
    C. extending the mastery of general cultural materials
    D. observing the classroom work of skilled teachers and in practice teaching
    E. providing advanced and intensive instruction in professional subjects

11. Written tests employed for the purpose of selecting educational personnel are NOT completely satisfactory CHIEFLY because, in general, they   11.____
    A. do not allow for probing in depth into a candidate's background, emotional problems, etc.
    B. do not allow for a wide enough sampling of a candidate's skills and knowledge
    C. do not attempt to evaluate a candidate's personality
    D. do not measure ability to perform
    E. have been useful only in the evaluation of factual knowledge

12. The MOST important of the following reasons for reviewing the non-teaching experiences of an applicant for a teaching position is that non-teaching experiences may   12.____
    A. indicate the range of experience the applicant has had in dealing with people
    B. provide basic evidence of the patriotic or subversive thinking of the applicant through the groups or organizations with which he has been associated

C. reveal sources of potential maladjustment which may develop
D. provide evidence concerning the applicant's motivation in choosing teaching as his life work
E. show avocational interests which the examiner should consider in prognosticating the mental health of the candidate as a teacher

13. No educational system can live without teachers who are competent, qualified, and above all, enthusiastic. The public school system is starving because of a lack of this kind of teacher.
The problem implied in this statement
   A. is likely to confront educational leaders everywhere for a long time
   B. would tend to be solved if higher intellectual standards were set by teacher examining boards
   C. is limited for the most part in its more crucial aspects to the smaller communities and to rural areas
   D. would tend to be solved if there were more teacher education institutions
   E. is probably a temporary, natural aftermath of the war period

13.____

14. Of the following procedures, the one which would probably be MOST effective in reducing teacher criticism of the standards used on examinations for supervisory positions in a school system is to
   A. eliminate all controversial qualifying tests from the examination
   B. hold periodic public hearings for the discussion of standards used on examinations
   C. provide for teacher participation in determining standards
   D. publish a detailed statement of the standards in advance
   E. use a fixed standard for all examinations

14.____

15. Experience requirements for newly-appointed teachers at the elementary and junior high school levels are much less prevalent today than 30 years ago. Of the following, the MAJOR justification for elimination of experience requirements is the
   A. demonstrated low value of teaching experience in predicting efficiency in teaching
   B. difficulty in recruiting young men and women interested in teaching
   C. longer period of professional preparation now required for appointment
   D. prevalence of in-service training opportunities in most urban areas
   E. undesirable competitive situations among school systems which result from experience requirements tied to higher salaries

15.____

16. Buros' MENTAL MEASUREMENTS YEARBOOK is a valuable reference for administrators who want to
   A. identify the causes of failure on teacher-selection examinations
   B. know the group intelligence-test scores for teachers and other professional groups
   C. locate and to evaluate standardized tests and references on testing
   D. know the techniques for administering diagnostic tests
   E. measure the degree of efficiency of instruction among beginning teachers

16.____

17. To the maximum extent possible, each school should be permitted to have   17.____
the responsibility for planning its own program. Adoption of this policy would
MOST likely lead to
   A. *less effective* planning primarily because members of a central planning
      agency tend to have a more objective viewpoint than teachers in a school
   B. *more effective* planning primarily because plans would be conceived in
      terms of the actual situation, and the participants would have a greater
      will to succeed
   C. *less effective* planning primarily because if planning is left to the school,
      there will be no agency qualified to determine whether the plans are
      properly executed
   D. *more effective* planning primarily because the men and women in the
      schools tend to be better qualified technically than the members of a staff
      agency
   E. *less effective* planning primarily because schools are usually
      undermanned and, consequently, are in no position to assign staff for
      planning purposes

18. Of the following publications, the one which is MOST useful for a   18.____
comprehensive overview of most of the major research related to the selection
of educational personnel is:
   A. McCall's MEASUREMENT OF TEACHER MERIT
   B. Monroe's ENCYCLOPEDIA OF EDUCATIONAL RESEARCH
   C. The latest triennial issue of the REVIEW OF EDUCATIONAL RESEARCH
      which deals with "Teachers and Non-academic Personnel"
   D. THE IMPROVEMENT OF TEACHING, a monograph published by the
      National Commission on Teacher Education and Professional Standards
   E. PRINCIPLES AND PROCEDURES OF TEACHER SELECTION, a
      monograph published by the American Association of Examiners and
      Administrators of Educational Personnel

19. Verified evidence of deep emotional disturbances in the records of an applicant   19.____
for a teaching position should point to a rejection of his application MAINLY
because
   A. educational systems should not employ people for teaching positions who
      have a history of emotional disturbance
   B. every child has the right to be taught by healthy, well-adjusted teachers
   C. it is generally agreed that people once afflicted with mental or emotional
      disturbances cannot be inspiring teachers
   D. some emotional experiences tend to have lasting deleterious effects upon
      a person's mental health
   E. teachers having deep emotional disturbances are not capable of teaching
      logical organized subjects, such as mathematics

20. The consensus of research findings to date indicates that teacher   20.____
effectiveness
    A. is negatively related to the amount of professional preparation beyond the bachelor's degree for elementary school teachers, but positively related to such preparation for high school teachers
    B. consists of two primary factors – knowledge of children and knowledge of subject – the latter being closely related to supervisors' efficiency ratings
    C. is not a unitary quality and, as variously defined has shown little or no consistent positive relationship to the amount of professional preparation, length of teaching experience, or supervisors' efficiency ratings
    D. consists of three primary factors – knowledge of children, knowledge of subject, and knowledge of the learning process – and that a substantial positive correlation exists between the first and teacher-pupil relations, the second and teacher-parent relations, and the third and teacher-supervisory relations
    E. is positively correlated with both the amount of teaching experience and supervisors' efficiency ratings, but that there is a slight but consistent negative relationship between these two factors

21. The one of the following sets of tests which would provide, in general, the   21.____
MOST practical and useful battery in the selection of elementary school
teachers in a large metropolitan school system is:
    A. An analysis of teaching-learning situations observed in films, a personality interview, a speech test, and the National Teacher Examination
    B. A multiple-choice test on child psychology as applied to the school situation and on general education and cultural background, a summary of teaching experience and preparation, and an analysis of the applicant's teaching performance
    C. An autobiography, including a summary of teaching experience and preparation, written response to a cases or situation presented, and a speech test
    D. A multiple-choice test on subject matter and educational methods , a test of personality, a speech test, and an analysis of classroom work observed by the applicant and the administrator
    E. The National Teacher Examination, an objective test of personality, a summary of teaching experience and preparation, and letters of recommendation

22. Too often the school administrator does not realize that the organization chart   22.____
is only an idealized picture of his intentions, a reflection of his hopes and aims,
rather than a photograph of the operating facts within his organization.
This statement is BEST supported by the fact that the organization chart
    A. cannot be a photograph of the living organization but must be either a record of past organization or proposed future organization
    B. deals in terms of positions rather than of people
    C. defines too explicitly the jurisdiction assigned to each component unit
    D. does not indicate unresolved internal ambiguities
    E. sometimes contains unresolved internal ambiguities

23. When interviewing teacher candidates, to which of the following   23.____
characteristics should GREATEST weight or consideration be accorded?
    A. Fluency of verbal expression   B. Poise and self-assurance
    C. Interest in teaching   D. Speech pattern
    E. Tact and courtesy

24. A fifth-grade teacher experimented with a form of experience curriculum   24.____
which emphasized pupil-teacher planning to meet the psychological needs of
pupils. At the end of the year, a comprehensive achievement test revealed that
the scores of pupils were a good deal higher than usual for that school in
language, art, geography, history, and literature, but lower in arithmetic.
Of the following, the MOST acceptable action to be taken on the basis of these
findings is:
    A. Essentially the same plan should be used for another year to determine
       whether corrective measures need be applied, and where
    B. Less emphasis should be given in the future to language, art, etc. so that
       more time will be available for arithmetic
    C. No radical change should be made in the experimental program, but the
       supervisor should help the teacher in the teaching of arithmetic in the
       experience curriculum
    D. Not enough emphasis was given to arithmetic, so that the future
       arithmetic skills should be taught separately, not as part of the experience
       curriculum
    E. The experience curriculum should be abandoned or at least de-
       emphasized, and greater emphasis should be place don subject-matter
       teaching

25. Curriculum development has been furthered MOST by research on   25.____
    A. the application of more meaningful tests and other instruments for
       evaluating curriculum effectiveness
    B. the effectiveness of such learning materials as audio-visual aids and their
       relationship to the curriculum
    C. better construction of courses of study from the viewpoint of the learning
       process
    D. the effects of remedial programs on pupil achievement in new areas
    E. the influence of the maturation, growth, and development of the child in
       relation to the scope and sequence of the curriculum

26. The departmental chairman in a high school executes policy formulated at   26.____
higher levels. He does not make policy. He is the element of the
administrative structure closest to the teacher.
Accepting this description of the duties of the departmental chairman, it follows
that he BEST carries out his responsibilities when he
    A. assigns teachers to classes on the basis of their abilities and interests
    B. checks on the progress of the teachers in his department in order to make
       certain that they will complete teaching assignments
    C. disciplines teachers who break rules

D. interprets and executes policies in a manner that respects teacher needs and interests

E. suggests desirable changes in the curriculum on the basis of his department's experience

27. You have been assigned to conduct a classroom teaching test. The one of the following means of preparing for this assignment that would be of LEAST value is to

27.____

A. become acquainted with the teacher's plan for the day
B. clarify your own thinking regarding effective teaching
C. review the forms and rating blanks to be used in the appraisal
D. study records and other data about the learners
E. visit the classroom for several days prior to the day of appraisal

28. The mental hygiene concept in modern teacher training requires that the classroom teacher should

28.____

A. be able to cope with all types of emotional problems as they arise in the classroom
B. prevent pupils from experiencing frustration
C. be able to discuss behavior problems with parents in simple terms
D. structure learning situations so that they strengthen pupils' adjustive processes
E. be a thoroughly well-adjusted individual

29. An approach to personality that represents a new influence on personality measurement is to be found in

29.____

A. Adorno, THE AUTHORITARIAN PERSONALITY
B. Bales, INTERACTION PROCESS ANALYSIS
C. Cronbach, ESSENTGIALS OF PSYCHOLOGICAL TESTING
D. Symonds, DIAGNOSING PERSONALITY AND CONDUCT
E. Traxler, TECHNIQUES OF GUIDANCE

30. The Committee on the Criteria of Teacher Effectiveness of the American Educational Research Association has issued several reports on discussions of the subject that have been held.
The PRINCIPAL contribution of these reports is the

30.____

A. detailing of a program of cooperative research on the character and causes of good teaching
B. formulation of a conceptual frame of reference for the study of teacher effectiveness
C. keen analysis of the characteristics of the democratically oriented teacher
D. listing of the published and unpublished tests which, in the opinion of the Committee, have been found most valid in measuring teacher characteristics
E. searching critique of the limitations of the several techniques currently employed in teacher selection and retention

31. Teacher participation in developing plans which will affect administrative and supervisory personnel as well as teachers will contribute to greater understanding of the entire system. When possible, such teacher participation should be encouraged.
    This policy, in general, is
    A. *good*, primarily because it will enable the teacher to make intelligent suggestions for adjustment of the plans in the future
    B. *bad*, primarily because teachers can be given administrative background instruction more effectively in an in-service training course
    C. *good*, primarily because plans tend to be better when more persons participate in formulating them
    D. *bad*, primarily because teachers should participate only in those activities which affect their own level; otherwise, conflicts in authority may arise
    E. *good*, primarily because teachers will accept administrative decisions more readily if they are aware of the real reasons for making them

31.____

32. Legal proof that an applicant for a position in an educational system has served a sentence in a penal institution, no matter how early in his life, should constitute an automatic rejection of his application.
    This basis for rejection is
    A. *desirable*, primarily because children will not respect teachers who have broken the laws of adult society
    B. *undesirable*, primarily because applications for teaching positions cannot reasonably be expected to have higher standards of conduct that citizens in any other occupation or profession
    C. *desirable*, primarily because educational systems should not employ people for teaching responsibilities who have served a sentence for a lapse in responsibility
    D. *undesirable*, primarily because it indicates little discrimination in terms of type and extent of crime or of subsequent conduct
    E. *desirable*, primarily because payment of the legal price for an unlawful act is no certain guarantee of the exercise of good citizenship thereafter

32.____

33. It is generally considered desirable to attract more men into the teaching profession PRIMARILY because it is believed that
    A. men are generally better at maintaining discipline and coaching teams
    B. children usually respect men more than women, and commonly achieve greater maturity and self-control under the guidance of men teachers
    C. men are needed for eventual promotion into positions of administrative leadership
    D. children should have an opportunity to be associated with men as well as women in school
    E. men are needed to give greater continuity to the school program

33.____

34. The MOST justifiable and, probably, MOST effective of the following   34.____
proposals for increasing the supply of teachers of trade subjects in the near
future is:
   A. Allow increased salary credit for journeyman experience in the trade
   B. Induct the trade unions in each of the several trades to cooperate in a
   recruitment drive
   C. Reduce initial eligibility requirements to a minimum of education and three
   years of journeyman experience, and permit appointees to take the
   required courses in educational subjects after they have begun to serve
   D. Simplify the examination for the regular license so that it will consist only
   of an interview to evaluate personal qualifications and a trade
   competence test
   E. Sponsor legislation under which teachers of trade subjects would be paid
   on a higher salary schedule than that paid to teachers of academic
   subjects

35. Improvement of mental hygiene practices in the schools must be CHIEFLY   35.____
a matter of
   A. carefully selecting mentally healthy teachers in the first place because
   empathic relations with others depend almost entirely on innate personal
   qualities
   B. continuous training of the teacher, both pre-service and in-service, in
   mental hygiene theory and practice
   C. eliminating those candidates who are not aware of the best mental health
   practices
   D. insisting that training in mental health practices be provided to those
   teachers already on the job who are in need of it
   E. regular consultation with professional mental health practitioners on pupil
   personality problems before and after they arise

36. In a school system where the superintendent of schools habitually decides   36.____
on all policy changes without staff consultation, the MOST probable staff
reaction is to
   A. accept the decisions if they are rational
   B. resent and obstruct all policy changes
   C. appreciate the source of authority in the situation
   D. demand opportunity to participate in future policy changes
   E. feel insecure

37. Management of educational personnel, when compared with management   37.____
of personnel in business and industry,
   A. cannot be based on the same principles as essentially different kinds of
   people are involved
   B has been in the direction of permitting the teacher greater freedom
   C. has, in all ways, been quite similar
   D. has, in all ways, been quite dissimilar
   E. should be based on the same principles without appropriate modification

38. In general, policies within a school system should evolve from 38.____
    A. analysis by the supervisor and his immediate staff and then be communicated to the rest of the staff
    B. participation of the entire staff
    C. studies made by persons who, because they are not concerned, can be objective
    D. participation of those most concerned
    E. analysis by the supervisor and his immediate staff, and then be voted upon by the entire staff

39. The relationship between mental ability and school achievement is illustrated 39.____
by the fact that a relatively satisfactory mental ability test for school administrators would be
    A. a test consisting of achievement items in current events and mechanical comprehension
    B. a test consisting of achievement items in grammatical classification and American history
    C. a test consisting of achievement items in spelling and arithmetic computation
    D. a test consisting of achievement items in word meaning and arithmetic reasoning
    E. impossible to attain through the use of achievement test items

40. The superintendent of schools asks you to prepare a statement dealing 40.____
with a controversial matter for public distribution.
Of the following approaches, the one which would usually be MOST effective is to
    A. buttress the board of education's viewpoint with all the statistical data and research techniques which were used in arriving at it
    B. avoid taking a definite stand if at all possible
    C. develop the board of education's viewpoint from ideas and facts well-known to most readers
    D. avoid taking a definite stand where you know that your views conflict with those of the superintendent
    E. present the board of education's viewpoint as tersely as possible without any reference to any other matters

41. Of the following, the GREATEST danger the average administrator of a 41.____
school system faces is
    A. being too personal in his dealings with staff who work directly with him
    B. failure to delegate responsibility effectively
    C. delegating responsibility he should keep
    D. failure to keep channels of communication open
    E. questioning his basic policy of subordinates

42. Plans for the organization of the school of the future must be flexible; the kind of school which will develop depends to a great extent on the quality of teachers we will have.
In general, this statement is
    A. *not correct*, primarily because individual teachers should not be able to change the organization of a school
    B. *correct*, primarily because if we have high quality teachers, the problem of organization tends to solve itself
    C. *not correct*, primarily because it is the function of any good school system to train its teachers rather than let them change it
    D. *correct*, primarily because school organization cannot be considered apart from teacher qualifications
    E. *not correct*, primarily because school organization is only remotely affected by the quality of teachers

42.____

43. Teachers can BEST related mental hygiene to discipline in the school by
    A. helping children develop standards of conduct in the classroom which make for the best possible conditions for learning and development
    B. holding children to consistent and thoroughly-understood standards of group behavior at all times
    C. maintaining a highly permissive spirit in the classroom so that misbehavior ceases to have individual meaning
    D. relying on the exercise of self-discipline of group members based on democratic sanctions created by the group itself
    E. using sound and long-understood teaching methods with normally well-behaved children, referring deviates to disciplinary authorities

43.____

44. Of the following mental health principles for dealing with the common mental health problems of individual pupils, the MOST important is to
    A. depend almost entirely on recommendations of professional specialists who can make adequate diagnoses
    B. do nothing until a thorough case study can be made
    C. employ common techniques which experience has shown to be effective in most cases
    D. let the problems work themselves out in the give-and-take of wholesome classroom activity
    E. work in terms of the specific causes and effects operating upon the individual child

44.____

45. School administrators frequently interview people in order to obtain information. This means of obtaining information has limitations which should not be overlooked.
The MOST important limitation of those listed is that
    A. information, which can be obtained by this method, tends to be necessarily subjective
    B. during an interview, people frequently refuse to give information which they are willing to submit in writing
    C. it is more difficult to conduct an interview than to construct a questionnaire

45.____

    D. people who are interviewed frequently answer questions with guesses
rather than admit their ignorance
    E. the interview is usually of value for obtaining specific information only

46. The one of the following which is usually the FIRST step in the development   46.____
of a test to be used in selecting educational personnel is to
    A. prepare the job description
    B. determine attributes and competencies required for success on the job
    C. review tests previously used for this purpose
    D. determine the types of tests to be used
    E. set up minimum requirements to be met by all applicants

47. Announcements of examinations for teaching positions have been attacked   47.____
because they do not contain sufficient specific information concerning the
scope of the written test for candidates to prepare properly for the test.
Of the following, the CHIEF limitation on giving information to prospective
candidates is that
    A. candidates sometimes interpret the scope, as defined, differently from the
examiner, and conflicts arise
    B. some candidates who are not familiar with some of the fields listed will not
file for the examination
    C. the board of examiners may not be able to arrive at a decision on what
fields should be tested
    D. the examination will not be a proper test of candidates' abilities as they
will know in advance the areas to be tested
    E. the examiner assigned to prepare the examination may find himself
unduly restricted in test scope

48. It has been recommended that explicit information concerning appeal   48.____
procedures be made available to all candidates.
To put this recommendation into effect would be
    A. *desirable*, primarily because candidates will have a better understanding
of the procedures of the board of examiners
    B. *undesirable*, primarily because it would encourage more candidates to
appeal
    C. *desirable*, primarily because it would encourage greater confidence in the
selection procedure
    D. *undesirable*, primarily because there is no point in making information
about these procedures public as only appellants are interested
    E. *desirable*, primarily because this would tend to standardize the appeal
process, making it more efficient for both the appellants and the board of
examiners

49. In reviewing the experience record of a candidate for a supervisory position, 49.____
an examiner decides that he should give credit for the candidate's contributions
to the improvement of educational conditions in the school system.
This decision is MOST justified on the basis that
    A. this practice has been satisfactory in industrial firms, which seek to place
       a premium on administrative or supervisory ability
    B. such contributions constitute a reliable index of current professional
       growth and future promise
    C. recognition of successful experience in any teaching, administrative, or
       supervisory situation is a matter of equity
    D. such contributions were not require in the normal line of duty
    E. this is an important way in which this type of work can be encouraged

50. In the course of planning for a series of individual interview tests for a given 50.____
license, it is decided to rate applicants on a number of traits.
The MOST important consideration to be borne in mind in such planning is that
the traits selected should
    A. be carefully defined
    B. include those which research has demonstrated to be characteristic of
       good teachers generally
    C. be objectively measurable
    D. not overlap
    E. be weighted in terms of their relative importance

KEY (CORRECT ANSWERS)

1.	A	11.	D	21.	B	31.	A	41.	D
2.	B	12.	A	22.	B	32.	D	42.	D
3.	D	13.	A	23.	C	33.	D	43.	A
4.	E	14.	C	24.	C	34.	A	44.	E
5.	E	15.	C	25.	E	35.	B	45.	D
6.	C	16.	C	26.	D	36.	A	46.	A
7.	E	17.	B	27.	E	37.	E	47.	E
8.	B	18.	B	28.	D	38.	D	48.	C
9.	B	19.	B	29.	A	39.	D	49.	B
10.	C	20.	C	30.	B	40.	C	50.	D

TEST 2

Each question or incomplete statement is followed by several suggested answers or completions. Select the one that BEST answers the question or completes the statement. *PRINT THE LETTER OF THE CORRECT ANSWER IN THE SPACE AT THE RIGHT.*

1. In the administration of a teacher-selection program, the standardization of qualifications is important PRIMARILY because it

    A. eliminates the need for comparing candidates for teaching positions with each other

    B. enables examiners to eliminate subjective judgment as a factor in the selection process

    C. makes the task of comparing candidates easier and more reliable

    D. provides a basis for the development of sound teacher-education programs

    E. tends to dissuade lower-ranking college graduates from applying for available positions

1.____

2. An examiner has the task of evaluating the teaching experience of candidates who have served only as student-teachers.
Of the following sources, the one which would be of the MOST value to him in making the evaluations is the

    A. confidential ratings of critic-teachers

    B. candidates' ratings on a written test of teaching methods

    C. course grades they received

    D. candidates' written statements describing their successes and failures as student-teachers

    E. written comments of the principal in the school where their student-teaching was performed

2.____

3. Two assistant examiners who have been assigned to prepare the outline for the essay section of an examination for principal of a high school disagree over the form of the proposed test. One wants five long essays while the other wants thirty short essays.
The one of the following considerations which would tend to influence your decision in favor of the FIRST choice is that a principal should have

    A. a fine sense of discrimination   B. considerable organizing ability

    C. a good cultural background   D. the ability to reason logically

    E. a good command of language

3.____

4. You are preparing a written test for the selection of high school social science teachers. The test is designed to measure their knowledge of a specified area of content.
Once the items have been completed and edited, you should

    A. administer the test to a group of social science teachers of known capabilities to derive evaluative data

    B. ask a committee of experts in the field to examine the items to determine their validity

4.____

C. administer the test to the candidates and eliminate those items which are not reliable
D. check the items against texts used in teaching the course to make sure they have valid teaching content
E. administer the test to the candidates and eliminate those items which are not valid

5. In constructing objective-type tests for the purpose of selecting educational personnel, the multiple-choice type item is effective PRIMARILY because it

5._____

A. is familiar to the testee because of widespread usage
B. is reasonably free from the guessing element
C. constitutes a superior measure of verbal memory
D. is simple to construct in such a way that several responses appear plausible
E. is well adapted to the measurement of understanding and discrimination

6. To give "face-validity" to items of a written test, the examiner should

6._____

A. avoid use of items that attempt to forecast rather than measure acquired knowledge
B. disguise aptitude items by achievement content
C. emphasize local practice and reduce the weight of broad generalizations
D. frame questions so as to avoid insularity in content and philosophy
E. utilize the names of schools, localities, and persons generally known by candidates

7. The following practices have been recommended at various times to the board of education as ways to increase the number of applicants for licenses who are not residents of the city.
Of these, the practice that is likely to be MOST feasible is that the board of examiners should

7._____

A. change the character of its written tests so as to make it possible for out-of-town candidates who have not been coached for these tests to have an advantage over local candidates who have been coached
B. conduct and complete in July and August of each year license examinations especially designed for out-of-town teaches who are taking summer session courses in the city
C. conduct its experience tests in such a manner as to give more weight to regular teaching experience outside of the city than to local experience as substitute teacher
D. conduct its written and other tests in any city or college center in the United States at which twenty or more persons apply
E. schedule examinations during vacation periods and plan each examination so that out-of-town candidates can complete all examination procedures during a single two-day stay in the city

8. The board of education should increase its efforts to induce persons residing   8.____
outside of the city to apply for teaching licenses in the city MAINLY because
   A. an increase in the number of applicants will of itself make it possible to
      enforce higher standards of competence
   B. diversification within any teaching staff with respect to the general
      background, training, and experience of its members is salutary
   C. out-of-towners are less likely to have "crammed" for the license
      examinations and, as a result, their ratings would tend to be more valid
      than those achieved by local applicants
   D. the available local supply of competent applicants is inadequate for most
      licenses
   E. there is a strong presumption that any person who wishes to teach in a
      community other than the one in which he was reared or trained is
      possessed of enterprise, adaptability, and other qualities desirable in a
      teacher

9. The board of education is about to conduct interview tests for applicants for a   9.____
certain teaching license.
To meet the requirement of competitiveness, the MOST important
consideration to observe is that the
   A. entire record of the tests must be open to public inspection so that any
      interested party may satisfy himself that the same standards were applied
      to all applicants
   B. number of examining panels employed be reduced to a minimum, that, so
      far as possible, all applicants be asked the same questions, and that, if
      this is not possible, the test material used be of comparable difficulty for
      all applicants
   C. qualities measured by the test must be reasonably relevant to the position
      sought and must be precisely defined
   D. ratings on each item must be justified by objective data duly recorded by
      each of the examiners
   E. tests must conform to measures or standards which are sufficiently
      objective to be capable of being challenged or reviewed by other
      examiners of equal ability and experience

10. Of the common reasons which may disqualify a candidate for a teaching   10.____
license in a physical and/or medical examination, the LEAST important is:
   A. The possibility that the health or safety of students may be endangered
   B. Inability to complete the normal period of service
   C. Undesirable or unsettling influence on children
   D. Inability to render the quality of service normally required
   E. The possibility of frequent or prolonged absences

11. Interview tests are being conducted for license as teacher of common   11.____
branch subjects in elementary schools. Each examining panel consists of two
elementary school principals and a speech expert. All of the examiners have
had considerable experience in interviewing applicants and are known to be
competent in this work. The topic that the applicants are asked to discuss is an
aspect of the teaching of the language arts in the present elementary school
program. Each test is scheduled to least from 15 to 20 minutes. Each member
of the examining panel is to rate all aspects of the applicants' performance.
Under the circumstances, the factor for which the test is likely to achieve a
MOST valid appraisal is that of the applicants'
    A. general fitness   B. knowledge of subject matter
    C. overall personality   D. reasoning ability
    E. speech

12. Many precautions must be taken in order to assure a reasonably accurate   12.____
demonstration of a candidate's teaching ability through direct work with
learners.
The LEAST important of these is to make certain that the candidate has an
opportunity to
    A. observe the class he is to teach several times prior to his teaching
    B. learn a day in advance the area of work for which he will be responsible
    C. review the textbook which the class has been using
    D. learn what area has already been covered by the teacher whose place he
       is taking
    E. study the lesson plan of the teacher whose work he is to take

13. In devising a test to determine the competence of teachers, the one of the   13.____
following skills with which you would be LEAST concerned is skill in
    A. directing discussion
    B. handling behavior problems
    C. identifying pupil needs
    D. providing for individual differences
    E. selection of instructional materials

14. A recommendation has been made that an agency be set up within the   14.____
board of education, apart from the board of examiners, for the sole purpose of
dealing with all appeals by candidates from examination ratings from inception
to conclusion.
Of the following comments for an against the acceptance of this
recommendation, the one which is MOST valid is that it is
    A. *undesirable*, primarily because, before the appeal goes to a review body,
       the examiner responsible for the rating should be permitted to justify his
       rating
    B. *desirable*, primarily because no examiner will be in a position to pass
       upon an appeal from a rating he gave
    C. *undesirable*, primarily because the appeal process is an integral part of
       the selection process and should not, in the first instance, at least, be
       divorced from it

D. *desirable*, primarily because the handling of appeals will be expedited
E. *undesirable*, primarily because the handling of appeals will be needlessly complicated

15. Of the following administrative devices for preventing conflict within a board of examiners with respect to the extent of the authority of each of the examiners, the MOST effective, as far as is practicable, is to

    15.____

    A. assign all related work to the same examiner
    B. have the chairman of the board administratively responsible for resolving all disagreements
    C. set up a committee of senior members of the board to determine policy
    D. have the chairman of the board review examiners' assignments periodically
    E. assign wok to the examiners on a rotation basis

16. Of the following, the MOST effective method of interesting qualified persons not already employed in the city public school system to apply for the directorship of a special subject, e.g., home economics, music, health education, in the city school system, would be for the board of examiners to

    16.____

    A. obtain from the Office of Education at Washington, D.C. a list of directors and supervisors of the special subject throughout the United States, and to mail circulars of announcement directly to such persons
    B. place advertisements in appropriate professional journals, giving full details concerning the scope of the examination and making it clear that applications from out-of-town applicants will be especially welcome
    C. request local universities specializing in offering graduate courses for out-of-town educators to furnish the board of examiners with lists of the names of persons preparing for supervisory positions in the specialty, and to circularize such persons
    D. send a representative to an appropriate professional convention to provide publicity for the examination and to search out and talk to prospective applicants
    E. send letters to the school superintendents in other cities, asking them to call the attention of qualified persons in their schools to the city's need and to the prospective examination to be held for the position

17. In analyzing the discriminatory power of a test, one item shows that equal proportions of high-scoring and low-scoring persons have succeeded on it. In general, this indicates that the item

    17.____

    A. contributes to the reliability of the test
    B. has a high discriminatory coefficient
    C. does not contribute to score differentiation
    D. has no validity because it is of doubtful reliability
    E. is probably ambiguous

18. A board of qualified persons is to assist an examiner by conducting oral examinations of a group of candidates.
Of the following, the examiner's BEST procedure with the board members would be to
    A. provide each member of the board with a detailed description of the duties of the position and a list of specific subject-matter questions which cover the entire field
    B. allow them to structure each interview s they wish in order to stimulate optimum interaction between candidates and interviewers
    C. provide each member of the board with a statement of the behaviors he should observe and suggested standard questions designed to provide opportunities for observing these behaviors
    D. call them together for an advance briefing at which the correct answers the examiner wants them to elicit from each candidate will be discussed and provide them with a rank-order listing of the candidates on the written test
    E. provide the board with a detailed list of specific questions to fit into any situation so the interviews will not lag or be open to possible interviewer bias

18.____

19. On a test consisting of 200 items, taken by 80 persons, an individual scored at the 60th percentile.
This means, in general, that
    A. he answered 120 questions correctly
    B. his score surpassed those attained by 48 persons
    C. higher scores than his were attained by 48 persons
    D. his score was more than six-tenths of one standard deviation from the mean
    E. he answered 80 items correctly

19.____

20. In order to achieve objectivity in the selection of education personnel, it is MOST important that
    A. only those dimensions be tested which are known to be related to teacher effectiveness
    B. testing for factual knowledge only be avoided
    C. the attributes deemed essential be clearly set forth
    D. the candidates be tested for factual knowledge as far as possible
    E. the types of tests to be used be clearly set forth

20.____

21. Skill in written test construction is BEST demonstrated by the
    A. ability to apply knowledge of scoring techniques
    B. manner in which statistical techniques are applied
    C. ability to maintain a constructively critical attitude toward the facets of the area to be covered
    D. manner in which the materials to be tested are converted into test items
    E. ability to standardize test items

21.____

22. It has been proposed that a curvilinear relationship be set up between varying lengths of similar experience and credit for that experience.
This proposal would tend to be acceptable if it is true that
   A. a single formula for scoring different kinds of experience could be developed
   B. people benefit more from some kinds of experience than from other kinds
   C. experience cannot be scored objectively and, consequently, corrective factors must be introduced
   D. people benefit more from their initial years of experience than from later experience
   E. prediction of job success should be based on recent experience

22.____

23. After two sessions of preliminary training, six panels, each consisting of three assistant examiners, interviewed applicants for the license of teacher of mathematics in junior high schools. Each panel interviewed six applicants. All applicants were rated numerically with a maximum of 20 points and with 12 as a passing grade. The results were:

23.____

Panel	Passed	Rejected	Rated Doubtful
A	4	2	0
B	6	0	0
C	2	3	1
D	5	1	0
E	2	4	0
F	3	3	0
	22	13	1

Of the following, the MOST suitable procedure for the examiner-in-charge to follow would be:
   A. Arrange for re-examination by new panels of all applicants who failed or were rated doubtful
   B. Compare the interview test ratings of these applicants with their ratings in the written test and with the official reports on the quality of their services, if any, and recall for a second interview test those applicants in whose cases the examiner-in-charge discovers obvious discrepancies
   C. Personally retest the applicants who were not passed by Panels C, E, and F to make sure that these panels were not unduly severe, and make appropriate revisions of their ratings if justified by the performance of the applicants in the retests
   D. Present these figures to the assistant examiners for appropriate discussion and consideration, and, unless there is a disposition on the part of one or more panels to reconsider their ratings, he should accept all ratings as final for that test
   E. Statistically work out a coefficient reflecting the degree of leniency or severity of each panel. Apply these coefficients to the ratings of all applicants.

24. Of the following test parts of an examination for teachers, the type of test
    for which rating on a qualifying, rather than competitive, basis can be BEST
    justified is the _____ test.
    A. classroom teaching   B. interview
    C. medical   D. speech
    E. written essay

24.____

25. When an applicant has been rated "unsatisfactory" in a personal test, such
    as an interview or a teaching test, it is the practice of some examining officials
    to prepare for the applicant, as part of the record of the test, a separate
    statement setting forth in detail the reason for his rejection.
    Such a statement is MOST worthwhile if it serves the purpose of
    A. indicating to the applicant the areas in which self-improvement is
       desirable
    B. protecting the examining authority in the event of litigation
    C. providing the applicant with a concrete basis for formulating an appeal
    D. requiring the examiner who conducted the test to crystallize his thinking
       and justify the rating
    E. satisfying the applicant that his rejection was justified

25.____

26. For the board of examiners to plan its work schedule so as to provide a
    constant backlog of work would be
    A. undesirable, primarily because it is almost impossible to plan for this type
       of backlog
    B. desirable, primarily because the board would be in a better position to
       change its plans if no deadlines were involved
    C. undesirable, primarily because lists of persons eligible for appointment
       would not be ready when required
    D. desirable, primarily because the procedure would tend to insure continuity
       of work flow
    E. undesirable, primarily because the board would be under constant
       pressure to get work out

26.____

27. Of the following statements, the one which BEST describes factory analysis
    is that factor analysis
    A. is a means of determining the abilities which cover the whole range of
       human capacity
    B. applied to a group of variables indicates the degree to which they are
       independent of each other
    C. is a method which has been suggested to replace present methods
       employed for purposes of prediction
    D. applied to complex processes such as organization and integration of
       materials, yields valid evaluations
    E. provides an adequate substitute for the psychological analysis of mental
       processes

27.____

28. In the preparation of valid examinations for selection or advancement of teachers, the MOST essential ingredient among the following is: 28.____
    A. Careful and detailed administrative review within the examining agency of the final draft of the questions to be used in the examination
    B. A job analysis or description of duties of the positions involved
    C. Collaboration of persons in the preparation of examinations who are thoroughly familiar with the types of jobs being filled
    D. Preliminary trial and statistical analysis of the questions to be used in the examination by persons administratively responsible for filling the positions
    E. Production of standard directions and copy for administration of examinations to the candidates

29. To ascertain the probability with which the assignment of papers to two raters, A and B, represents a random or chance allocation of the papers. the MOST suitable of the following statistical measures to use is the 29.____
    A. average standard error of each of the distributions of ratings of the two raters
    B. closeness of fit to the normal curve of the combined distributions of the scores given by the two raters
    C. coefficient of correlation between the scores given by the two raters
    D. critical ratio of the difference between the distributions of the ratings of the two raters
    E. skewness of the combined distribution

30. You have only one form of a test of 200 items to be used in selecting teachers. 30.____
    In experimenting with it to determine its reliability, the BEST method to use would be to
    A. obtain the bi-serial correlation of each item with the total score on the test
    B. correlate scores of a norm group on the first 100 items with those obtained on the second 100 items (second half)
    C. rank the items in order of difficulty, split into odd-numbered and even-numbered, and correlate scores thus obtained
    D. correlate the scores from two administrations to a control group a week apart
    E. split the items according to odd-numbered ones and even-numbered ones, and correlate the two scores thus obtained

31. Observed teaching performance should not be the determining factor in teacher selection PRIMARILY because 31.____
    A. effectiveness in teaching can vary greatly according to size of class, level of student intelligence, and other factors not always properly weighted
    B. one or two "perfect" or "near perfect" performances do not reveal potentialities as to skill, understanding, or personality
    C. many teachers do not demonstrate their most effective teaching when under observation by administrators or examiners

D. one or two teaching performances cannot possibly include all or most of the important facts of good teaching for a term or semester

E. temporary illness or incapacity may prevent best performance at the time of observation

32. A young woman about to graduate from a state teachers college in a nearby state applies to an examiner for advice. She states that her family will soon move to the city. She would like to apply for a license as teacher of common branch subjects in elementary schools for which applications are being accepted at present. However, she is concerned over the fact that, as a condition of her admission to the state teachers college, she subscribed to an agreement to teach in that state for a minimum of two years.
Knowing that the license is usually valid for three years and that it normally takes a year to publish the eligible list, the examiner should

A. advise her to obtain a position in the schools of the state in which she now resides and to apply for the city license in the examination to be held a year hence

B. explain to her that she may apply at once for the city license

C. make it clear to her that the agreement she entered into is no longer binding since, as soon as she is graduated, it will not be enforceable

D. suggest that she serve the two years required as she agreed, and to apply in the city after completing her obligation

E. urge her to seek a release from her agreement and to return to the board of examiners to file an application if she is successful

Questions 33-34.

DIRECTIONS: Questions 33 and 34 are to be answered on the basis of the following situation.

An examiner is puzzled by the fact that when two of his most trusted assistant examiners work together in conducting an oral examination, they agree much better in their ratings for most candidates than do other pairs of assistant examiners, but that, nevertheless, they give widely divergent ratings to a few candidates. In making their ratings, all assistant examiners employ rating guide sheets which the examiner has recently prepared himself after thorough study of more than twenty different rating sheets and review of some seventy books and articles on techniques of rating in the oral interview.

33. Of the following, the MOST probable explanation for the divergent ratings is:

A. One of the assistant examiners is reacting to certain of the candidates much more subjectively than the other assistant examiner.

B. The format of the rating guide sheets does not make adequate provision for careful checking by the assistant examines.

C. The general agreement is due to chance and the rating guide sheets do not, in general, promote objectivity.

D. The ratings of one or both of the assistant examiners are affected by some circumstances external to the interviews themselves, such as fatigue, anxiety over home problems, dissatisfaction with job outlook, etc.

E. The two assistant examines are interpreting their rating guide sheets differently on some points which are crucial in rating some candidates.

34. Of the following steps, the one which is MOST likely to be profitable for the examiner to take in an effort to correct this situation is:

   34.____

   A. Assign a third assistant examiner to work with the pair so as to identify which one of them deviates most often from his usual standards and why these deviations occur.
   B. Confer with each of the assistant examiners separately, take careful notes while each gives in detail his reasons for his rating of a candidate on whom the two were in marked disagreement, and then compare the notes taken to identify discrepancies.
   C. Hold a conference with the two assistant examiners, describe the situation to them frankly and objectively, and tell them to resolve their differences.
   D. Recall the candidates in whose ratings the disagreements have been found and examine them himself in order to resolve the disagreements.
   E. Rewrite the rating guide sheets after having examined them carefully to discover the possible causes for the disagreements which have been noted.

35. Fewest candidates would probably be discouraged from applying to take a scheduled examination for an elementary school license by the statement that

   35.____

   A. background knowledge as well as the fields of knowledge taught in the elementary school will be tested in the examination
   B. poor speech has been the major cause of failure on the examination in the past
   C. teaches who can meet high standards are preferred
   D. the examination will be composed entirely of objective test questions
   E. the examination will include a competitive performance test in music and art

36. In the development of standards for evaluation of non-teaching work experience of candidates, the one of the following on which MAJOR emphasis should be placed is the

   36.____

   A. closeness of relationship between non-teaching experiences and the teaching position under consideration
   B. elements of persistence and dependability in these work experiences
   C. relationship between scholastic preparation and types of employment obtained
   D. social status of such non-teaching experiences
   E. variety of non-teaching experience

37. In the selection of teacher personnel, the personal interview should be structured so as to reveal PRIMARILY

   37.____

   A. the ability of the candidate to stand up under emotional tensions
   B. the candidate's degree of insight into himself
   C. whether or not the candidate has any emotional problems
   D. the candidate's native intelligence
   E. the candidate's personal biases and prejudices

38. In the course of an examination for license as principal of a vocational high school, a total of 14 applicants appear before the entire board of examiners for interview tests in a period of three successive days. The examiners make running notes of the substance of the applicants' presentation and responses. In addition, wire recordings are made.
Of the following, these wire recordings are likely to be of GREATEST value in
   A. aiding the member of the board designated to draft an official statement of the reasons for the rejection in the case of any applicant who failed in the test
   B. determining the accuracy of any allegations made by an applicant as to the substance and manner of his responses
   C. helping any member of the board who is not able to recall the details of a specific interview
   D. justifying the action of the board in granting a licenses to an applicant in the event that this action is questioned by other educational authorities
   E. settling disagreements among the members of the board as to how an applicant should be rated

38.____

39. The group oral test has been increasingly utilized during recent years in examinations MAINLY because
   A. the applicants come away from the examination with a greater degree of confidence in the operation of the merit system
   B. it has been found possible by this method to examine a larger number of applicants per time unit
   C. the group test has been found to be a valuable means of checking on the reliability of the individual interview test
   D. it is believed that, by this type of test, certain traits may be more accurately evaluated than by any other form of examination
   E. the situation provided in the group test is more realistic and more natural than in the case of an individual test

39.____

40. A significant trend in aptitude and achievement tests is
   A. allowing a choice of questions rather than having all examinees answer all questions
   B. the arrangement by different publishers to use the same norms population
   C. the inclusion of a larger number of shorter questions to increase reliability
   D. setting time limits so that most examinees can finish
   E. the use of scores on fewer items as a basis of separate interpretation

40.____

41. To determine appropriate training and experience qualification requirements for elementary school principals at the entrance level, the MOST effective of the following methods is to
   A. get questionnaire responses from representative samples of successful and unsuccessful elementary school principals as to their status in these items at the time when they became principals
   B. check national surveys of characteristics of persons employed in such positions and from these make the necessary determinations

41.____

C. have a committee of principals meet with the board of examiners and, through discussion, arrive at acceptable standards
D. check the membership roster of the National Education Association's division of elementary school administrators to determine norms for acceptable training and experience
E. seek the judgments of professors of education engaged in the preparation of school administrators

Questions 42-43.

DIRECTIONS: Questions 42 and 43 are to be answered on the basis of the following information.

An examiner reviews the scores achieved by 260 candidates on an objective test of teaching methods composed of 15 five-choice items. The test has been scored by the standard formula to correct for guessing. The examiner finds that the highest raw score attained is 147, and the lowest raw score is 58. The mean raw score is 100.2, the standard deviation is 14.3, and the distribution is not significantly skewed. The examiner is aware that most candidates have completed their pre-service preparation in institutions which give course marks or grades on a percentage scale for which 70 is passing. His review of the candidates' credentials and his judgment on their raw score performance convinces him that about 80 percent of the candidates should pass the objective test. The examiner has responsibility for determining the form in which individual performance on the test will be reported to each candidate.

42. The formula used to score this test was: Raw Score equals Rights minus   42.____
    A. 1/5 Wrongs   B. Wrongs
    C. Omits minus 1/5 Wrongs   D. Wrongs plus 30
    E. 1/4 Wrongs

43. The examiner should set the passing mark at a raw score of APPROXIMATELY   43.____
    A. 70   B. 78   C. 85   D. 93   E. 100

44. During a meeting of the board of examiners, the chairman stated that it is   44.____
    of utmost importance that we communicate to assistant examiners the
    desirability of achieving our goals and the importance of the jobs they are
    performing toward reaching these.
    In general, the MOST important result of adopting this point of view would be
    that
    A. assistant examiners would be better prepared to take over the duties of
       an examiner when necessary
    B. avenues of communication would be more clearly defined
    C. assistant examiners would be in a better position to evaluate the
       objectives of the board
    D. less supervision of the work of an assistant examiner would be required
    E. assistant examiners would know what the general objectives of the board
       are

45. It has been decided to set up a special license for the principalship of   45.____
    elementary schools located in high delinquency areas. In the rating of
    candidates for this license, special attention should be given to the candidate's
    A. emotional stability, as measured by one of the better-known paper-and-
       pencil tests of personality adjustment
    B. performance on some type of projective technique
    C. reaction in a stress interview
    D. record of experience in a similar situation
    E. score on the Minnesota Attitude Inventory Test

46. The distribution of scores on the written test for a teacher of common branches   46.____
    in the elementary schools is skewed considerably in the direction of low scores.
    Of the following, the SOUNDEST interpretation of this finding is that the
    A. candidates were not able, for the most part, to finish the test
    B. correlation between test score and teaching performance will probably be
       low
    C. reliability of the test was attenuated by outside influences
    D. test did not discriminate among the best candidates, probably because
       the test was too easy
    E. test is not homogeneous in nature, either with respect to difficulty or with
       respect to content

47. During a periodic review of appeal procedures, the question is raised as to   47.____
    whether either representative answers or perfect answers should or should not
    be shown to candidates.
    This question should be decided in favor of
    A. *showing* this information to candidates primarily because many appeals
       would not be made if candidates knew what had been expected of them
    B. *not showing* this information to candidates primarily because candidates
       tend to interpret their answers on the basis of the representative answer
       in order to make a case
    C. *showing* this information to candidates primarily because the time
       examiners spend reviewing papers with candidates would be sharply
       reduced
    D. *not showing* this information to candidates primarily because candidates
       may question the correctness of the representative answers
    E. *showing* this information to candidates primarily because, without
       something with which answers can be compared, a meaningful appeal
       cannot be made

48. In the conduct of speech tests, the MOST important of the following   48.____
    considerations is that
    A. applicants be given the opportunity of silently reviewing in advance of the
       test the material on which they are to be tested
    B. a record be made in phonetic script of the applicant's errors and
       shortcomings in speech
    C. provision should be made for an unrehearsed talk or free conversation
       with the examiner

D. standardized speech tests be employed
E. the test material used include a substantial number of words frequently mispronounced

49. The BEST way to reduce the errors caused by variations in the marking standards of raters of essay questions is for the supervising examiner to

49.____

    A. arrange for sessions at which marking keys may be developed, applied, and discussed
    B. instruct the raters beforehand as to the number of papers to be passed by each rater on each question
    C. read and re-grade any papers for which ratings appear to be out of line
    D. reduce the distribution of the scores given by each rater to the form of the normal curve through the use of the T score or one of the other standard score techniques
    E. transmute the raw scores into percents of maximum score

50. In the process of appraising a teacher candidate, LEAST consideration should be given to

50.____

    A. his character and personality ratings
    B. the quality of his professional experience
    C. the extent of his participation in community activities
    D. the quality of his professional preparation
    E. his understanding of and interest in children

KEY (CORRECT ANSWERS)

1.	C	11.	E	21.	D	31.	A	41.	A
2.	A	12.	E	22.	D	32.	B	42.	E
3.	B	13.	A	23.	D	33.	E	43.	C
4.	A	14.	C	24.	C	34.	B	44.	D
5.	E	15.	A	25.	A	35.	D	45.	D
6.	B	16.	D	26.	D	36.	B	46.	D
7.	E	17.	C	27.	B	37.	B	47.	E
8.	B	18.	C	28.	C	38.	B	48.	C
9.	E	19.	B	29.	D	39.	D	49.	A
10.	B	20.	C	30.	C	40.	D	50.	C

EXAMINATION SECTION
TEST 1

DIRECTIONS: Each question or incomplete statement is followed by several suggested answers or completions. Select the one that *BEST* answers the question or completes the statement. *PRINT THE LETTER OF THE CORRECT ANSWER IN THE SPACE AT THE RIGHT.*

1. The Coleman Report, EQUALITY OF EDUCATIONAL OPPORTUNITY devoted a major section to achievement in the public schools.
   Which of the following was NOT among the findings of the report?

   A. With some exceptions, average minority pupil scores were distinctly lower than average white pupil scores.
   B. The schools provide little opportunity for minority groups to overcome their initial deficiency.
   C. Black students in the South score below black students in the North.
   D. There was no notable difference between scores of various ethnic groups.

   1._____

2. Which of the following did the Coleman Report, EQUALITY OF EDUCATIONAL OPPOR-TUNITY, find to be MOST significantly related to pupil achievement?

   A. Degree of parent participation
   B. Socio-economic background of the students
   C. Quality of the curriculum
   D. Class size

   2._____

3. The one of the following that is the CHIEF obstacle to establishing a system of measuring teacher competence is that

   A. tenure provisions make it difficult to get rid of incompetent teachers
   B. methods of training teachers vary widely
   C. the ability of pupils varies widely from district to district
   D. there is neither a common definition of competence nor a substantial empirical base for building one

   3._____

4. Benjamin S. Bloom is credited with having influenced attitudes toward day care and planning of day care programs. In his writing, as exemplified by his book STABILITY AND CHANGE IN HUMAN CHARACTERISTICS, he has

   A. stressed the need to make day care an integral part of the school program
   B. recommended a structureed approach for preschool children
   C. pointed to the family as the major influence and the preschool years as the crucial ones for mental development
   D. stressed the need for thorough evaluation of all day care centers

   4._____

5. The one of the following which has been LEAST emphasized by the *alternative school movement* in recent years has been the need to

   A. provide special education for the handicapped
   B. be more responsive to change
   C. be more responsive to communities
   D. be more humane to students and teachers

   5._____

6. Efforts to improve inner city school districts are often handicapped by the absence of   6.____
adequate housing, health care, recreation facilities and other social services in the area.
Of the following, the federal program aimed at coordinating and supporting the broad
spectrum of urban services in a given area is

   A. Housing and Redevelopment
   B. Title III of the Elementary and Secondary Education Act
   C. Urban Renewal
   D. Model Cities

7. The term *pupil mobility factor* refers to the   7.____

   A. problems encountered in zoning pupils into other than neighborhood schools
   B. pupils who leave their schools to go to other schools
   C. unwillingness of parents to move once their children have started school
   D. transportation problems related to educational parks

8. Which of the following statements is INCORRECT regarding publication of scores of the   8.____
city-wide reading tests in the city?

   A. Law mandates that the reading tests be given.
   B. Publication of poor results often raises children's anxiety.
   C. Percentage scores related to national norms are easily understood and interpreted
by most parents.
   D. Scores on these reading tests can be used as the basis for planning reading pro-
grams.

9. Which of the following statements concerning school boards in the United States is the   9.____
MOST accurate?

   A. The decisions of school boards are often reached only after bargaining and com-
promising.
   B. Most school board members today receive salaries for their services.
   C. Most of the activities of school boards are mandatory rather than discretionary.
   D. States are now beginning to set educational qualifications for board membership.

10. Which of the following statements concerning federal aid to education is MOST valid?   10.____

   A. Federal aid to education will result in loss of control by the states over their
schools.
   B. The tax system of the federal government is generally more efficient and equitable
than those of state and local governments.
   C. Aid to nonpublic schools has not been an issue in the debate on federal aid to education.
   D. The strong support given by the states to vocational education has been used as
an argument against federal aid.

11. Which of the following is a well-known proponent of the *comprehensive high school con-*   11.____
cept?

   A. Jerome Bruner   B. James B. Conant
   C. Robert J. Havighurst   D. Hyman Rickover

12. The one of the following which would be LEAST useful in facilitating the learning of edu-   12.____
cable mentally retarded children is

   A. insuring that the child's successful experiences are balanced with unsuccessful experiences

   B. teaching new concepts with an emphasis on drill rather than on transfer to a new situation

   C. conducting a day-to-day program aimed at the completion of easy short range goals

   D. eliminating school experiences that tend to cause frustration

13. According to research on learning as applied to the education of educable mentally   13.____
retarded children, which one of the following practices should NOT be used by a teacher
of such children?

   A. They should be asked to learn and retain materials in very small units or sequences.

   B. Massed practice, rather than distributed practice should be used to facilitate learning.

   C. Devices should be found to encourage the children to focus on the material to be learned.

   D. They should be taught how to memorize by repeating many times what they are asked to retain.

14. The one of the following whose work has provided the MAJOR theoretical basis for the   14.____
open classroom is

   A. Frederick Froebel   B. John Holt
   C. Maria Montessori   D. Jean Piaget

15. In introducing the *open classroom* into a school system, the one of the following which is   15.____
necessary in order for the *open classroom* to function effectively and become a successful educational experience is that it should

   A. be implemented in larger, rather than smaller schools

   B. use advisors from inside the school rather than from outside the school, working directly with the teachers in implementing the school's goals

   C. redefine slowly, rather than all at once, the roles of the administrator, teachers,and children

   D. involve, from its inception, the whole school and the whole school day

16. The one of the following concepts which is NOT specified in the Bereiter and Englemann   16.____
approach for preschool education of the disadvantaged is

   A. direct instruction   B. discovery conditioning
   C. sensory stimulation   D. verbal processes

17. When a teacher's focus of interest is on the response patterns of the pupil in a given sit-   17.____
uation, she is, knowingly or unknowingly, using the *concept* of _____ learning.

   A. classical   B. operant   C. signal   D. type-S

18. In his book, BEYOND FREEDOM AND DIGNITY, B. F. Skinner implied that   18.____

    A. to control or change human behavior, it is necessary only to control or change the environment
    B. since man is an autonomous agent, prediction and control of his behavior are impossible
    C. man's behavior is controlled by his wishes, perceptions, and ideas
    D. we need less rather than more *intentional* control in order to survive

19. In the Guilford structure-of-intellect model, which one of the following operations is considered to be the MOST closely related to creative thinking in children?   19.____

    A. Evaluation B   B. Cognition
    C. Convergent thinking   D. Divergent thinking

20. Arthur Jensen has hypothesized two genotypically distinct basic processes of learning. They are associative learning (Level I) and conceptual learning (Level II). His theory about the relationship of these two processes of learning to socio-economic status (SES) is that middle SES children are _____ to low SES children in _____ learning.   20.____

    A. superior; associative
    B. superior; conceptual
    C. equal; conceptual
    D. inferior; associative

21. Piaget has conceptualized four basic stages of intellectual development. Which of the following reflects the PROPER *order* of these different stages?   21.____

    A. Formal Operations, Concrete Operations, Sensorimotor, Preoperational
    B. Concrete Operations, Formal Operations, Sensorimotor, Preoperational
    C. Sensorimotor, Preoperational, Concrete Operations, Formal Operations
    D. Preoperational, Sensorimotor, Concrete Operations, Formal Operations

22. Which one of the following intellectual tasks would be the MOST advanced according to Piaget's theory and observations?   22.____

    A. Conserve quantities
    B. Construct and use propositions
    C. Reciprocate logical relations
    D. Understand superordinate-subordinate classes

23. According to Christopher Jencks, evaluation of a school should be based PRIMARILY on whether or not   23.____

    A. the students and teachers find it a satisfying place to be
    B. school reform has long-term cognitive effects on the students
    C. school reform has any significant effect on the degree of inequality among the students as adults
    D. the school budget, its policies, and its teachers have any effect on the cognitive inequality among students

24. The one of the following which is the MAJOR aim of computer-managed instruction is   24.____

    A. elimination of grade levels
    B. decrease in expenditure for books and other instructional materials
    C. reduction in number of teachers needed
    D. individualization of instruction

25. Which one of the following statements describes the fundamental difficulty in the evaluation of teacher behavior for certification purposes?   25.____

    A. Specific teacher behaviors do not sum to a measure of competent teaching.
    B. The specific behaviors to be measured are too numerous.
    C. Behavioral objectives exist at only one level of specificity.
    D. Behavioral objectives cannot be logically derived from a theory of teaching.

KEY (CORRECT ANSWERS)

1.	D		11.	B
2.	B		12.	A
3.	D		13.	B
4.	C		14.	D
5.	A		15.	C
6.	D		16.	C
7.	B		17.	B
8.	C		18.	A
9.	A		19.	D
10.	B		20.	B

21. C
22. B
23. A
24. D
25. A

TEST 2

1. The MOST important role that evaluation could play in a competency-based teacher education program is that of   1.____

    A. assessing teacher education students for the appropriateness of their attitudes about children
    B. examining curriculum, physical facilities, library, personnel, and other resources
    C. conducting follow-up studies of teachers on the job in order to produce desired changes in teacher education programs
    D. developing state-monitored certification agencies

2. Which of the following ways of assessing a teacher trainee's competencies are *likely* to be ACCEPTABLE in a competency-based teacher certification program?   2.____

    A. Microteaching and simulation tests *only*
    B. Microteaching and paper-and-pencil tests *only*
    C. Simulation tests and paper-and-pencil tests *only*
    D. Microteaching, simulation tests, and paper-and-pencil tests

3. State education departments are requiring new programs in teacher education to be competency-based in order to gain state approval for certification of graduates of these programs.   3.____
The one of the following which is an ESSENTIAL element for a program to be accredited as competency-based is that the program

    A. include program units developed in module form
    B. be highly individualized
    C. include a teacher center for students' practice teaching
    D. provide for instruments to assess a trainee's performance in the classroom

4. A long-term goal in planning for competency based teacher certification is to certify only teachers who can   4.____

    A. demonstrate acceptable professional attitudes in the classroom
    B. present evidence of general background knowledge, subject matter knowledge and teaching skill
    C. produce specified learning gains for pupils they are to teach
    D. demonstrate that they have participated in a field-centered teacher education program

5. A MAJOR trend in teacher certification policy reflected in *most* state plans for competency-based teacher certification is the   5.____

    A. elimination of permanent certificates and the substitution of renewable certificates
    B. establishment of uniform statewide standards for permanent certification
    C. emphasis on university-based graduate study for permanent certification
    D. elimination of the baccalaureate requirement for provisional certification

6. Which of the following groups of educational personnel are *likely* to be included under competency-based certification? Teachers,   6.____

    A. *only*
    B. and counselors *only*
    C. and administrators *only*
    D. administrators, and counselors

7. The MAJOR obstacle to implementing competency-based teacher certification is the inability to   7.____

    A. develop competency-based teacher education instructional materials and methods
    B. specify the relationship between teacher competencies and measured pupil performance
    C. develop teacher centers for the distribution of instructional modules
    D. persuade taxpayers and legislators of the essential validity of the process

8. Competency-based certification might not be acceptable under the Guidelines on Employee Selection Procedures of the Equal Employment Opportunity Commission if fewer minority group teachers are certified on this basis than would be certified by use of the National Teachers Examination (NTE).   8.____
In order to be acceptable under the Guidelines, competency-based certification would have to demonstrate that

    A. the teachers certified under the competency-based certification are more effective than those certified under the NTE
    B. it yields more reliable assessments of teacher competency than the NTE
    C. the costs of administering competency based certification are lower than the costs of administering the NTE
    D. minority group members have no objection to this procedure

9. An important distinction on certification made in most state plans is that   9.____

    A. the employer and NOT the teacher education institution should certify the teacher
    B. the teacher education institution and NOT the employer should certify the teacher
    C. either the teacher education institution or the employer should certify the teacher
    D. neither the teacher education institution nor the employer snould certify the teacher

10. Assume that the following measures have been suggested to assess teacher competency.   10.____
The one which is the MOST objective is a

    A. judgement as to the clarity with which a teacher presents material
    B. record of the frequency with which a teacher asks questions
    C. record of the frequency with which a teacher asks questions which are at the right difficulty for pupils
    D. record of the extent to which a teacher uses student ideas

11. A MAJOR issue in current teacher education programs is the apparent conflict between advocates of   11.____

    A. a systems-analytic approach and advocates of a humanistic approach
    B. a performance-based approach and advocates of a systems-analytic approach

C. a humanistic approach and advocates of a person-centered approach
D. microteaching and advocates of simulation training

12. Which of the following teacher training techniques has been the BEST example of a *systems approach* to teacher education?   12.____

    A. Field experience in a community agency
    B. Training student teachers to use audio-visual equipment
    C. Assigning student teachers to two or more schools in a system
    D. Microteaching

13. Which of the following would it be essential to include in a systems approach to teacher training?   13.____
    I. Precise specification of the desired teaching behavior and a training program designed to develop this behavior
    II. Measurement of the results of training in terms of behavioral objectives
    III. Feedback to the learner and instructor of measurement results
The correct combination is:

    A. I *only*   B. I and II
    C. II and III   D. I, II, and III

14. Which of the following combinations of approaches to continuing education for teachers is receiving INCREASED emphasis?   14.____

    A. Teacher centers and university graduate courses
    B. Teacher centers and career development centers
    C. Career development centers and university graduate courses
    D. Career development centers, teacher centers, and university graduate courses

15. A recent trend in teacher education is early, direct involvement in the professional roles to be acquired. This trend is BEST demonstrated by the INCREASED emphasis on   15.____

    A. minicourses in the culminating student teaching experience
    B. classroom simulation and sensitivity training laboratories
    C. school and community participation in the design of teacher education programs
    D. the master of arts in teaching program

16. A new approach in teacher effectiveness research is the   16.____

    A. use of simulation techniques to study teacher behavior
    B. description of classroom observations in everyday language
    C. use of pupil gain as the major criterion
    D. application of personaltiy theory to the descriptions of effective teacher behavior

17. Under the Equal Employment Opportunity Act of 1972, sex should NOT normally be an occupational qualification. However, jobs may be restricted to members of one sex when   17.____

    A. prior employment practices can be cited as a precedent
    B. the job involves heavy physical labor (e.g., laborer)
    C. there is a need for authenticity (e.g., female to model women's clothing)
    D. the job requires personal charm (e.g., receptionist)

18. Which of the following is NOT a basic merit system factor in the development of an effec-   18._____
    tive Affirmative Action Plan for women?
    Reviewing

    A. job requirements to assure that unnecessary sex qualifications are eliminated
    B. salary and pay scales to assure that men and women receive equal pay for equal
       work
    C. selection processes to assure that they are bias-free
    D. job performance standards to assure that they will be met by both men and women

19. Of the following, the FIRST step in establishing an effective program to combat discrimi-   19._____
    nation against women in employment in any organization is to

    A. develop a quota system for future employment
    B. obtain top management support for the program
    C. recognize that there is no difference between men and women
    D. determine those jobs for which women are best suited

20. Discrimination in employment because of age, sex, or physical requirements may be   20._____
    defensible if

    A. there are a large number of highly qualified applicants for a job
    B. the requirements represent a bona-fide qualification necessary to fulfill a job prop-
       erly
    C. a change in requirements would be detrimental to long-standing employment poli-
       cies
    D. it can be proved that a change in requirements for employment would so disturb
       present employees that their performance would be impaired

21. The BASIC purpose in developing an Affirmative Action Plan for equal opportunity in   21._____
    employment is to

    A. create new jobs specifically for members of minority groups
    B. accept responsibility for past discriminatory actions
    C. take positive steps to promote equal opportunity
    D. give preferential treatment to minority groups discriminated against in the past

22. Which one of the following steps is NOT advisable in the development of recruitment and   22._____
    upward mobility practices for an Affirmative Action Plan?

    A. Placing special emphasis on the identification and development of sources of
       minority group members and women for positions in which they are currently
       under-represented
    B. Establishing production standards so that those employees who are recruited will
       be fully productive workers within a minimum time period
    C. Providing for the establishment of training and education programs to give employ-
       ees maximum opportunity to advance to their highest potential
    D. Planning for participation in community efforts to improve conditions which affect
       employability and employment opportunities

23. Under Equal Employment Opportunity Commission Guidelines on Employee Selection Procedures, the use of any test which results in a disproportionate number of persons of one race who are appointed or promoted constitutes discrimination unless the test

    23._____

    A. has been validated and has a reliability of .80 or higher
    B. is reliable and differential validity has been proven
    C. is job-related, has been validated, and alternative selection procedures are unavailable
    D. has been validated, has a high degree of reliability, and has equal cut-off scores for minority and non-minority groups

24. According to Equal Employment Opportunity Commission Guidelines on Employee Selection Procedures, *satisfactory* assessment of the utility of a test is defined as

    24._____

    A. testimony by at least two competent authorities that the test is job-related
    B. the cost and feasibility of test administration
    C. a statistically significant relationship between the test and at least one relevant criterion
    D. a relationship between test and criterion that is both statistically significant and practically significant

25. The first and most basic step in the development of a job-related test is to

    25._____

    A. make a job analysis to determine skills, knowledge, and abilities necessary to perform the job
    B. conduct a criterion-validity study to determine how well the test predicts success on the job
    C. prepare an outline for the test plan according to psychological principles
    D. select a sample of subjects for a pilot test representative of the minority population available for the job

---

KEY (CORRECT ANSWERS)

1.	C		11.	A
2.	D		12.	D
3.	D		13.	D
4.	C		14.	B
5.	A		15.	B
6.	D		16.	C
7.	B		17.	C
8.	A		18.	D
9.	D		19.	B
10.	B		20.	B

21.	C
22.	B
23.	C
24.	D
25.	A

EXAMINATION SECTION
TEST 1

DIRECTIONS: Each question or incomplete statement is followed by several suggested answers or completions. Select the one that BEST answers the question or completes the statement. *PRINT THE LETTER OF THE CORRECT ANSWER IN THE SPACE AT THE RIGHT.*

1. Which of the following items of federal legislation was designed to encourage the growth of labor unions and restrain management from interfering with that growth?   1._____

    A. Wagner Act
    B. Taft–Hartley Act
    C. Fair Labor Standards Act
    D. Sherman Antitrust Act

2. The _____ training approach to employee training involves a simulation of the real working environment.   2._____

    A. apprenticeship   B. classroom
    C. vestibule   D. step

3. Company A is conducting a wage survey in order to determine its external competitive-ness. In order to be useful and informative, the survey results must include each of the following EXCEPT   3._____

    A. the names and sizes of the companies surveyed
    B. a brief description of job duties
    C. data from companies that are in the same geographic location
    D. the dates on which listed wages and salaries were in effect

4. In forecasting an organization's demand for employees, which of the following is a *bottom–up* technique?   4._____

    A. Trend projection   B. Unit demand forecasting
    C. Modeling   D. Expert estimate

5. What is the term for the method in which a manager continually ranks his or her employ-ees from most valuable to least valuable?   5._____

    A. Object classification   B. Alteration ranking
    C. Subject categorization   D. Forced–choice rating

6. In order to be effective, the criteria on which performance evaluations are based should be designed with each of the following in mind EXCEPT   6._____

    A. relevance   B. practicality
    C. comprehensiveness   D. sensitivity

7. Historically, the personnel function was considered to be concerned almost exclusively with blue–collar or operating employees, until about the   7._____

    A. 1890s   B. 1920s   C. 1960s   D. 1990s

8. During an employment interview, the solicitation of information about _____, in ANY sit-   8._____
uation, no matter what the perceived relationship to the job, is unlawful.

    A. religion   B. handicaps
    C. race or color   D. national origin

9. What is the term for the process of unionized employees voting to drop the union?   9._____

    A. Decertification   B. Opening shop
    C. Exposure   D. Closing shop

10. All written sexual harassment policies presented by an employer need to contain the fol-   10._____
lowing EXCEPT a(n)

    A. statement encouraging people to come forward with complaints
    B. definition of sexual harassment
    C. alternative channel for filing complaints
    D. promise to make a case public once it has been confirmed and resolved

11. To human resource professionals, the primary advantage associated with computer–   11._____
aided job evaluations is that they

    A. decrease the bureaucratic burdens associated with the process
    B. produce results that are more widely accepted
    C. are much more efficient than other kinds of processes
    D. are nearly always less expensive than other methods

12. In order for the National Labor Relations Board to be appropriately petitioned to hold a   12._____
representation election to determine whether employees in a bargaining unit can be represented by a union, at least _____% of the bargaining unit's employees must sign an
authorization card.

    A. 10   B. 30   C. 50   D. 75

13. Which of the following items of federal legislation was designed to audit and regulate the   13._____
internal affairs of unions?

    A. Civil Rights Act of 1964
    B. Landrum–Griffin Act
    C. Fair Labor Standards Act
    D. Robinson–Patman Act

14. Which of the following unions is currently experiencing the most rapid growth rate?   14._____

    A. Service Employees International Union
    B. United Steel Workers
    C. American Federation of Government Employees
    D. United Auto Workers

15. Which of the following is NOT a potential disadvantage associated with a flexible–benefits plan?

    A. It requires intensive administrative effort.
    B. It often results in erratic cost patterns for the organization.
    C. For employees, contributions and deductibles are often increased.
    D. It tends to raise the costs of introducing new forms of benefits.

15.____

16. Under the Hazard Communications Standard of the Occupational Safety and Health Act, either of the following may complete Material Safety Data Sheets on chemicals imported into, produced, or used in the workplace EXCEPT

    A. employees   B. manufacturers
    C. employers   D. importers

16.____

17. The term *halo effect* is most often used to refer to cases when a human resources manager

    A. allows a single prominent characteristic of an interviewee to dominate judgment of all other characteristics
    B. projects the behaviors and attitudes of one prominent employee onto other employees
    C. typifies an employee's work habits by one exceptional example, good or bad
    D. considers all of the employees in his or her charge together as one unit, rather than as individuals

17.____

18. Approximately how much time should be scheduled by a human resources department to develop a behaviorally anchored rating scale (BARS) for performance evaluation?

    A. 1 working day   B. 2–4 days
    C. 2 weeks   D. 6 weeks

18.____

19. Each of the following actions, if taken by a human resources manager, is likely to have a positive effect on employee motivation EXCEPT

    A. treating employees as members of a group
    B. encouraging participation
    C. relating rewards to performance
    D. making work interesting

19.____

20. Which of the following federal laws prohibited a union to require that a person be a member of a union before he or she is hired?

    A. Sherman Antitrust Act   B. Clayton Act
    C. Taft–Hartley Act   D. Landrum–Griffin Act

20.____

21. Among the different types of retirement plans, 401(k) plans are classified as

    A. employee stock ownership plans (ESOPs)
    B. private pensions
    C. tax reduction stock ownership plans (TRASOPs)
    D. asset income

21.____

22. The strictness of a company's employee discipline policy depends most on   22.____

    A. the supportiveness of the work group
    B. the nature of the supervisor
    C. the nature of the prevailing labor markets
    D. existing legal statutes

23. The first union in the United States to achieve significant size and influence was the   23.____

    A. United Garment Workers
    B. American Federation of Labor
    C. Knights of Labor
    D. Congress of Industrial Organizations

24. What is the term for a diagram which vertically represents the activities to be performed,   24.____
and horizontally represents the time required to perform them?

    A. Nomograph   B. Gantt chart
    C. Layout chart   D. Flow–process chart

25. The age discrimination provisions of the Age Discrimination in Employment Act apply to   25.____
all employers of _____ or more people.

    A. 5   B. 15   C. 20   D. 100

KEY (CORRECT ANSWERS)

1.	A		11.	A
2.	C		12.	B
3.	A		13.	B
4.	B		14.	A
5.	B		15.	D
6.	C		16.	A
7.	C		17.	A
8.	C		18.	B
9.	A		19.	A
10.	A		20.	C

    21. D
    22. C
    23. C
    24. B
    25. C

TEST 2

DIRECTIONS: Each question or incomplete statement is followed by several suggested answers or completions. Select the one that BEST answers the question or completes the statement. *PRINT THE LETTER OF THE CORRECT ANSWER IN THE SPACE AT THE RIGHT.*

1. Which of the following is NOT a disadvantage commonly associated with skill–based pay structures?

   A. They often result in bloated staffing.
   B. Their compliance with the Equal Pay Act is still undecided on many points.
   C. They are based mostly on job content.
   D. They often become expensive if not properly managed.

1.____

2. The number of applicants hired at an organization, divided by the total number of applicants, yields a statistic known as a _____ ratio.

   A. turnover   B. market pay
   C. selection   D. recruitment success

2.____

3. Job _____ is the term for the formal process by which the relative worth of various jobs in the organization is determined for pay purposes.

   A. analysis   B. specification
   C. evaluation   D. enlargement

3.____

4. Which of the following is NOT an effective means of counteracting commonly–occurring career problems in a new employee?

   A. Give the employee a challenging initial assignment
   B. De–emphasize a job's negative aspects
   C. Give the employee as much authority as possible
   D. Assign new employees initially to demanding supervisors

4.____

5. In the factor comparison method of job evaluation, which of the following is typically performed LAST?

   A. Benchmark or key jobs are evaluated according to compensable factors.
   B. Key jobs are displayed in a job comparison chart.
   C. Comparison factors are selected and defined.
   D. Evaluators allocate a part of each key job's wage to each job factor.

5.____

6. Concerning discipline, employees _____ are usually the easiest to work with and adjust.

   A. with alcohol–or drug–related problems
   B. whose performance are due to factors directly related to work
   C. whose performance are due to problems caused by the work group
   D. with family problems

6.____

7. Among individual performance assessment techniques, the oldest and most commonly used is the

   A. critical incident technique
   B. forced–choice evaluation
   C. weighted checklist
   D. graphic rating scale

7.____

8. The *traditional* theory of human resources management holds that _____ is the primary motivator of people.

    A. money   B. approval
    C. achievement   D. safety

8.____

9. Generally, under the child labor provisions of the Fair Labor Standards Act, children must be at LEAST _____ years old to be employed in interstate commerce of any kind.

    A. 12   B. 14   C. 16   D. 18

9.____

10. Benefits are typically evaluated by human resource professionals in terms of their objectives. Which of the following objectives tends to be LEAST important in these evaluations?

    A. Impact on employee families
    B. Fairness or equity with which they are viewed by employees
    C. Cost effectiveness of benefit decisions
    D. Impact on employee work behaviors

10.____

11. Which of the following performance assessment techniques tends to involve the highest developmental costs?

    A. Graphic rating scale
    B. Performance testing
    C. Field review
    D. Management by objectives (MBO)

11.____

12. Which of the following types of employees is NOT typically classified as *exempt* under the Fair Labor Standards Act?

    A. Line workers   B. Administrators
    C. Outside sales personnel   D. Executives

12.____

13. Which of the following is a typical guideline to be followed in the process of orienting a new employee to the workplace?

    A. The most significant part of orientation deals with necessary job skills and work habits, rather than the nature of the relationship between the new employee and supervisors and/or co-workers.
    B. New employees should be allowed a generous amount of time to adjust to the new workplace before their responsibilities are increased.
    C. New employees should be *sponsored* or directed in the immediate environment by a group of experienced workers.
    D. Orientation should begin with the more general policies of the organization.

13.____

14. The _____ theory of employee motivation is based on the assumption that employees are motivated to satisfy a number of needs and that money can satisfy, directly or indirectly, only some of these needs.

    A. traditional
    B. behavioral/reinforcement
    C. need hierarchy
    D. achievement–power–affiliation

14.____

15. Which of the following is a grouping of a variety of jobs that are similar in terms of work   15.____
    difficulty and responsibility?

    A. Pay class   B. Job classification
    C. Broadband   D. Rate change

16. Which of the following statements is TRUE of recruitment that is performed using realistic   16.____
    job previews (RJPs)?

    A. RJPs tend to reduce the flow of highly capable applicants into the organization.
    B. RJPs tend to generate an extremely high rate of job offer acceptance.
    C. RJPs make a job look unattractive to some or many applicants.
    D. Employees hired after receiving RJPs tend to have a lower rate of job survival than
       those using traditional previews.

17. The theory of human behavior based on the belief that people attempt to increase plea-   17.____
    sure and decrease displeasure is the _____ theory.

    A. input–output
    B. achievement–power–affiliation
    C. preference–expectancy
    D. behavioral

18. The agencies most responsible for enforcing equal employment opportunity regulations   18.____
    include each of the following EXCEPT the

    A. Occupational Health and Safety Administration (OSHA)
    B. Equal Employment Opportunity Commission (EEOC)
    C. federal courts
    D. Office of Federal Contract Compliance Programs (OFCCP)

19. The majority of top–level managers consider _____ as the most important workplace   19.____
    activity for dealing with employee substance abuse.

    A. employee assistance programs
    B. drug testing
    C. supervisory training programs
    D. drug education programs

20. In the performance evaluation process, which of the following functions is typically under-   20.____
    taken exclusively by the human resource manager, rather than the operating manager?

    A. Training the raters
    B. Setting the policy on evaluation criteria
    C. Discussing the evaluation with the employee
    D. Choosing the evaluation system

21. Which of the following characteristics is LEAST likely to influence the acceptance of variable pay plans by employees of an organization?   21.____

    A. Ratio of variable pay to base pay (leverage)
    B. Amount of base pay
    C. Risk
    D. Procedural justice

22. Which of the following is a performance simulation test used in the personnel selection process?   22.____

    A. Wonderlic Personnel Test
    B. Wechsler Adult Intelligence Scale
    C. California Test of Mental Maturity
    D. Revised Minnesota Paper Form Board Test

23. The extent to which a technique for selecting employees is successful in predicting important elements of job behavior is known as   23.____

    A. construct validity
    B. job correlation
    C. normative probability
    D. criterion–related validity

24. Critics of the *rotation and transfer* method of on–the–job training for managers argue that this method   24.____

    A. creates generalists who may not be able to manage in many specialized situations
    B. discourages new ideas in the work environment
    C. does not provide authentic work experiences
    D. slows the promotion of highly competent individuals

25. According to the Theory X/Theory Y concept of leadership attitudes, which of the following is a Theory X assumption?   25.____

    A. Commitment to objectives is a function of the rewards associated with their achievement.
    B. The average person learns, under proper conditions, not only to accept but to seek responsibility.
    C. Under the conditions of modern industrial life, the intellectual potentials of the average person are only partially utilized.
    D. The average person prefers to be directed.

KEY (CORRECT ANSWERS)

1.	A	11.	B
2.	C	12.	A
3.	C	13.	B
4.	B	14.	C
5.	B	15.	A
6.	B	16.	C
7.	D	17.	C
8.	A	18.	A
9.	C	19.	A
10.	A	20.	A

21.	B
22.	D
23.	D
24.	A
25.	D

EXAMINATION SECTION
TEST 1

DIRECTIONS: Each question or incomplete statement is followed by several suggested answers or completions. Select the one that BEST answers the question or completes the statement. *PRINT THE LETTER OF THE CORRECT ANSWER IN THE SPACE AT THE RIGHT.*

1. The Public Services Careers Program is a manpower program   1.____

    A. designed to develop permanent employment opportunities for the disadvantaged
    B. designed to encourage college graduates to enter the field of public administration
    C. run by the federal government for private organizations
    D. designed to prepare physically handicapped persons for new positions

2. The Intergovernmental Personnel Act (P.L. 91-648) provides federal assistance to state   2.____
and local governments for improving and strengthening personnel administration.
The one of the following which is NOT provided for in this Act is

    A. creation of a new personnel system for upper-level personnel
    B. expanded training programs
    C. improved personnel management
    D. interchange of employees between federal government and state and local governments

3. Kepner-Tregoc management training courses are MOST closely involved with   3.____

    A. management by objectives
    B. development of overall leadership qualities
    C. leadership style
    D. problem-solving techniques

4. The BASIC purpose of the Managerial Grid for training program is to train managers to   4.____

    A. have concern for both production and the people who produce
    B. utilize scientific problem-solving techniques
    C. maximize efficient communication
    D. improve the quality of their leadership in *brainstorming* sessions

5. In establishing employee development objectives, management must make sure that   5.____
they are

    A. stated in broad terms
    B. relevant to job performance
    C. developed by a training expert
    D. written in the vocabulary of the training field

6. In order that group conferences serve their purpose of developing professional staff, it is   6.____
essential that

    A. discussion of controversial matters be limited
    B. notes be taken by the participants
    C. participants be encouraged to take part in the discussions
    D. chairmanships be rotated at the meetings

7. A personnel officer receives a request to conduct a course for interested employees who   7.____
have filed for a promotion examination. The request that the course be given on agency
time is turned down.
This action is

   A. *justified;* such courses do not contain content that serve to improve employee per-
      formance
   B. *justified;* the course is designed to benefit the individual primarily, not the agency
   C. *unjustified;* regardless of objective, any training related to City operations will have
      an affect on employee performance tangibly or intangibly
   D. *unjustified;* if productivity has been based on full use of employee time, productivity
      will suffer if time is allocated for such a course

8. Of the following, the PRIMARY objective of sensitivity training is to   8.____

   A. teach management principles to participants
   B. improve and refine the decision-making process
   C. give the participants insight as to how they are perceived by others
   D. improve the emotional stability of the participants

9. In considering the functions of a manager, it is clear that the FIRST step in building a   9.____
quality work force is the manager's need to

   A. design jobs to meet the realities of the labor market
   B. examine the qualification requirements for his positions and eliminate those which
      appear to be controversial
   C. determine the methods to be used in reaching that special public deemed most
      suitable for the agency
   D. establish controls so that there is reasonable assurance that the plans established
      to staff the agency will be properly consummated

10. Based on data documenting the differences between healthy and unhealthy organiza-   10.____
tions, which statement describes a healthy, as contrasted with an unhealthy, organization?

   A. Innovation is not widespread but exists in the hands of a few.
   B. Risks are not avoided but accepted as a condition of change.
   C. Decision-making is not dispersed but delegated to organizational levels.
   D. Conflict is not overt but resolved without confrontation.

11. Which of the following management actions is NOT conducive to greater job satisfaction?   11.____

   A. Diversifying tasks in the unit as much as feasible
   B. Permitting workers to follow through on tasks rather than carry out single segments
      of the process
   C. Avoiding the use of *project teams* or *task forces*
   D. Delegating authority to each layer of the hierarchy to the maximum extent possible

12. When the span of control of a manager or administrator is widened or increased, a MOST likely result is

    A. greater specificity of operational procedures
    B. a decrease in total worker-administrator contacts
    C. a blurring of objectives and goals
    D. an increase in responsibility of subordinates

12.____

13. Although *superagencies* may have value in assisting the chief executive to supervise operations more efficiently, a MAJOR shortcoming is that they

    A. may not provide more effective delivery of services to the public
    B. may limit the chief executive in his ability to find out what is happening within the agencies
    C. tend to reduce the responsibility of component agency heads for their own operations
    D. add costs that have little relation to the efforts to achieve administrative effectiveness

13.____

14. Business and psychological literature on managerial effectiveness is based for the MOST part on

    A. job analyses or descriptions about the management process
    B. field studies or observations about the outcome of effective management
    C. personal experiences or opinions about the traits good managers possess
    D. attitudes or perceptions of managers about organizational goals and strategies

14.____

15. The impression MOST likely to be gained from published surveys of traits necessary for management is that the lists

    A. limit identified traits to obvious human virtues
    B. lack precision in pinpointing behavioral elements
    C. emphasize negative rather than positive variables
    D. exclude attitudinal and motivational factors

15.____

16. Management concepts in public and private organizations have been undergoing drastic shifts as a consequence of a new view emerging from the recent synthesis of learning in the sciences. While still in its infancy, this development has challenged much of what has been considered accepted management theory for a long time.
This change is frequently referred to in current management literature as

    A. systems thinking   B. scientific management
    C. behavioral science   D. multivariate analysis

16.____

17. Assuming more and more importance every day, the subject of management has under-   17.____
gone prodigious change in recent times.
With respect to this development, the MOST valid expression concerning the current
status of management would be:

    A. Authoritative texts have progressed to the point where differences in the formal
       treatment of the process of management are comparatively rare
    B. The generalized theory of management which has been synthesized recently by
       scholars in the field has given the term *management* a fixed meaning and definition
       from which revolutionary progress may now be anticipated
    C. Unity of conception, thought, and view about the process of management is still a
       long way off
    D. Unity of conception, thought, and view about the process of management has
       been achieved in administrative circles under the revolutionary concepts brought
       into being as a result of the latest developments in computer technology

18. That there is no average man, the manager would be first to acknowledge. Yet the exi-   18.____
gencies of organized enterprise require that the assumption be made.
Of the following, the procedure or process that is PRIMARILY based on this assumption is the

    A. administration of discipline
    B. establishment of rules and regulations
    C. policy of job enlargement
    D. promotion policy

19. There are four or more phases in the process of manpower planning.   19.____
Of the following, the one which should be scheduled FIRST is

    A. gathering and analyzing data through manpower inventories and forecasts
    B. establishing objectives and policies through personnel and budget control units
    C. designing plan and action programs
    D. establishing production goals for the agency

20. When ranked in order of frequency of performance, studies show which of the following   20.____
ranks LOWEST among the functions performed by central personnel offices in local governments?

    A. Planning, conducting, and coordinating training
    B. Certifying or auditing payrolls
    C. Conducting personnel investigations
    D. Engaging in collective bargaining

21. Which of the following activities of an agency personnel division can BEST be consid-   21.____
ered a control function?

    A. Scheduling safety meetings for supervisory staff
    B. Consultation on a disciplinary problem
    C. Reminders to line units to submit personnel evaluations
    D. Processing requests for merit increases

22. Which of the following interview styles is MOST appropriate for use in a problem-solving situation?   22.____

    A. Directed   B. Non-directive
    C. Stress   D. Authoritarian

23. Which of the following is a COMMONLY used measure of morale in an organization?   23.____

    A. Turnover rate
    B. Espirit de corps
    C. Specialized division of labor
    D. Job satisfaction

24. According to studies in personnel and industrial psychology, information that travels along the *grapevine* or informal communication system in an organization usually follows a pattern BEST classified as   24.____

    A. cluster—key informants tell several individuals, one of whom passes it on in the same way
    B. wheel—around through successive informants until it reaches the source
    C. chain—double informants linked to successive pairs
    D. random probability—informant tells anyone he happens to encounter, and so forth

25. A carefully devised program has been developed in a certain city for combining performance evaluation and seniority into a formula to determine order of layoff. The essence of this plan is first to group employees of a particular job class into *seniority blocks* and then to use performance evaluation as a basis for determining layoff order within each seniority block.
The BEST of the following inferences which can be made from the above paragraph is that   25.____

    A. this plan is unfair since seniority is not given sufficient weight in the selection process
    B. this city is probably behind most civil service jurisdictions in the evaluation of employee performance
    C. combining performance and seniority cannot be done since it is like *combining apples and oranges*
    D. under this plan, it is conceivable that a person with high seniority could be laid off before a person with lower seniority

26. With any decentralization of personnel functions, specific procedures and rules are developed to assure conformance with relevant provisions of the Civil Service Law and the Rules and Regulations of the central personnel agency.
To the extent that these procedures are specific and detailed,   26.____

    A. agency involvement in the execution of the decentralized function will be limited
    B. agency discretion in the administration of the decentralized function will be limited
    C. size and composition of agency personnel staff will tend to become fixed
    D. flexibility of application to bolster agency performance will be provided

27. While decentralization of personnel functions to give operating agencies more authority   27.____
in personnel matters relating to their operations has been a goal of personnel policy,
recentralization is an ever-present possibility. Of the following, the factor which is the
BEST indicator of the desirability of recentralization is that

    A. inconsistent policies or inconsistent application of policies resulted when decentral-
ized operations were instituted
    B. costs in terms of personnel and procedures increased significantly when decentral-
ization was introduced
    C. the decentralization did not serve any real identifiable need
    D. agency personnel units were not prepared to handle the responsibilities delegated
to them

28. Although the Department of Personnel has developed and maintains an Executive Ros-   28.____
ter, its use by agency heads to fill managerial positions has been disappointing.
Of the following, the one that is the LEAST likely reason for NOT using the roster is
that

    A. personal factors essential to the relationship of manager and administrator are not
revealed in the roster record
    B. most agencies prefer to advance their own employees rather than use a general
roster
    C. some agency heads think of experienced City managerial employees as superan-
nuated administrative deadwood
    D. use of the roster implies a reduction of the scope of administrative discretion in
selection

29. During one program year, an examiner found a number of occasions in which a special   29.____
task, a special report, or some activity outside of planned programs had to be assigned.
One staff member continually offered to undertake these assignments whenever the
administrative examiner requested a volunteer. He handled these jobs in timely fashion
even though he had begun the year with a full-time workload.
Of the following, the conclusion MOST warranted from the information given is that the

    A. staff member was much more efficient than other examiners in the division in plan-
ning and executing work
    B. staff member's regular workload actually was less than a full-time assignment for
him
    C. commitment and will to serve was greater in this member than in others
    D. quality of work of other examiners may have been higher than that of this staff
member

30. An examiner has three subordinate supervisors, each responsible for a major program in   30.____
his division. He finds that one supervisor is much weaker than the other two, both in his
planning of work and in his follow-through to achieve timely completion of tasks. To bol-
ster the *weak* supervisor, the administrative examiner reassigns his best examiners to
this unit.
This decision is POOR primarily because

    A. the performance of the competent examiners is likely to suffer eventually
    B. the assigned examiners will be expected to make more decisions themselves
    C. the ineffective supervisor might have done better by assignment elsewhere
    D. indicated disciplinary action was not taken

31. Because of the frustrations felt by many public administrators who have been unable to   31.____
    motivate their subordinates, the classic civil service reform movement has been con-
    demned by observers of the public government scene. Those condemning that move-
    ment believe that the system has failed to develop a quality public service precisely
    because of the policies implemented as a result of the reform movement.
    They suggest that the remedy lies in

    A. centralizing the personnel functions in the hands of an elite group of professional
       personnel practitioners who would be best equipped to initiate needed remedies
    B. changing the concept of personnel management to a generalist approach, thus
       guaranteeing a broader and more integrated resolution of employee problems
    C. finding and implementing more practical personnel techniques in dealing with the
       various functional personnel areas
    D. completely decentralizing personnel administration to the responsible agency
       heads

32. The British scholar and statesman Harold J. Laski has stated that the expert was too   32.____
    likely to *make his subject the measure of life, instead of making life the measure of his
    subject.*
    When applying this comment to the modern public service administrator, it is meant
    that the administrator should

    A. expand the jurisdiction of his authority so that better integration among functional
       areas is possible
    B. personally be receptive to the concept of change and not merely concerned with
       protecting the methods of the past
    C. develop a group of specialists in functional subject matter areas in order to give
       better service to the operating department heads
    D. see the relationship of his own particular area of jurisdiction to other governmental
       activities and to the private sector

33. Suppose that, as an examiner, you are asked to prepare a budget for the next fiscal year   33.____
    for a division performing personnel functions.
    Of the following, the consideration which is LEAST important to your development of
    the division budget involves

    A. adequacy of the current year's budget for your division
    B. changes in workload that can be anticipated
    C. budget restrictions that have been indicated in a memorandum covering budget
       preparation
    D. staff reassignments which are expected during that fiscal year

34. Suppose you have been designated chairman of an intra-departmental committee to implement a major policy decision. The one of the following which is LEAST desirable as a subject for a planning meeting is 34._____

   A. determination of details of execution by each bureau
   B. specific allocation of responsibility for the phases of administration
   C. provision of means for coordination and follow-up
   D. formulation of sub-goals for each bureau

35. Collective bargaining challenges the concept of the neutrality of the personnel function in the public service. Which one of the following statements BEST reflects this observation? 35._____

   A. Personnel offices must clearly serve as a bridge between management and employees.
   B. In most cases, negotiation involves a tripartite group—labor relations, fiscal or budget, and the employee organization.
   C. Personnel bureaus must be identified openly with the public employer.
   D. Personnel units cannot make policy or commitments in labor relations; their primary function is to execute personnel decisions made by others.

36. Changes in the field of public employee labor relations have been both numerous and significant in recent years. Below are four statements that an examiner preparing a report on developments in this area of personnel management might possibly include as correct: 36._____
   I. At least one-third of the states give some type of bargaining rights to their employees
   II. Less than half the states have granted public employees the right to organize
   III. Since 1959, at least eight states have enacted comprehensive labor relations laws affecting public employees
   IV. By 1966, state and local governments had entered into more than 1,000 separate agreements with employee organizations
   Which of the following choices lists the statements that are CORRECT?

   A. I, II, and III are correct, but not IV
   B. I, III, and IV are correct, but not II
   C. I and III are correct, but not II and IV
   D. II and III are correct, but not I and IV

37. Which of the following is NOT a major goal of unions in contract negotiations? 37._____

   A. Establishing management prerogatives
   B. Preserving and strengthening the union
   C. Promoting social and economic objectives
   D. Promoting the status of the union representatives

Questions 38–39.

DIRECTIONS: Answer Questions 38 and 39 on the basis of the following paragraph.

An impending reorganization within an agency will mean loss by transfer of several professional staff members from the personnel division. The division chief is asked to designate the persons to be transferred. After reviewing the implications of this reduction of staff with his assistant, the division chief discussed the matter at a staff meeting. He adopts the recommendations of several staff members to have volunteers make up the required reduction.

38.   The decision to permit personnel to volunteer for transfer is   38._____

    A.   *poor;* it is not likely that the members of a division are of equal value to the division chief
    B.   *good;* dissatisfied members will probably be more productive elsewhere
    C.   *poor;* the division chief has abdicated his responsibility to carry out the order given to him
    D.   *good;* morale among remaining staff is likely to improve in a more cohesive framework

39.   Suppose one of the volunteers is a recently appointed employee who has completed his   39._____
probationary period acceptably, but whose attitude toward division operations and agency administration tends to be rather negative and sometimes even abrasive. Because of his lack of commitment to the division, his transfer is recommended.
If the transfer is approved, the division chief should, prior to the transfer,

    A.   discuss with the staff the importance of commitment to the work of the agency and its relationship with job satisfaction
    B.   refrain from any discussion of attitude with the employee
    C.   discuss with the employee his concern about the employee's attitude
    D.   avoid mention of attitude in the evaluation appraisal prepared for the receiving division chief

40.   It is time to make position classification a real help to line officials in defining programs   40._____
and objectives and structuring tasks to meet those objectives, rather than continuing to act as a post auditor and controller.
Of the following, the statement which BEST reflects the sense of this passage is that

    A.   post audit and control procedures should be related to the prior processes of objectives and goals determination
    B.   position classification should be part of management decisions rather than an evaluation of them
    C.   program definition requires prior determination of position characteristics and performance factors to facilitate management program decisions
    D.   primary responsibility for position classification and grade or level allocation is that of line management, not that of the classification specialist

41. Pencil and paper objective testing procedures have tremendous advantages of quantifi-   41.____
cation and empiricism. They are economical in production and use. But the procedures
have a great disadvantage in that they are designed primarily for statistical prediction.
A conclusion that is MOST consistent with the above statement is that

    A. statistical prediction becomes meaningless if the applicants tested constitute a
stratified sample and not a representative sample of the population
    B. predictions of adequate performance by any one group of successful applicants
will follow the normal curve
    C. if the group is small, statistical indices cannot have high validity
    D. such test procedures cannot predict the job success or failure of a specific appli-
cant

42. It has been stated that in the public service, the use of written tests is more appropriate   42.____
for selecting from among those outside the organization than from those within the organization.
This is so since

    A. written tests serve to reduce the number of final competitors to manageable pro-
portions
    B. vouchering of prospective employees from outside the organization is deemed to
be invalid and not reliable
    C. written tests are in effect substitutes for direct observation on the gob
    D. testing outside applicants for aptitude and achievement has served a useful pur-
pose in the elimination of extraneous prejudicial factors in the selection process

43. The *Test Validation Board* is a recent innovation.   43.____
The MAJOR purpose of this board is to review

    A. and approve questions to be used before the written test is held
    B. and approve the test questions and the proposed key answers immediately after
the test is held
    C. the test items and protests and then establish the final key answers
    D. the test items and protests and then recommend adoption of a final rating key

44. *Brainstorming* sessions include each of the following EXCEPT   44.____

    A. free-wheeling or wild ideas
    B. criticism of any idea
    C. great quantities of ideas
    D. combining or building on ideas

45. It has been ascertained that a certain top-level position should NOT be placed in the   45.____
competitive class.
What determines whether the new position should be placed in the non-competitive
class rather than in the exempt class?

    A. Subordinate positions are in the competitive class.
    B. An executive in a specific field is needed.
    C. The position can be subjected to examination.
    D. The position is policy making.

46. Personnel practice in most governmental organizations provides that a new employee must serve a probationary period generally not to exceed six months. During this period, he is to be given special attention in such matters as instruction, indoctrination, and general adjustment to his job. The theory behind this practice is that this period is the last phase of the testing process, but the consensus is that the probationary period is not living up to its possibilities as a testing opportunity.
The MAJOR reason for this opinion is that the

    A. techniques used by personnel practitioners to encourage supervisors to pass objective judgments on probationers are not effective
    B. probationary period is too short and marginal employees can maintain their best behavior for this length of time
    C. supervisors are not living up to their obligation to conduct vigorous probationary appraisals
    D. supervisors try to avoid making unpleasant personal judgments about their employees

46._____

47. Plans were recently announced to require one year of college for entrance into the police service and eventually a college degree for promotion in the police force.
Of the following, the one that will NOT present problems in implementing these plans is

    A. changing the Civil Service requirements for entrance or promotion
    B. overcoming police union objections to the promotion requirements
    C. providing sufficient time for affected individuals to meet these educational requirements
    D. retaining college graduates in the police service over a period of years

47._____

Questions 48–50.

DIRECTIONS: Answer Questions 48 through 50 on the basis of the following paragraph.

The increase in the extent to which each individual is personally responsible to others is most noticeable in a large bureaucracy. No one person decides anything; each decision of any importance is the product of an intricate process of brokerage involving individuals inside and outside the organization who feel some reason to be affected by the decision, or who have special knowledge to contribute to it. The more varied the organization's constituency, the more outside "veto-groups" will need to be taken into account. But even if no outside consultations were involved, sheer size would produce a complex process of decision. For a large organization is a deliberately created system of tensions into which each individual is expected to bring work–ways, viewpoints, and outside relationships markedly different from those of his colleagues. It is the administrator's task to draw from these disparate forces the elements of wise action from day to day, consistent with the purposes of the organization as a whole.

48. This passage is ESSENTIALLY a description of decision-making as

    A. an organization process
    B. the key responsibility of the administrator
    C. the one best position among many
    D. a complex of individual decisions

48._____

49. Which one of the following statements BEST describes the responsibilities of an adminis-   49._____
    trator?
    He

    A. modifies decisions and goals in accordance with pressures from within and outside
       the organization
    B. creates problem-solving mechanisms that rely on the varied interests of his staff
       and *veto-groups*
    C. makes determinations that will lead to attainment of his agency's objectives
    D. obtains agreement among varying viewpoints and interests

50. In the context of the operations of a central public personnel agency, a *veto-group* would   50._____
    LEAST likely consist of

    A. employee organizations
    B. professional personnel societies
    C. using agencies
    D. civil service newspapers

KEY (CORRECT ANSWERS)

1.	A	11.	C	21.	C	31.	D	41.	D
2.	A	12.	D	22.	B	32.	D	42.	C
3.	D	13.	A	23.	A	33.	D	43.	D
4.	A	14.	C	24.	A	34.	A	44.	B
5.	B	15.	B	25.	D	35.	C	45.	B
6.	C	16.	A	26.	B	36.	B	46.	C
7.	B	17.	C	27.	C	37.	A	47.	C
8.	C	18.	B	28.	D	38.	A	48.	A
9.	A	19.	A	29.	B	39.	C	49.	C
10.	B	20.	D	30.	A	40.	B	50.	B

TEST 2

DIRECTIONS: Each question or incomplete statement is followed by several suggested answers or completions. Select the one that BEST answers the question or completes the statement. *PRINT THE LETTER OF THE CORRECT ANSWER IN THE SPACE AT THE RIGHT.*

1. The definition of merit system as it pertains to the public service is that a person's worth to the organization is the factor governing both his entrance and upward mobility within that service. The main ingredient used to accomplish entrance and mobility has been competition based on relative qualifications of candidates.
The burgeoning demands of new occupations and critical social and economic urgencies in the public service make it imperative that now

   A. greater emphasis be placed on the intellectual and technical capacities of applicants in order to improve the high standards achieved by some professionals
   B. current methods be strengthened in order to make them more valid and reliable indicators among applicants for government positions
   C. public personnel officials work more closely with representatives of the various professions and occupations to establish more equitable minimum standards in order to improve the quality of its practitioners
   D. the system adapt to the new changes by establishing alternative methods more suitable to current needs

1.____

2. Civil service systems need to be reexamined from time to time to determine whether they are correctly fulfilling stated merit obligations. Frequently, inspection determines that what was once a valid practice ... has ceased to be an effective instrument and has become, instead, an unrealistic barrier to the implementation of merit principles. Which one of the following practices would be considered to be such an unrealistic barrier?

   A. Disqualifying candidates with poor work history for positions involving the operation of trains or buses
   B. Disqualifying candidates for police work who have records of serious arrests
   C. Requiring a degree or license for medical, scientific, and professional positions
   D. Requiring a high school diploma for custodial, maintenance, and service positions

2.____

3. It is generally accepted that work attitudes and interpersonal relationships contribute at least as much as knowledge and ability to job performance. Several personality measuring and appraisal devices have been found useful in predicting personality and work attitudes.
A MAJOR drawback in their use in competitive selection, however, is the

   A. *fakeability* of responses possible in such selection situations
   B. cost of the materials and their interpretation
   C. inability of these measures to predict actual job performance
   D. lack of reviewability of these devices

3.____

4. Human Relations School discoveries having a major impact on modern personnel prac-   4._____
   tices include all of the following EXCEPT that

   A. social as well as physical capacity determines the amount of work an employee
      does
   B. non-economic rewards play a central role in employee motivation
   C. the higher the degree of specialization, the more efficient the division of labor
   D. workers react to management as members of groups rather than as individuals

5. Studies of the relationship between creativity and intelligence indicate that creativity   5._____

   A. is one of several special intelligence factors
   B. consists primarily of general intelligence as measured by standardized tests
   C. involves non-intellective factors as well as minimums of intelligence
   D. relates more directly to quantitative than to verbal aptitudes and skills

6. Strategies of data collection applicable to personnel work can be grouped into two broad   6._____
   categories: the mechanical method in which data be collected according to pre-established guidelines, rules, or procedures, and the clinical method in which the manner of
   data collection may differ from candidate to candidate at the discretion of the professional person collecting it.
   An argument that has proved VALID in support of the clinical method is that

   A. no sound basis exists for writing any single set of rules for collecting data
   B. no known mechanical procedure can fully anticipate all potentially relevant data
   C. mechanical processes stress the use of techniques such as synthetic validation
   D. mechanical methods are inadequate for formulating optimal individualized predic-
      tion rules

7. Which one of the following actions appears LEAST mandated by the Griggs vs. Duke   7._____
   Power Company decision of the U.S. Supreme Court on discriminatory employment
   practice?

   A. Study of certification and appointment policies and procedures
   B. Determination of job performance standards as related to successful performance
   C. Review of personal history forms, applications, and interviews involved in employ-
      ment procedures
   D. Test validation by correlation of individual test items with total test scores

8. In decision-making terminology, the type of action taken on a problem when the deci-   8._____
   sion–maker finds that he cannot do anything to eliminate the cause is MOST often called
   _____ action.

   A. corrective   B. adaptive
   C. stopgap   D. interim

9. The Intergovernmental Personnel Act became law recently. This Act does NOT provide for

    A. temporary assignment of personnel between governmental jurisdiction
    B. grants for improving personnel administration and training
    C. interstate compacts for personnel and training activities
    D. a National Advisory Council to study federal personnel administration and make recommendations to the President and Congress

9.____

10. Following are three kinds of performance tests for which arrangements might be made to give the candidates a pretest warm-up period:
    I. typing
    II. truck driving
    III. stenography
Which one of the following choices lists all of the above tests that should be preceded by a warm-up session?

    A. I, III
    C. I, II, III

    B. II *only*
    D. None of the above

10.____

Questions 11–12.

DIRECTIONS: Answer Questions 11 and 12 on the basis of the following paragraph.

Your role as human resources utilization experts is to submit your techniques to operating administrators, for the program must in reality be theirs, not yours. We in personnel have been guilty of encouraging operating executives to believe that these important matters affecting their employees are personnel department matters, not management matters. We should hardly be surprised, as a consequence, to find these executives playing down the role of personnel and finding personnel "routines" a nuisance, for these are not in the mainstream of managing the enterprise—or so we have encouraged them to believe.

11. The BEST of the following interpretations of the above paragraph is that

    A. personnel people have been guilty of *passing the buck* on personnel functions
    B. operating officials have difficulty understanding personnel techniques
    C. personnel employees have tended to usurp some functions rightfully belonging to management
    D. matters affecting employees should be handled by the personnel department

11.____

12. The BEST of the following interpretations of the above paragraph is that

    A. personnel departments have aided and abetted the formulation of negative attitudes on the part of management
    B. personnel people are labor relations experts and should carry out these duties
    C. personnel activities are not really the responsibility of management
    D. management is now being encouraged by personnel experts to assume some responsibility for personnel functions

12.____

13. Employee training can be described BEST as a process that   13.____

    A. increases retention of skills
    B. changes employees' knowledge, skills, or aptitudes
    C. improves the work methods used
    D. improves the work environment

14. With respect to the use of on-the-job training methods, the theory is that it is possible to   14.____
create maximally favorable conditions for learning while on the job. In actual practice, it
has been found that these favorable conditions are difficult to achieve.
The MAIN reason militating against such ideal conditions is that

    A. the primary function on the job is production, and training must, therefore, take
second place
    B. an adequate number of skilled and knowledgeable employees is usually not avail-
able to engage in effective person-to-person training
    C. expensive equipment and work space are tied up during training, which is not
advantageous to establishing good rapport between trainer and trainee
    D. an appraisal of trainee learning under pressure of job demands is not conducive to
showing the trainee the reasons for his mistakes

15. In most major studies directed toward identification of productive scientific personnel, the   15.____
MOST effective predictor has been

    A. biographical information
    B. motivational analysis
    C. tests of ideational flexibility
    D. high-level reasoning tests

16. Because interviewing is a difficult art, MOST personnel people who conduct interviews   16.____

    A. break the interview into specific units with pauses in between
    B. remain fairly constant in the technique they use despite differences of purpose and
persons interviewed
    C. utilize non-directive techniques during their first few years of interviewing
    D. vary their style and technique in accordance with the purpose of the interview and
the personality of the persons interviewed

17. When using the *in-basket* technique, it is NOT possible to obtain measures of the   17.____

    A. amount of work done in a given time
    B. extent to which the candidate seeks guidance before making decisions
    C. proportion of decisions that lead to actual cost savings
    D. proportion of work time devoted to prepatory activities

18. The MOST appropriate people to develop the definition for specific classes of positions in   18.____
order that they may serve as useful criteria for allocating positions to classes are the

    A. personnel experts in the area of job evaluation
    B. program practitioners
    C. job analysts working within other occupations under study
    D. organization and methods analysts

19. By its very nature and in order to operate effectively, a job classification system which groups jobs into broad occupational categories and then subdivides them into levels of difficulty and responsibility requires

    A. the upgrading of positions in order to raise the pay rates of incumbents
    B. a process in which lengthy job descriptions covering the allocation criteria are pre-requisites
    C. a certain amount of central control
    D. the transfer of classification authority from an *inside-track priesthood to* the operating official

19.____

20. A plan of classifying positions based on duties and responsibilities is not the same thing as a pay plan. Although the classification arrangement may be a vital element upon which a compensation structure is based and administered, there are differences between the two plans. The MAJOR distinction between these plans can be illustrated best by the fact that

    A. a uniform accounting system requires a uniform job terminology, which can be accomplished best by a classification plan
    B. the compensation plan can be changed without affecting the classification plan, and classes of positions can be rearranged on a pay schedule without changing the schedule
    C. job evaluation results in a common understanding of the job for which a rate is being set and for job-to-job comparison
    D. the classification principle of *equal pay for equal work* was instrumental in evolving pay reform

20.____

21. By stretching higher grade duties over as many jobs as possible, the position classifier makes for

    A. economy
    B. more effective performance
    C. effective use of the labor market
    D. higher operational costs

21.____

22. Contemporary information about what people want that is pertinent to potential entrants to the public service labor market indicates that a MAJOR want is

    A. more time for play and less time for work
    B. more personal privacy and fewer creature comforts
    C. more employee relationships and less organizational hierarchy
    D. more political participation and less partisan neutrality

22.____

23. An occupational rather than an organizational commitment to personnel administration as a professional field is MOST likely to prevail among personnel workers who perceive their work as part of a function that is

    A. designed to serve the employees of their agency
    B. dominated by necessary but uninteresting tasks
    C. dedicated to obtaining compliance with the law
    D. devoted to the human problems of organizations

23.____

24. The FIRST major strike by city employees which tested the Condon-Wadlin Act was by   24.____
    employees of the

    A. Sanitation Department   B. Police Department
    C. Fire Department   D. Department of Welfare

25. In the aftermath of the city transit strike of 1966, study groups were appointed to recom-   25.____
    mend ways in which such strikes could be avoided.
    The recommendations made at that time by the Governor's Committee and the Ameri-
    can Arbitration Association were especially significant in that they both

    A. included machinery for the settlement of labor disputes which was to be set up out-
       side the regular civil service establishment
    B. advocated the retention of the legal prohibition against strikes by public employees
    C. agreed to imposition of heavy fines on the union in case of a strike
    D. opted for repeal of the section in the Condon-Wadlin Act which prohibited strikes

26. Of the following, which country was the pioneer in employee-management relationships   26.____
    within the public service?

    A. Canada   B. France   C. Australia   D. Mexico

27. There are notable similarities and differences between collective bargaining in industry   27.____
    and government.
    In which of the following areas are the similarities GREATEST?

    A. Negotiable subjects   B. Bargaining processes
    C. Mediation and arbitration   D. Strikes

28. Traditionally, white-collar and professional workers resisted unionization both in govern-   28.____
    ment and in industry. This attitude has changed drastically among these workers since
    the late 1950's, however, particularly among public employees.
    The BASIC cause behind this change among public employees was that

    A. organized labor trained its big union recruitment guns on organizing these workers
       in the face of the dwindling proportion of blue-collar people in the labor force
    B. these employees generally identified with middle-class America, which had now
       become union-oriented
    C. they felt deep frustration with the authoritarianism of public administrators who
       believed that the *merit system* process gave the employee all the protection he
       needed
    D. the continual upward spiral of inflation resulted in making these workers among
       those deemed economically disadvantaged and necessitated their joining in
       unions for their own protection

29. Union efforts to improve retirement benefits for public employees have caused concern in the State legislature. Recently, a special legislative committee was ordered to determine whether retirement benefits should remain a subject for collective bargaining or whether they should be regulated by

    A. a bipartisan pension commission
    B. a board designated by management and labor
    C. large commercial insurance carriers
    D. the State Insurance Fund

29.____

30. The performance of personnel functions which are part of a comprehensive and integrated program of personnel management is conditioned significantly by personnel policies. Which one of the following is the LEAST valid criterion of what positive policies can accomplish?

    A. Functions are governed by rules which permit their being performed in line with the desired goals of the organization.
    B. Guidance for executives restrains them from mishandling the specified functions with which they have been entrusted.
    C. Standard decisions make it unnecessary for subordinates to ask their supervisors how given problems should be handled.
    D. Goals are enunciated for the purpose of selecting candidates best equipped to prove successful in the particular organizational milieu.

30.____

31. The GREATEST handicap of personnel systems which are predicated on the *corps of people* concept rather than on job analysis is lack of facility for

    A. conducting program evaluation studies
    B. developing sound programs for the direction and control of productivity
    C. manpower planning
    D. determining the limits of authority and responsibility among managerial personnel

31.____

32. It is an anomaly that one of the greatest threats to maintaining classification plans adequately is slowness in adjusting salaries to keep up with the changing labor market.
Thus, distortions of many classification plans occur.
This is MAINLY due to

    A. pressure from management officials to upgrade employees who have not received salary range increases
    B. inability to maintain an adequate file of pertinent pay data
    C. conflict in the pay philosophy between maintaining external alignment and comparability with union rates
    D. difficulty in distinguishing between the pay program and the fringe benefit package

32.____

33. A personnel agency charged with identifying candidates with the kind of creative talent   33.____
that can be used in an organizational setting should look for a high degree of certain
attributes among the candidate population. Below are listed four characteristics which
may qualify as desirable attributes for the purpose indicated:
    I.   Self-confidence
    II. Social conformity
    III. Mobility aspirations
    IV. Job involvement
Which of the following choices lists ALL of the above attributes which the personnel
agency should look for?

    A. I, II, IV   B. I, III, IV
    C. II, III, IV   D. III, IV

34. With regard to educational standards for selection purposes, the U.S. Supreme Court   34.____
has held that such requirements should be

    A. eliminated in most cases
    B. related to job success
    C. maintained whenever possible
    D. reduced as far as possible

35. In surveying job series which would be most conducive to job restructuring, most atten-   35.____
tion has focused on P, T, and M positions.
The benefits claimed for job restructuring include all of the following EXCEPT

    A. creating more interesting and challenging P, T, and M jobs
    B. increasing promotional opportunities for P, T, and M employees
    C. providing more job opportunities for the lesser skilled
    D. creating new promotional opportunities for those in low-skill or dead-end jobs

36. We must restructure as many job series as possible to allow entry into the service and to   36.____
permit successful job performance without previous training and experience. In the type
of restructuring alluded to, it is ESSENTIAL that

    A. job duties be rearranged to form a learning progression as well as a means of
       reaching work objectives
    B. educational achievement be minimized as a factor in determining progression to
       higher position rank
    C. separate and distinctive job series be created independent of existing job series
    D. lateral entry opportunities be emphasized

37. From the standpoint of equal opportunity, the MOST critical item operating personnel   37.____
must focus on is

    A. hiring more minority applicants for top-level positions
    B. helping existing minority employees upgrade their skills so they may qualify for
       higher skilled positions
    C. placing minority candidates in job categories where, there is little minority repre-
       sentation
    D. eliminating merit system principles

38. Most of the jobs opened up in human services through new career development efforts have been filled by women.
Of the following, the MAIN reason for this result is that the

    A. need to develop suitable careers for women is the major focus of the program
    B. majority of new career jobs are in fields where the work normally has been done by women
    C. labor shortages are found in fields that draw heavily on womanpower
    D. legislation and funds provide guides which emphasize the employment of women who are disadvantaged or underemployed

38.____

39. Thirty years ago, the Federal District Court granted a preliminary injunction restraining the city school system's board of examiners from conducting supervisory examinations or issuing lists based on them.
The reason given for this judicial action was that the

    A. disadvantaged and minority group members were given preferential treatment
    B. eligibility requirements were too high
    C. rating used was based on a *pass–fail* scoring system
    D. tests discriminated against Blacks and Puerto Ricans

39.____

40. The city recently began making thousands of jobs available to the unemployed and underemployed. This program, administered by the Human Resources Administration, implements the Federal Emergency Employment Act.
The federal statute provides that FIRST priority for such jobs be given to

    A. heads of households
    B. persons living alone
    C. veterans of the Indochina or Korean War
    D. youths entering the labor market

40.____

41. According to the Equal Employment Opportunity Act of 1966, a covered employer may NOT

    A. discriminate against an individual because he is a member of the Communist Party in the United States
    B. indicate preference for or limitation to national origin in printing a notice or advertisement for employment
    C. employ only members of a certain religion if the employer is an educational institution owned or supported by that religion
    D. apply different pay scales, conditions, or facilities of employment according to the location of various plants or facilities

41.____

42. Data received by the Equal Employment Opportunity Commission from firms employing 100 or more people suggest that emphasis in the area of equal opportunity has shifted from one of detection of conscious discrimination to one of

    A. human resources utilization
    B. passive resistance
    C. unconscious discrimination
    D. education

42.____

43. According to surveys pertaining to equal employment opportunities, available information   43.____
indicates that discriminatory patterns in job placement of minority group members is

    A. higher in craft unions than in industrial unions
    B. greater in the East than in the West
    C. higher in new plants than in old plants
    D. higher among young executives than among old executives

44. The area of criticism on which Congress concentrated its attention in its recent investiga-   44.____
tions of testing was

    A. cultural bias
    B. depersonalization of the individual
    C. increase in *meritocracy*
    D. invasion of privacy

45. If accepted criteria of a profession are applied, which of the following work groupings   45.____
ranks LOWEST in the distinctiveness of its character as a profession?

    A. Social service or community work
    B. Managerial or administrative work
    C. Health or health services work
    D. Teaching or educational work

46. Surveys of factors contributing to job satisfaction indicate, according to employees, that   46.____
the factor having HIGHEST priority among those listed is

    A. opportunity for advancement
    B. good pay schedules
    C. concern for training employees for better job performance
    D. good work environment

47. Job enrichment is intended to increase employee motivation and interest by increasing   47.____
the accountability of employees for their work, by introducing more complex tasks, and
by granting authority to make job decisions.
A MAJOR hazard that ma.y result from application of such restructuring is to

    A. increase complaints of work pressure
    B. reduce the effectiveness of task specialization
    C. stimulate demand for salary increases
    D. limit the status of the immediate supervisor

48. Which of the following statements concerning performance appraisal systems is NOT   48.____
correct?
They

    A. require line management participation
    B. provide for periodic discussions of performance between the supervisor and the
       employee
    C. are used primarily to uncover employee weaknesses
    D. require supervisor training to assure uniform appraisals

49. In the forced-choice technique of performance evaluation, the rater is forced to judge   49.____
which of several alternative statements is most descriptive of an employee's performance. It forces the rater to discriminate on the basis of concrete aspects of a subordinate's work behavior rather than to rely on an impression of his total worth.
The one of the following which is NOT considered a value of this technique is that it

    A. increases rater ability to produce a desired outcome
    B. is relatively free of the usual pile-up at the top of the scale
    C. tends to minimize subjective elements
    D. produces results that correlate positively with other variables associated with effec-
tive job performance

50. Of the following, the one which is NOT an advantage of the proper delegation of work by   50.____
a manager is that it

    A. increases planning time
    B. relieves the tension of seeing to details
    C. increases the manager's familiarity with routine work
    D. increases understanding of the responsibilities of subordinates

---

KEY (CORRECT ANSWERS)

1.	D	11.	C	21.	D	31.	C	41.	B
2.	D	12.	A	22.	C	32.	A	42.	A
3.	A	13.	B	23.	D	33.	B	43.	A
4.	C	14.	A	24.	D	34.	B	44.	D
5.	C	15.	D	25.	A	35.	B	45.	B
6.	B	16.	B	26.	A	36.	A	46.	A
7.	D	17.	C	27.	B	37.	B	47.	D
8.	B	18.	A	28.	C	38.	B	48.	C
9.	D	19.	C	29.	A	39.	D	49.	A
10.	C	20.	B	30.	D	40.	C	50.	C

EXAMINATION SECTION
TEST 1

DIRECTIONS: Each question or incomplete statement is followed by several suggested answers or completions. Select the one that BEST answers the question or completes the statement. *PRINT THE LETTER OF THE CORRECT ANSWER IN THE SPACE AT THE RIGHT.*

1. The task of developing data necessary for intelligent budgeting should be shared by the line department and the central budget agency.
The central budget agency should provide data on

    A. manpower utilization   B. operating costs
    C. personnel needs   D. price and wage factors

1.____

2. Under a system of responsibility accounting, the school transportation of handicapped children should be a charge against a department of

    A. child care   B. education
    C. health   D. transportation

2.____

3. Cost-benefit analysis

    A. *can* always be expressed in dollars
    B. *can* seldom provide complete answers
    C. *should* always have a single criterion for evaluation
    D. *should* be restricted to factors that can be qualified

3.____

4. Which measure among the following FAILS to relate programs to government objectives?

    A. Accident rates on highways
    B. Mortality rates
    C. Number of firemen per 1,000 population
    D. Unemployment rate

4.____

5. The MOST difficult type of activity measurement is that of

    A. economy   B. effectiveness
    C. performance   D. production

5.____

6. Assuming adequate authority and funds to support the decision, what would normally be the BEST method of coping with poor performance by units within a department?

    A. Appointing staff aides to the unit head, who can install better methods
    B. Assigning a team of administrative analysis from the central office to improve methods
    C. Replacing the unit head whenever a unit performs inadequately
    D. Training existing personnel in better management methods

6.____

7. Of the following programs for methods improvement, the program that is likely to be MOST effective is

    A. employee suggestion awards
    B. production standards
    C. time study
    D. work simplification training

7.____

8. In developing a program structure for PPBS, the one of the following that need NOT be a basic consideration is:

    8.____

    A. All functions should be included regardless of organizational placement
    B. Classifications should focus on objectives
    C. Formal organization of government agencies need not correspond to program structure
    D. Program structures should be the same as budget categories

9. PERT is MOST closely related to

    9.____

    A. Critical Path Method
    B. Efficiency and Economy Studies
    C. Operations Research
    D. Organization and Methods Studies

10. In PPBS, the role of the central budget bureau shifts from an emphasis on control to an emphasis on

    10.____

    A. economy   B. efficiency
    C. management   D. policy

11. A properly administered budget should provide assurance that certain conditions will prevail.
Which of the following is NOT appropriate to this statement?

    11.____

    A. All agency heads will express their financial assumptions in the same terms.
    B. Diverse statements of expenses will be reviewed and coordinated by responsible officials.
    C. The agency head will be able to look to the budget director, after final acceptance of the budget, to defend and support his individual role and contribution to the overall budget plan.
    D. It will be possible to review and analyze variances between anticipated and actual financial results to determine what (if anything) went wrong.

12. The quality of a public service is MOST difficult to measure in terms of its

    12.____

    A. characteristics   B. content
    C. payroll   D. objectives

13. In the analysis of processes, we are concerned with three types of variables: input, process, and output.
Which of the following is a process variable?

    13.____

    A. Social adaptation
    B. Student-teacher ratio
    C. Student time in classroom
    D. Teaching personnel

14. Which one of the following may BEST be considered an objective of BOTH the public and private sectors of the economy?

    14.____

    A. Increasing the national income
    B. Maintaining a smoothly running free enterprise system by preserving competition
    C. Provision of public goods
    D. Redistribution of income

15. Which of the following methods of dealing with incorrect decisions on the part of subordi-   15.____
nates is MOST constructive for the erring employee?

    A. Correct mistakes when they are found and say nothing
    B. Correct mistakes and warn the subordinate to be more careful
    C. Help the subordinate discern the nature of his errors
    D. Order the supervisor to review all decisions of his subordinates

16. In dealing with subordinates, some supervisors tend to issue orders which cannot be   16.____
questioned or discussed.
This method of supervision is likely to

    A. encourage open discussion and new ideas
    B. insure that subordinates clearly understand directions
    C. make the supervisor occasionally question his own decisions
    D. result in considerably faster action in completing an assignment

Questions 17-23.

DIRECTIONS: Questions 17 through 23 are to be answered SOLELY on the basis of the information contained in the following paragraphs, which is the fee schedule of a
hypothetical college.

FEE SCHEDULE

    a. A candidate for any baccalaureate degree is not required to pay tuition fees for under-
graduate courses until he exceeds 128 credits. Candidates exceeding 128 credits in undergraduate courses are charged at the rate of $100 a credit for each credit of undergraduate
course work in excess of 128. Candidates for a baccalaureate degree who are taking graduate courses must pay the same fee as any other student taking graduate courses.

    b. Non-degree students and college graduates are charged tuition fees for courses,
whether undergraduate or graduate, at the rate of $180 a credit. For such students there is an
additional charge of $150 for each class hour per week in excess of the number of course
credits. For example, if a three-credit course meets five hours a week, there is an additional
charge for the extra two hours. Graduate courses are shown with a (G) before the course
number.

    c. All students are required to pay the laboratory fees indicated after the number of cred-
its given for that course.

    d. All students must pay a $250 general fee each semester.

    e. Candidates for a baccalaureate degree are charged a $150 medical insurance fee for
each semester. All other students are charged a $100 medical insurance fee each semester.

17. Miss Burton is not a candidate for a degree. She registers for the following courses in the spring semester: Economics 12, 4 hours a week, 3 credits; History (G) 23, 4 hours a week, 3 credits; English 1, 2 hours a week, 2 credits.
The TOTAL amount in fees that Miss Burton must pay is

    17._____

    A. less than $2000
    B. at least $2000 but less than $2100
    C. at least $2100 but less than $2200
    D. $2200 or over

18. Miss Gray is not a candidate for a degree. She registers for the following courses in the fall semester: History 3, 3 hours a week, 3 credits; English 5, 3 hours a week, 2 credits; Physics 5, 6 hours a week, 3 credits, laboratory fee $60; Mathematics 7, 4 hours a week, 3 credits.
The TOTAL amount in fees that Miss Gray must pay is

    18._____

    A. less than $3150
    B. at least $3150 but less than $3250
    C. at least $3250 but less than $3350
    D. $3350 or over

19. Mr. Wall is a candidate for the Bachelor of Arts degree and has completed 126 credits. He registers for the following courses in the spring semester, his final semester at college: French 4, 3 hours a week, 3 credits; Physics (G) 15, 6 hours a week, 3 credits, laboratory fee $80; History (G) 33, 4 hours a week, 3 credits.
The TOTAL amount in fees that this candidate must pay is

    19._____

    A. less than $2100
    B. at least $2100 but less than $2300
    C. at least $2300 but less than $2500
    D. $2500 or over

20. Mr. Tindall, a candidate for the B.A. degree, has completed 122 credits of undergraduate courses. He registers for the following courses in his final semester: English 31, 3 hours a week, 3 credits; Philosophy 12, 4 hours a week, 4 credits; Anthropology 15, 3 hours a week, 3 credits; Economics (G) 68, 3 hours a week, 3 credits.
The TOTAL amount in fees that Mr. Tindall must pay in his final semester is

    20._____

    A. less than $1200
    B. at least $1200 but less than $1400
    C. at least $1400 but less than $1600
    D. $1600 or over

21. Mr. Cantrell, who was graduated from the college a year ago, registers for graduate courses in the fall semester. Each course for which he registers carries the same number of credits as the number of hours a week it meets. If he pays a total of $1530 including a $100 laboratory fee, the number of credits for which he is registered is

    21._____

    A. 4   B. 5   C. 6   D. 7

22. Miss Jayson, who is not a candidate for a degree, has registered for several courses   22.____
including a lecture course in History. She withdraws from the course in History for which
she had paid the required course fee of $690.
The number of hours that this course is scheduled to meet is

    A. 4   B. 5   C. 2   D. 3

23. Mr. Van Arsdale, a graduate of a college in Iowa, registers for the following courses in   23.____
one semester: Chemistry 35, 5 hours a week, 3 credits; Biology 13, 4 hours a week, 3
credits, laboratory fee $150; Mathematics (G) 179, 3 hours a week, 3 credits.
The TOTAL amount in fees that Mr. Van Arsdale must pay is

    A. less than $2400
    B. at least $2400 but less than $2500
    C. at least $2500 but less than $2600
    D. at least $2600

24. Which of the following is LEAST important in successfully implementing organizational   24.____
changes?

    A. Assigning responsibility for current failure
    B. Careful assessment of the *human consequences* of change
    C. Realistic goals for change
    D. Support and interest on the part of top management

25. Of the following, the one which is the MOST appropriate purpose for a conference of   25.____
administrative staff in a government organization is to

    A. solve unusual and complex problems arising out of administrative reorganization in
        the agency
    B. provide detailed and specific information needed in the preparation of a study of
        proposed changes in departmental procedures
    C. check on progress in implementing recent changes in operating procedures in var-
        ious divisions of the agency
    D. assign specific tasks to various individuals in connection with implementation of a
        new program

26. The MOST likely result of over-standardized and over-proceduralized regulations in an   26.____
organization is

    A. deterioration of organizational structure
    B. inhibition of individual initiative
    C. resistance to delegation of authority
    D. resistance to the flow of communications

27. The concept that decision should be made at the lowest level in an organization where all   27.____
the required information and competence are available is a GENERAL rule in

    A. communications theory
    B. decentralization of authority
    C. incremental decision-making
    D. span of control

28. The FIRST step in selecting a sample for a research project is to determine   28.____

    A.   the characteristics of the population
    B.   the extent to which you wish to generalize your findings
    C.   the accessibility of the sample data
    D.   whether every element of the population will have the same opportunity of being included in the sample

29. Direction, accompanied by authority, of the work of others is BEST defined as   29.____

    A.   coordination   B.   domination
    C.   planning   D.   supervision

30. Measures of central tendency, variability, and correlation of data are   30.____

    A.   examples of descriptive statistics
    B.   examples of inferential statistics
    C.   procedures to determine the dependability of data
    D.   unrelated statistics

31. In general, state and local debt in a state is incurred   31.____

    A.   for the financing of capital acquisition and construction
    B.   to balance all expense budget deficits
    C.   when tax resistance is very high
    D.   when tax resistance is relatively low

32. The MAJORITY of capital improvements undertaken by local governments are financed   32.____

    A.   by borrowed funds
    B.   by earmarked taxes
    C.   by grants from higher levels of government
    D.   on a pay-as-you-go basis

33. You have been asked to set up a system of reporting on activities to help the department's planning section. To propose as policy that no overlap or duplication be permitted, even if it meant that some areas of work would be left uncovered, would, GENERALLY, be   33.____

    A.   *desirable;* overlapping and duplication in reporting indicates poor planning
    B.   *undesirable;* inflexibility may result from establishment of general policy before the specific reporting system has been developed
    C.   *desirable;* complete coverage is not essential in order to be able to plan operations
    D.   *undesirable;* overlap or duplication is preferable to leaving a possible important area uncovered

34. PPBS CANNOT be applied if   34.____

    A.   objectives are not comparable
    B.   the difference in costs of two alternatives is very great
    C.   there is a fixed budget ceiling
    D.   utility is fixed

35. The BEST measure of effectiveness or results of a refuse collection program in terms of end products is the

    A. cleanliness of city streets
    B. number of men employed in the refuse collection process
    C. number of trucks used to collect refuse
    D. tons of refuse collected

35.____

36. Of the following, the budget process is MOST essentially concerned with

    A. allocating manpower to various units
    B. resolving the distribution of scarce resources among a variety of competing claims
    C. showing how much money is being spent for non-essentials
    D. showing which department is most efficient

36.____

37. The MAJOR value of performance budgeting is that it

    A. distinguishes between programs and performance
    B. enables program planning
    C. relates output to input
    D. requires the participation of top officials

37.____

38. The success of a budget allotment program depends PRIMARILY on the budget examiner's knowledge of

    A. departmental accounting procedures
    B. departmental budget codes
    C. seasonal patterns of departmental expenditures
    D. work flow charts of departmental activities

38.____

39. Costing of programs becomes MOST difficult when

    A. a program is conducted jointly by more than one agency
    B. performance cannot be measured in terms of end product
    C. salaries account for a major part of the program
    D. work standards do not exist

39.____

40. In analyzing the costs and benefits associated with a proposed municipal program, a budget examiner encounters certain factors which cannot be measured in dollar terms. His BEST course of action should be to

    A. assume that the non-measurable costs and benefits will balance out against one another
    B. give them weight equal to the weight given to measurable costs and benefits
    C. ignore such factors
    D. list them and describe what he believes their importance to be

40.____

KEY (CORRECT ANSWERS)

1.	D	11.	C	21.	C	31.	C
2.	B	12.	C	22.	A	32.	D
3.	B	13.	C	23.	C	33.	C
4.	C	14.	A	24.	A	34.	A
5.	B	15.	C	25.	A	35.	B
6.	D	16.	D	26.	B	36.	B
7.	D	17.	B	27.	B	37.	C
8.	D	18.	A	28.	B	38.	C
9.	A	19.	B	29.	D	39.	A
10.	D	20.	B	30.	A	40.	D

TEST 2

DIRECTIONS: Each question or incomplete statement is followed by several suggested answers or completions. Select the one that BEST answers the question or completes the statement. *PRINT THE LETTER OF THE CORRECT ANSWER IN THE SPACE AT THE RIGHT.*

1. A personnel utilization report for an activity indicates that efficiency for the fiscal year exceeded 100 percent. As a budget examiner, you may MOST logically infer that

   A. a study of the activity should be undertaken
   B. employees are overworked
   C. employees in this activity were very highly motivated
   D. the activity is well supervised

   1.____

2. The one of the following which is LEAST likely to be a tool used by the budget examiner is

   A. analysis   B. balance sheet
   C. economic forecast   D. standards

   2.____

3. In analyzing changes in productivity measured in terms of units per man-hour, it is NOT necessary to consider changes in

   A. price level   B. quality of labor
   C. quality of output   D. technology

   3.____

4. In contrast with traditional object line-item budgeting, the PPBS information system MAINLY emphasizes

   A. measurement   B. people
   C. projects   D. purposes

   4.____

5. It is estimated that prices will rise by 5 percent during the corning year.
   Interest on the current outstanding debt for the coming year may be expected to

   A. depend on new capital programs
   B. increase by about 5 percent
   C. increase by more than 5 percent because of the generally more rapid increase in construction costs
   D. remain unchanged

   5.____

6. Which of the following terms BEST describes a tax that places a greater burden on those less able to pay than on those more able to pay?
   _____ tax.

   A. Escalator   B. Progressive
   C. Regressive   D. Reversal

   6.____

7. The MOST important phase of the budget cycle, from a legal point of view, is

   A. appropriation   B. classification
   C. execution   D. formulation

   7.____

8. The BEST reason for prescribing definite procedures for certain work in an agency is to   8.____

    A. enable supervision to keep on top of details of work
    B. enable work to be processed speedily and consistently
    C. prevent individual discretion
    D. reduce training periods

9. Good program planning should start with   9.____

    A. analysis of costs and benefits
    B. definition of objectives
    C. last year's program
    D. setting a top limit for spending

10. A decrease in manpower needs for an appropriation unit because of declining activity   10.____
may BEST be provided for in the budget by

    A. a transfer of funds from other activities
    B. elimination of a vacant position
    C. elimination of backlog
    D. improved methods of work

11. Historical data are often used to estimate work standards.   11.____
The MOST serious short-coming of this procedure is that it(s)

    A. involves the use of data difficult to obtain
    B. may tend to perpetuate existing inefficiencies
    C. requires an accurate accounting system
    D. use is difficult to sell to department officials

12. Of the following, the one which is NOT a basic concept of administrative organization is   12.____
to

    A. assemble jobs into units which serve a common goal
    B. group like functions into the same job or jobs
    C. provide appropriate lines of authority and communication
    D. replace men with machines wherever machines can be built to do the work

13. Within organizations, the BASIC functions of communication are to   13.____

    A. build a permanent record of the organizational activities
    B. give and receive directions and information
    C. stimulate closer relationships between management and workers
    D. inform each employee of all significant events which may affect the organization

14. Automatic data processing does NOT necessarily   14.____

    A. assure more valid results
    B. facilitate data handling
    C. permit extensive manipulation of data
    D. permit the use of complex models of activities

15. The head of the agency has issued instructions that employees preparing letters for his   15.____
signature use no more words than are needed to convey adequately the required information.
To follow this rule in letter writing is GENERALLY

   A. *desirable;* typing of the correspondence will be less time-consuming
   B. *undesirable;* letters will be so terse that unfavorable attitudes toward government
   agencies may result
   C. *desirable;* the purpose of the letter will be carried out without obscuring the meaning or tiring the reader
   D. *undesirable;* it is usually necessary to elaborate on an explanation in order to make
   sure that the reader will understand the meaning

16. When preparing a long report on a study prepared for your superior, the one of the fol-   16.____
lowing which should usually come FIRST in your report is a(n)

   A. brief description of the working procedure followed in your study
   B. review of the background conditions leading to the study
   C. summary of your conclusions
   D. outline of suggested procedures for implementing the report

17. The MAIN function of a research report is usually to   17.____

   A. convince the reader of the adequacy of the research
   B. report as expeditiously as possible what was done, why it was done, the results,
   and the conclusions
   C. contribute to the body of scientific knowledge
   D. substantiate an a priori conclusion by presenting a set of persuasive quantitative
   data

18. Which one of the following terms BEST describes operating agencies which directly   18.____
serve the public?

   A. Administrative   B. Line
   C. Specialist   D. Staff

19. The budget in a democracy is primarily an expression of which one of the following types   19.____
of authority?

   A. Administrative   B. Executive
   C. Legislative   D. Managerial

20. The *item veto,* as applied to budgeting, is the   20.____

   A. power of the chief executive to veto legislative riders
   B. power of the chief executive to veto the entire appropriation bill
   C. requirement for a chief executive to itemize the reasons for his veto of the appropri-
   ation bill
   D. right of a chief executive to approve an appropriation bill as a whole but disapprove
   certain details

21. An experiment was conducted to measure the error rate of typists. The results follows: 21._____

| | | ERROR RATE |
TYPISTS	PERCENT OF TOTAL OUTPUT	(IN PERCENT)
A	30	1.00
B	30	1.50
C	40	0.50

The error rate, in percent, for the three typists combined

A. is 0.95
B. is 1.00
C. is 3.00
D. cannot be calculated from the given data

22. It is found that for the past three years the average weekly number of inspections per   22._____
inspector ranged from 20 inspections to 40 inspections.
On the basis of this information, it is MOST reasonable to conclude that

A. on the average, 30 inspections per week were made
B. the average weekly number of inspections never fell below 20
C. the performance of inspectors deteriorated over the three year period
D. the range in average weekly inspections was 60

Questions 23-25.

DIRECTIONS: Questions 23 through 25 are to be answered on the basis of the following information.

*The number of students admitted to University X in 2018 from High School Y was 268
students. This represented 13.7 percent of University X's entering freshman classes. In 2019,
it is expected that University X will admit 591 students from High School Y, which is expected
to represent 19.4 percent of the 2019 entering freshman classes of University X.*

23. Which of the following is the CLOSEST estimate of the size of University X's expected   23._____
2019 entering freshman classes?
_____ students.

A. 2000   B. 2500   C. 3000   D. 3500

24. Of the following, the expected percentage of increase from 2018 to 2019 in the number   24._____
of students graduating from High School Y and entering University X as freshmen is
HOST NEARLY

A. 5.7%   B. 20%   C. 45%   D. 120%

25. Assume that the cost of processing each freshman admission to University X from High   25._____
School Y in 2018 was an average of $28. Also, that this was 1/3 more than the average
cost of processing each of the other 2018 freshman admissions to University X.
Then, the one of the following that MOST closely shows the total processing cost of all
2018 freshman admissions to University X is

A. $6,500   B. $20,000   C. $30,000   D. $40,000

Questions 26-28.

DIRECTIONS: Answer Questions 26 through 28 on the basis of the following information.

Assume that in order to encourage Program A, the State and Federal governments have agreed to make the following reimbursements for money spent on Program A, provided the unreimbursed balance is paid from City funds.

During Fiscal Year 2018-2019 - For the first $2 million expended, 50% Federal reimbursement and 30% State reimbursement; for the next $3 million, 40% Federal reimbursement and 20% State reimbursement; for the next $5 million, 20% Federal reimbursement and 10% State reimbursement. Above $10 million expended, no Federal or State reimbursement.

During Fiscal Year 2019-2020 - For the first $1 million expended, 30% Federal reimbursement and 20% State reimbursement; for the next $4 million, 15% Federal reimbursement and 10% State reimbursement. Above $5 million expended, no Federal or State reimbursement.

26. Assume that the Program A expenditures are such that the State reimbursement for Fiscal Year 2018-2019 will be $1 million.
Then, the Federal reimbursement for Fiscal Year 2018-2019 will be

     A. $1,600,000   B. $1,800,000
     C. $2,000,000   D. $2,600,000

26.____

27. Assume that $8 million were to be spent on Program A in Fiscal Year 2019-2020, the total amount of unreimbursed City funds required would be

     A. $3,500,000   B. $4,500,000
     C. $5,500,000   D. $6,500,000

27.____

28. Assume that the City desires to have a combined total of $6 million spent in Program A during both the Fiscal Year 2018-2019 and the Fiscal Year 2019-2020.
Of the following expenditure combinations, the one which results in the GREATEST reimbursement of City funds is _____ million in Fiscal Year 2018-2019 and _____ million in Fiscal Year 2019-2020.

     A. $5; $1   B. $4; $2   C. $3; $3   D. $2; $4

28.____

29. The term PPBS relates most directly to one of the systems PRINCIPALLY designed to do which one of the following?

     A. Reduce the number of mistakes resulting in spoilage and wasted effort to zero
     B. Obtain greater cost effectiveness
     C. Assure that all operations are performed at the highest quality level that is technically attainable at the present time
     D. Assure that all output units are fully verified prior to being sent out

29.____

30. Assume that you are working with a computer programmer to solve a complex problem. Together, you have defined your problem in everyday English clearly enough to proceed. In the next step, you both start breaking down the information in the definition so that you both can decide on the operations needed for programming the problem.
This next step of getting from the definition of the problem to the point where you can begin laying out the steps actually to be taken in solving the problem is MOST appropriately called

30.____

A. completing the documentation   B. implementing the solution
C. identifying the problem statement   D. analyzing the problem

31. Assume that during the fiscal year 2018-2019, a bureau produced 20% more work units than it produced in the fiscal year 2017-2018. Also, assume that during the fiscal year 2018-2019 that bureau's staff was 20% SMALLER than it was in the fiscal year 2017-2018.
On the basis of this information, it would be MOST proper to conclude that the number of work units produced per staff member in that bureau in the fiscal year 2018-2019 exceeded the number of work units produced per staff member in that bureau in the fiscal year 2017-2018 by which one of the following percentages?

31.____

    A. 20%   B. 25%   C. 40%   D. 50%

32. Assume that during the following five fiscal years (FY), a bureau has received the following appropriations:
         FY 2014-2015 - $200,000
         FY 2015-2016 - $240,000
         FY 2016-2017 - $280,000
         FY 2017-2018 - $390,000
         FY 2018-2019 - $505,000
The bureau's appropriation for which one of the following fiscal years showed the LARGEST percentage of increase over the bureau's appropriation for the immediately previous fiscal year?
FY

32.____

    A. 2015-2016   B. 2016-2017   C. 2017-2018   D. 2018-2019

33. Which one of the following statements is MOST generally supported by modern industrial and behavioral research?

33.____

    A. High productivity and high quality each show a substantial negative correlation with high morale.
    B. Where professional employees participate in defining how much and what caliber of their service should be considered acceptable, they generally will set both types of goals substantially below those which management alone would have set.
    C. Professional employees get greatest satisfaction out of work that challenges them to exert their capacities fully.
    D. The participative approach to management relieves the manager of the need to be a decision-maker.

34. A bureau has a very large number of clerical personnel engaged in very similar duties, and only a limited portion can be absent at any one time if the workload is to be handled properly.
Which one of the following would generally be the bureau head's BEST approach toward scheduling the annual leave time (vacation, etc.) to be taken by the employees of that bureau?
The bureau head

34.____

    A. personally receives from each employee his preferred schedule of leave time, personally decides on when the employee can most conveniently be spared from the viewpoint of the office workload, and issues his decisions to all concerned in the form of a binding memorandum

B. advises his subordinate supervisors and employees of the parameters and constraints in time and numbers upon annual leave. The employees and subordinate supervisors prepare a proposed annual leave schedule within those limitations and submit it to the bureau head for approval or modification, and for promulgation

C. initially asks his subordinate supervisors to prepare a proposed annual leave schedule for employees with a minimum of consultation with the employees. He then circulates this schedule to the employees over his signature as a proposed schedule and invites employee reaction directly to him

D. asks employee or union representatives to prepare a proposed schedule with all leave to be taken spread evenly over the entire vacation period. He personally reviews and accepts or modifies this proposal,

35. An agency head desires to have an estimate of the *potential* of a middle-level administrative employee for development for higher-level administrative positions. He also desires to try to minimize possible errors or capriciousness which might creep into that estimate. Of the following, it would generally be MOST desirable to have the estimate   35._____

A. result from the pooled judgment of three or more past or present substantial-level supervisors of the subject employee and of persons with lateral or service contacts with the subject employee

B. made solely by substantial-level executives outside the past or present direct line of supervision above the subject employee

C. result from the pooled judgment of substantial-level personnel staff members rather than line executives

D. made solely by the present immediate line supervisor of the subject employee

36. If we total all of the occasions in which all government positions are filled with new faces (persons who did not occupy those specific positions previously), we generally would find that a GREATER number will result from   36._____

A. new accessions from the outside than from movement of personnel within the organization

B. movement of personnel within the organization than from new accessions from the outside

C. promotion of staff personnel to higher staff jobs than from promotion of line personnel to higher line jobs

D. filling of Exempt and Non-Competitive Class positions than from filling of Competitive Class positions

37. Which one of the following is generally the BEST criterion for determining the classification title to which a position should be allocated?   37._____
The

A. personal qualifications possessed by the present or expected appointee to the position

B. consequences of the work of the position or the responsibility it carries

C. number of work units required to be produced or completed in the position

D. consequences of inadequate overall governmental pay scales upon recruitment of outstanding personnel

38. The MAJOR decisions as to which jobs shall be created and who shall carry which responsibilities should generally be made by

    38.____

    A. budgetary advisers
    B. line managers
    C. classification specialists
    D. peer-level rating committee

39. Which one of the following generally BEST characterizes the basic nature of budget making and budget administration from a managerial viewpoint?

    39.____

    A. Budget administration is control, while budget making is planning.
    B. Budget administration is planning, while budget making is control.
    C. Both budget making and budget administration are only control functions; neither is a planning function.
    D. Both budget making and budget administration are only planning functions; neither is a control function.

40. In preparing his annual budget request for a large bureau with both substantial continuing and anticipated new activities, the bureau head must consider various factors (e.g., retaining credibility and obtaining required funds).
Of the following, the BEST long-range budgeting strategy would normally be for the bureau head to request

    40.____

    A. twice what is actually needed on the assumption that higher authorities will generally cut the requested amount in half
    B. ten percent less than he actually estimates to be needed and to submit a supplementary request later for that ten percent
    C. what is needed for the continuing activities plus twenty-five percent to allow some slack funds
    D. what he estimates is needed to continue existing essential programs and to fund needed new activities

---

KEY (CORRECT ANSWERS)

1.	A	11.	B	21.	A	31.	D
2.	B	12.	D	22.	B	32.	C
3.	A	13.	B	23.	C	33.	C
4.	D	14.	A	24.	D	34.	B
5.	D	15.	C	25.	D	35.	A
6.	C	16.	C	26.	B	36.	B
7.	A	17.	B	27.	D	37.	B
8.	B	18.	B	28.	A	38.	B
9.	B	19.	C	29.	B	39.	A
10.	B	20.	D	30.	D	40.	D

EXAMINATION SECTION
TEST 1

DIRECTIONS: Each question or incomplete statement is followed by several suggested answers or completions. Select the one that BEST answers the question or completes the statement. *PRINT THE LETTER OF THE CORRECT ANSWER IN THE SPACE AT THE RIGHT.*

1. As a supervisor in a bureau, you have been asked by the head of the bureau to recommend whether or not the work of the bureau requires an increase in the permanent staff of the bureau.
   Of the following questions, the one whose answer would MOST likely assist you in making your recommendation is: Are

   A. some permanent employees working irregular hours because they occasionally work overtime?
   B. the present permanent employees satisfied with their work assignments?
   C. temporary employees hired to handle seasonal fluctuations in work load?
   D. the present permanent employees keeping the work of the bureau current?

   1.____

2. In making job assignments to his subordinates, a supervisor should follow the principle that each individual GENERALLY is capable of

   A. performing one type of work well and less capable of performing other types well
   B. learning to perform a wide variety of different types of work
   C. performing best the type of work in which he has had experience
   D. learning to perform any type of work in which he is given training

   2.____

3. Assume that you are the supervisor of a large number of clerks in a unit in a city agency. Your unit has just been given an important assignment which must be completed a week from now. You know that, henceforth, your unit will be given this assignment every six months.
   You or any one of your subordinates who has been properly instructed can complete this assignment in one day. This assignment is of a routine type which is ordinarily handled by clerks. There is enough time for you to train one of your subordinates to handle the assignment and then have him do it. However, it would take twice as much time for you to take this course of action as it would for you to do the assignment yourself. The one of the following courses of action which you should take in this situation is to

   A. do the assignment yourself as soon as possible without discussing it with any of your subordinates at this time
   B. do the assignment yourself and then train one of your subordinates to handle it in the future
   C. give the assignment to one of your subordinates after training him to handle it
   D. train each of your subordinates to do the assignment on a rotating basis after you have done it yourself the first time

   3.____

4. You are in charge of an office in which each member of the staff has a different set of duties, although each has the same title. No member of the staff can perform the duties of any other member of the staff without first receiving extensive training. Assume that it is necessary for one member of the staff to take on, in addition to his regular work, an assignment which any member of the staff is capable of carrying out.
The one of the following considerations which would have the MOST weight in determining which staff member is to be given the additional assignment is the

    A. quality of the work performed by the individual members of the staff
    B. time consumed by individual members of the staff in performing their work
    C. level of difficulty of the duties being performed by individual members of the staff
    D. relative importance of the duties being performed by individual members of the staff

4.____

5. The one of the following causes of clerical error which is usually considered to be LEAST attributable to faulty supervision or inefficient management is

    A. inability to carry out instructions
    B. too much work to do
    C. an inappropriate recordkeeping system
    D. continual interruptions

5.____

6. Suppose you are in charge of a large unit in which all of the clerical staff perform similar tasks.
In evaluating the relative accuracy of the clerks, the clerk who should be considered to be the LEAST accurate is the one

    A. whose errors result in the greatest financial loss
    B. whose errors cost the most to locate
    C. who makes the greatest percentage of errors in his work
    D. who makes the greatest number of errors in the unit

6.____

7. Assume that under a proposed procedure for handling employee grievances in a public agency, the first step to be taken is for the aggrieved employee to submit his grievance as soon as it arises to a grievance board set up to hear all employee grievances in the agency. The board, which is to consist of representatives of management and of rank and file employees, is to consider the grievance, obtain all necessary pertinent information, and then render a decision on the matter. Thus, the first-line supervisor would not be involved in the settlement of any of his subordinates' grievances except when asked by the board to submit information.
This proposed procedure would be generally UNDESIRABLE chiefly because the

    A. board may become a bottleneck to delay the prompt disposition of grievances
    B. aggrieved employees and their supervisors have not been first given the opportunity to resolve the grievances themselves
    C. employees would be likely to submit imaginary, as well as real, grievances to the board
    D. board will lack first-hand, personal knowledge of the factors involved in grievances

7.____

8. Sometimes jobs in private organizations and public agencies are broken down so as to permit a high degree of job specialization.
Of the following, an IMPORTANT effect of a high degree of job specialization in a public agency is that employees performing

8.____

A. highly specialized jobs may not be readily transferable to other jobs in the agency
B. similar duties may require closer supervision than employees performing unrelated functions
C. specialized duties can be held responsible for their work to a greater extent than can employees performing a wide variety of functions
D. specialized duties will tend to cooperate readily with employees performing other types of specialized duties

9. Assume that you are the supervisor of a clerical unit in an agency. One of your subordinates violates a rule of the agency, a violation which requires that the employee be suspended from his work for one day. The violated rule is one that you have found to be unduly strict, and you have recommended to the management of the agency that the rule be changed or abolished. The management has been considering your recommendation but has not yet reached a decision on the matter.
In these circumstances, you should

A. not initiate disciplinary action but, instead, explain to the employee that the rule may be Changed shortly
B. delay disciplinary action on the violation until the management has reached a decision on changing the rule
C. modify the disciplinary action by reprimanding the employee and informing him that further action may be taken when the management has reached a decision on changing the rule
D. initiate the prescribed disciplinary action without commenting on the strictness of the rule or on your recommendation

10. Assume that a supervisor praises his subordinates for satisfactory aspects of their work only when he is about to criticize them for unsatisfactory aspects of their work.
Such a practice is UNDESIRABLE primarily because

A. his subordinates may expect to be praised for their work even if it is unsatisfactory
B. praising his subordinates for some aspects of their work while criticizing other aspects will weaken the effects of the criticisms
C. his subordinates would be more receptive to criticism if it were followed by praise
D. his subordinates may come to disregard praise and wait for criticism to be given

11. The one of the following which would be the BEST reason for an agency to eliminate a procedure for obtaining and recording certain information is that

A. it is no longer legally required to obtain the information
B. there is no advantage in obtaining the information
C. the information could be compiled on the basis of other information available
D. the information obtained is sometimes incorrect

12. In determining the type and number of records to be kept in an agency, it is important to recognize that records are of value PRIMARILY as

A. raw material to be used in statistical analysis
B. sources of information about the agency's activities
C. by-products of the activities carried on by the agency
D. data for evaluating the effectiveness of the agency

13. Aside from requirements imposed by authority, the frequency with which reports are submitted or the length of the interval which they cover should depend PRINCIPALLY on the

    A. availability of the data to be included in the reports
    B. amount of time required to prepare the reports
    C. extent of the variations in the data with the passage of time
    D. degree of comprehensiveness required in the reports

13.____

14. Organizations that occupy large, general, open-area offices sometimes consider it desirable to build private offices for the supervisors of large bureaus.
The one of the following which is generally NOT considered to be a justification of the use of private offices is that they

    A. lend prestige to the person occupying the office
    B. provide facilities for private conferences
    C. achieve the maximum use of office space
    D. provide facilities for performing work requiring a high degree of concentration

14.____

15. The LEAST important factor to be considered in planning the layout of an office is the

    A. relative importance of the different types of work to be done
    B. convenience with which communication can be achieved
    C. functional relationships of the activities of the office
    D. necessity for screening confidential activities from unauthorized persons

15.____

16. The one of the following which is generally considered to be the CHIEF advantage of using data processing equipment in modern offices is to

    A. facilitate the use of a wide variety of sources of information
    B. supply management with current information quickly
    C. provide uniformity in the processing and reporting of information
    D. broaden the area in which management decisions can be made

16.____

17. In the box design of office forms, the spaces in which information is to be entered are arranged in boxes containing captions.
Of the following, the one which is generally NOT considered to be an acceptable rule in employing box design is that

    A. space should be allowed for the lengthiest anticipated entry in a box
    B. the caption should be located in the upper left corner of the box
    C. the boxes on a form should be of the same size and shape
    D. boxes should be aligned vertically whenever possible

17.____

18. As a management tool, the work count would generally be of LEAST assistance to a unit supervisor in

    A. scheduling the work of his unit
    B. locating bottlenecks in the work of his unit
    C. ascertaining the number of subordinates he needs
    D. tracing the flow of work in the unit

18.____

19. Of the following, the FIRST step that should be taken in a forms simplification program is to make a

19.____

A. detailed analysis of the items found on current forms
B. study of the amount of use made of existing forms
C. survey of the amount of each kind of form on hand
D. survey of the characteristics of the more effective forms in use

20. The work-distribution chart is a valuable tool for an office supervisor to use in conducting   20.____
work'simplification programs.
Of the following questions, the one which a work-distribution chart would generally be
LEAST useful in answering is:

A. What activities take the most time?
B. Are the employees doing many unrelated tasks?
C. Is work being distributed evenly among the employees?
D. Are activities being performed in proper sequence?

21. Assume that, as a supervisor, you conduct, from time to time, work-performance studies   21.____
in various sections of your agency. The units of measurement used in any study depend
on the particular study and may be number of letters typed, number of papers filed, or
other suitable units.
It is MOST important that the units of measurement to be used in a study conform to
the units used in similar past studies when the

A. units of measurement to be used in the study cannot be defined sharply
B. units of measurement used in past studies were satisfactory
C. results of the study are to be compared with those of past studies
D. results of the study are to be used for the same purpose as were those of past
studies

22. As it is used in auditing, an internal check is a   22.____

A. procedure which is designed to guard against fraud
B. periodic audit by a public accounting firm to verify the accuracy of the internal
transactions of an organization
C. document transferring funds from one section to another within an organization
D. practice of checking documents twice before they are transmitted outside an orga-
nization

23. Of the following, the one which can LEAST be considered to be a proper function of an   23.____
accounting system is to

A. indicate the need to curtail expenditures
B. provide information for future fiscal programs
C. record the expenditure of funds from special appropriations
D. suggest methods to expedite the collection of revenues

24. Assume that a new unit is to be established in an agency. The unit is to compile and tab-   24.____
ulate data so that it will be of the greatest usefulness to the high-level administrators in
the agency in making administrative decisions. In planning the organization of this unit,
the question that should be answered FIRST is:

A. What interpretations are likely to be made of the data by the high-level administrators in making decisions?
B. At what point in the decision-making process will it be most useful to inject the data?
C. What types of data will be required by high-level administrators in making decisions?
D. What criteria will the high-level administrators use to evaluate the decisions they make?

25. The one of the following which is the CHIEF limitation of the organization chart as it is generally used in business and government is that the chart   25.____

    A. engenders within incumbents feelings of rights to positions they occupy
    B. reveals only formal authority relationships, omitting the informal ones
    C. shows varying degrees of authority even though authority is not subject to such differentiation
    D. presents organizational structure as it is rather than what it is supposed to be

26. The degree of decentralization that is effective and economical in an organization tends to vary INVERSELY with the   26.____

    A. size of the organization
    B. availability of adequate numbers of competent personnel
    C. physical dispersion of the organization's activities
    D. adequacy of the organization's communications system

27. The one of the following which usually can LEAST be considered to be an advantage of committees as they are generally used in government and business is that they   27.____

    A. provide opportunities for reconciling varying points of view
    B. promote coordination by the interchange of information among the members of the committee
    C. act promptly in situations requiring immediate action
    D. use group judgment to resolve questions requiring a wide range of experience

28. Managerial decentralization is defined as the decentralization of decision-making authority.
    The degree of managerial decentralization in an organization varies INVERSELY with the   28.____

    A. number of decisions made lower down the management hierarchy
    B. importance of the decisions made lower down the management hierarchy
    C. number of major organizational functions affected by decisions made at lower management levels
    D. amount of review to which decisions made at lower management levels are subjected

29. Some policy-making commissions are composed of members who are appointed to overlapping terms.
    Of the following, the CHIEF advantage of appointing members to overlapping terms in such commissions is that   29.____

A. continuity of policy is promoted
B. the likelihood of compromise policy decisions is reduced
C. responsibility for policy decisions can be fixed upon individual members
D. the likelihood of unanimity of opinion is increased

30. If a certain public agency with a fixed number of employees has a line organizational structure, then the width of the span of supervision is   30.____

   A. inversely proportional to the length of the chain of command in the organization
   B. directly proportional to the complexity of tasks performed in the organization
   C. inversely proportional to the competence of the personnel in the organization
   D. directly proportional to the number of levels of supervision existing in the organization

31. Mr. Brown is a supervisor in charge of a section of clerical employees in an agency. The   31.____
    section consists of four units, each headed by a unit supervisor. From time to time, he
    makes tours of his section for the purpose of maintaining contact with the rank and file
    employees. During these tours, he discusses with these employees their work produc-
    tion, work methods, work problems, and other related topics. The information he obtains
    in this manner is often incomplete or inaccurate. At meetings with the unit supervisors,
    he questions them on the information acquired during his tours. The supervisors are
    often unable to answer the questions immediately because they are based on incom-
    plete or inaccurate information. When the supervisors ask that they be permitted to
    accompany Mr. Brown on his tours and thus answer his questions on the spot, Mr. Brown
    refuses, explaining that a rank and file employee might be reluctant to speak freely in the
    presence of his supervisor. This situation may BEST be described as a violation of the
    principle of organization called

   A. span of control   B. delegation of authority
   C. specialization of work   D. unity of command

Questions 32-36.

DIRECTIONS: Each of Questions 32 through 36 consists of a statement which contains one
               word that is incorrectly used because it is not in keeping with the meaning that
               the quotation is evidently intended to convey. For each of these questions, you
               are to select the INCORRECTLY used word and substitute for it one of the
               words lettered A, B, C, or D, which helps BEST to convey the meaning of the
               statement.

32. There has developed in recent years an increasing awareness of the need to measure   32.____
    the quality of management in all enterprises and to seek the principles that can serve as
    a basis for this improvement.

   A. growth   B. raise   C. efficiency   D. define

33. It is hardly an exaggeration to deny that the permanence, productivity, and humanity of   33.____
    any industrial system depend upon its ability to utilize the positive and constructive
    impulses of all who work and upon its ability to arouse and continue interest in the neces-
    sary activities.

   A. develop   B. efficiency
   C. state   D. inspirational

34. The selection of managers on the basis of technical knowledge alone seems to recognize that the essential characteristic of management is getting things done through others, thereby demanding skills that are essential in coordinating the activities of subordinates.

    A. training   B. fails
    C. organization   D. improving

34._____

35. Only when it is deliberate and when it is clearly understood what impressions the ease of communication will probably create in the minds of employees and subordinate management, should top management refrain from commenting on a subject that is of general concern.

    A. obvious   B. benefit   C. doubt   D. absence

35._____

36. Scientific planning of work requires careful analysis of facts and a precise plan of action for the whims and fancies of executives that often provide only a vague indication of the work to be done.

    A. substitutes   B. development
    C. preliminary   D. comprehensive

36._____

37. Within any single level of government, as a city or a state, the administrative authority may be concentrated or dispersed.
Of the following plans of government, the one in which administrative authority would be dispersed the MOST is the _____ plan.

    A. mayor   B. mayor-council
    C. commission   D. city manager

37._____

38. In general, the courts may review a decision of an administrative agency with rule-making powers. However, the courts will usually REFUSE to review a decision of such an agency if the only question raised concerning the decision is whether or not the

    A. decision contravenes public policy
    B. agency has abused the powers conferred upon it
    C. decision deals with an issue which is within the jurisdiction of the agency
    D. agency has applied the same rules of evidence as are used in the courts

38._____

39. A legislature sometimes delegates rule-making powers to the administrators of a public agency.
Of the following, the CHIEF advantage of such delegation is that

    A. the frequency with which the legality of the agency's rules is contested in court will be reduced
    B. the agency will have the flexibility to adjust to changing conditions and problems
    C. mistakes made by the administrators or the legislature in defining the scope of the agency's program may be easily corrected
    D. the legislature will not be required to approve the rules formulated by the agency

39._____

40. Some municipalities have delegated the functions of budget preparation and personnel selection to central agencies, thus removing these functions from operating departments.
Of the following, the MOST important reason why municipalities have delegated these functions to central agencies is that

40._____

A. the performance of these functions presents problems that vary from one operating department to another
B. operating departments often lack sufficient funds to perform these functions adequately
C. the performance of these functions by a central agency produces more uniform policies than if these functions are performed by the operating departments
D. central agencies are not controlled as closely as are operating departments and so have greater freedom in formulating new policies and procedures to deal with difficult budget and personnel problems

41. Of the following, the MOST fundamental reason for the use of budgets in governmental administration is that budgets   41._____

    A. minimize seasonal variations in work loads and expenditures of public agencies
    B. facilitate decentralization of functions performed by public agencies
    C. provide advance control on the expenditure of funds
    D. establish valid bases for comparing present governmental activities with corresponding activities in previous periods

42. In some governmental jurisdictions, the chief executive prepares the budget for a fiscal   42._____
period and presents it to the legislative branch of government for adoption. In other jurisdictions, the legislative branch prepares and adopts the budget.
Preparation of the budget by the chief executive rather than by the legislative branch is

    A. *desirable*, primarily because the chief executive is held largely accountable by the public for the results of fiscal operations and should, therefore, be the one to prepare the budget
    B. *undesirable*, primarily because such a separation of the legislative and executive branches leads to the enactment of a budget that does not consider the overall needs of the government
    C. *desirable*, primarily because the preparation of the budget by the chief executive limits legislative review and evaluation of operating programs
    D. *undesirable*, primarily because responsibility for budget preparation should be placed in the branch that must eventually adopt the budget and appropriate the funds for it

43. The one of the following which is generally the FIRST step in the budget-making process   43._____
of a municipality that has a central budget agency is

    A. determination of available sources of revenue within the municipality
    B. establishment of tax rates at levels sufficient to achieve a balanced budget in the following fiscal period
    C. evaluation by the central budget agency of the adequacy of the municipality's previous budgets
    D. assembling by the central budget agency of the proposed expenditures of each agency in the municipality for the following fiscal period

44. It is advantageous for a municipality to issue serial bonds rather than sinking fund bonds   44._____
CHIEFLY because

A. an issue of serial bonds usually includes a wider range of maturity dates than does an issue of sinking fund bonds

B. appropriations set aside periodically to retire serial bonds as they fall due are more readily invested in long-term securities at favorable rates of interest than are appropriations earmarked for redemption of sinking fund bonds

C. serial bonds are sold at regular intervals while sinking fund bonds are issued as the need for funds arises

D. a greater variety of interest rates is usually offered in an issue of serial bonds than in an issue of sinking fund bonds

45. Studies conducted by the Regional Plan Association of the 22-county New York Metropolitan Region, comprising New York City and surrounding counties in New York, New Jersey, and Connecticut, have defined Manhattan, Brooklyn, Queens, the Bronx, and Hudson County in New Jersey as the *core*. Such studies have examined the per capita personal income of the core as a percent of the per capita personal income of the entire Region, and the population of the core as a percent of the total population of the entire Region.
These studies support the conclusion that, as a percent of the entire Region,   45._____

A. both population and per capita personal income in the core were higher in 1970 than in 1940

B. both population and per capita personal income in the core were lower in 1970 than in 1940

C. population was higher and per capita personal income was lower in the core in 1970 than in 1940

D. population was lower and per capita personal income was higher in the core in 1970 than in 1940

KEY (CORRECT ANSWERS)

1.	D	11.	B	21.	C	31.	D	41.	C
2.	B	12.	B	22.	A	32.	B	42.	A
3.	C	13.	C	23.	D	33.	C	43.	D
4.	B	14.	C	24.	C	34.	B	44.	A
5.	A	15.	A	25.	B	35.	D	45.	B
6.	C	16.	B	26.	D	36.	A		
7.	B	17.	C	27.	C	37.	C		
8.	A	18.	D	28.	D	38.	D		
9.	D	19.	B	29.	A	39.	B		
10.	D	20.	D	30.	A	40.	C		

EXAMINATION SECTION
TEST 1

DIRECTIONS: Each question or incomplete statement is followed by several suggested answers or completions. Select the one that BEST answers the question or completes the statement. *PRINT THE LETTER OF THE CORRECT ANSWER IN THE SPACE AT THE RIGHT.*

1. The number of subordinates that can be supervised directly by one person tends to   1.____

    A. *increase* as the level of supervision progresses from the first-line supervisory level to the management level
    B. *decrease* as the duties of the subordinates increase in difficulty and complexity
    C. *decrease* with an increase in the knowledge and experience of the subordinates
    D. *increase* as the physical distance between supervisor and subordinates, as well as between the individual subordinates, increases

2. A study of the supervision of employees in an agency reveals that the bureau chiefs are reluctant to delegate responsibility and authority to their assistants.   2.____
   This study is *most likely* to reveal, in addition, that

    A. the organizational structure of this agency should be centralized
    B. the bureau chiefs tend to spend too much of their time on minor aspects of their work
    C. the number of employees supervised by bureau chiefs is excessive
    D. significant deviations from planned performance are not called to the attention of the bureau chiefs

3. The delegation of responsibility and authority to subordinates by their superior generally does NOT   3.____

    A. facilitate a division of labor or the development of specialization
    B. permit the superior to carry out programs of work that exceed his immediate personal limits of physical energy and knowledge
    C. result in a downward transfer of work, both mental and manual
    D. involve a transfer of ultimate responsibility from superior to subordinate

4. Horizontal coordination is achieved when the various units of a bureau work with mutual harmony and assistance.   4.____
   The achievement of such coordination is generally made *more difficult* when the chief of a large bureau

    A. conducts periodic conferences with supervisors of his operating units
    B. delegates some of his coordinating tasks to a staff assistant
    C. increases the number of specialized units in his bureau and the degree of their specialization
    D. transfers, subordinates from one to another of his operating units to broaden their understanding of the bureau's work

5. Some subdivision of work is imperative in large-scale operation. However, in subdividing work the superior should adopt the methods that have the greatest number of advantages and the fewest disadvantages.
The one of the following that is *most likely* to result from subdivision of work is

    A. measuring work performed by employees is made more difficult
    B. authority and responsibility for performance of particular operations are not clearly defined
    C. standardizing work processes is made more difficult
    D. work is delayed in passing between employees and between operating units

    5.____

6. In developing a system for controlling the production of a bureau, the bureau chief should give consideration to reducing the fluctuations in the bureau's work load.
Of the following, the technique that is generally LEAST helpful in reducing fluctuations in work load is

    A. staffing the bureau so that it can handle peak loads
    B. maintaining a controlled backlog of work
    C. regulating the timing of work routed to the bureau
    D. changing the order of steps in work processes

    6.____

7. The flow of work in an organization may be divided and channeled according to either a serial method or a parallel method. Under the serial method, the work moves through a single channel with each job progressing step by step through various work stations where a worker at each station completes a particular step of the job. Under the parallel method, the jobs are distributed among a number of workers, each worker completing all the steps of a job. The MOST accurate of the following statements regarding these two methods of dividing the flow of work is that

    A. the training or break-in time necessary for workers to acquire processing skills is generally shorter under the parallel method
    B. the serial method enables the workers to obtain a fuller understanding of the significance of their work
    C. the parallel method tends to minimize the need for control devices to keep track of individual jobs in process
    D. flexibility in the use of available staff is generally increased under the serial method

    7.____

8. The executive who has immediate responsibility for a group of functions should have the right to decide what the structure of his organization shall be.
In making such decision, the executive should realize that

    A. the lower the competence of a staff, the more important it is to maintain a sound organizational structure
    B. the productivity of a competent staff will not be affected by an impairment in organizational structure
    C. the productivity of a staff whose level of competency is low cannot be improved by an improvement in organizational structure
    D. where there is a sound organizational structure there must of necessity be a sound organization

    8.____

9. Of the following means that a bureau chief may utilize in training his understudy, the LEAST acceptable one is for him to

    A. give the understudy assignments which other employees find too difficult or unpleasant
    B. discuss with the understudy the important problems that confront the bureau chief
    C. rotate the assignments given the understudy
    D. give the understudy an opportunity to attend some of the meetings of bureau chiefs

9.____

10. Of the following practices and techniques that may be employed by the conference leader, the one that the conference leader should ordinarily AVOID is

    A. permitting certain participants to leave the conference to get back to their work when the discussion has reached the point where their special interests or qualifications are no longer involved
    B. encouraging the participants to take full written notes for later comparison with the minutes of the meeting
    C. helping a participant extricate himself from an awkward position in which the participant has placed himself by an illadvised remark
    D. translating the technical remarks of a speaker for the benefit of some participants who would otherwise fail to grasp the meaning of the remarks

10.____

11. In assigning work to his subordinates, a supervisor is MOST likely to lose the respect of his subordinates if he

    A. reviews with a new employee the main points of an oral order issued to this employee
    B. issues written orders instead of oral orders when a subordinate has repeatedly failed to carry out oral orders
    C. gives oral orders regarding a task which the subordinate has performed satisfactorily in the past
    D. gives an oral order which he feels the subordinate will not carry out

11.____

12. Both Agency X and Agency Y have district offices in all areas of the city. In Agency X the activities of the various districts are administered under centralized control, whereas in Agency Y the activities of the various district offices are administered under decentralized control.
The one of the following which is MORE characteristic of Agency X than of Agency Y is that in Agency X

    A. activities of the district offices can more readily be adapted to meet the problems of the district served
    B. there are greater opportunities for district administrators to develop resourcefulness
    C. agency policies can be carried out with greater uniformity
    D. decisions are made by individuals closer to the points at which problems arise

12.____

13. Of the following training methods, the one that is generally MOST valuable in teaching employees new clerical skills is

    A. organized group discussion
    B. individual instruction on the job
    C. use of visual aids, such as charts and pictures
    D. supervised reading, research and inspection

13.____

14. Department X maintains offices in each district of the city. Data gathered by the district offices are submitted monthly to the main office on a standard set of forms which are somewhat complicated.
Of the following methods of issuing detailed instructions for filing out the forms properly, the one generally considered MOST acceptable is

14.____

   A. incorporating the instructions in the department's procedure manual
   B. including an instructions sheet with each package of blank forms sent to a district office
   C. printing the instructions on the back of each form
   D. conducting periodic staff conferences devoted exclusively to discussions of the proper method of filling out the form

15. The one of the following which is usually LEAST affected by an increase in the personnel of an organization is the

15.____

   A. problems of employee relationships
   B. average amount of work performed by an employee
   C. importance of coordinating the work of organizational units
   D. number of first-line supervisors required

16. As part of his program to simplify clerical procedures, the chief of the records management division has decided to make an analysis of the forms used by his agency and to establish a system of forms control. He has assigned the assistant bureau chief to perform the bulk of the work in connection with this project. This assistant will receive part-time help from four subordinate employees.
Of the following actions the bureau chief may take in planning the work on this project, the MOST appropriate one is for him to

16.____

   A. have the plans drawn up by the assistant and then submitted for final approval to the four part-time subordinates before work on the project is begun
   B. have the assistant work with him in drawing up the plans and then present the plans to the four part-time subordinates for their comments
   C. join with the five employees as a committee to formulate the plans for the project
   D. prepare the plans himself and then submit the plans for approval to all five employees who are to work on the project

17. Bureau X is composed of several clerical units, each supervised by a unit head accountable to the bureau chief. Assume that the bureau chief has a special task for an employee of one of the clerical units and wishes to issue instructions directly to the employee regarding this task.
The LEAST appropriate of the following procedures for the bureau chief to follow is to

17.____

   A. issue the instructions to the employee without notifying the employee's unit head
   B. give the instructions to the employee in the presence of the unit head
   C. ask the unit head to send the employee to him for instructions on this special task
   D. tell the employee to inform his unit head of the bureau chief's instructions

18. A bureau chief has scheduled a conference with the unit heads in his bureau to obtain their views on a major problem confronting the bureau.
The LEAST appropriate action for him to take in conducting this conference is to

18.____

A. present his own views on the solution of the problem before asking the unit heads for their opinions
B. call upon a participant in the conference for information which this participant should have as part of his job
C. weigh the opinions expressed at the conference in the light of the individual speaker's background and experience
D. summarize briefly at the conclusion of the conference, the important points covered and the conclusions reached

19. Of the following, the greatest stress in selecting employees for office supervisory positions should ordinarily be placed on   19.____

A. intelligence and educational background
B. knowledge of the work and capacity for leadership
C. sincere interest in the activities and objectives of the agency
D. skill in performing the type of work to be supervised

20. The MOST acceptable of the following guides in preparing the specifications for a form is that   20.____

A. when forms are to be printed on colored paper, the dark shades of colored paper should be used
B. *tumble* or *head-to-foot* should be used if forms printed on both sides of the sheet are to be placed in binders with side binding
C. provision for ballot-type entries should be made if items requiring *yes* or *no* entries are to appear on the form
D. all-rag ledger paper rather than all-wood pulp bond paper should be used for forms which will receive little handling and will be kept for a short time

21. Suppose you are the chief of a bureau which contains several operating units. On one occasion you observe one of your unit heads severely reprimand a subordinate for violating a staff regulation. This subordinate has a good record for observing staff regulations, and you believe the severe reprimand will seriously undermine the morale of the employee.   21.____
Of the following, the BEST action for you to take in this situation is to

A. call both the unit head and the subordinate into your office at the same time and have each present his views on the matter to you
B. refrain from intervening in this matter because the unit head may resent any interference
C. take the subordinate aside, inform him that the unit head had not intended to reprimand him severely, and suggest that the matter be forgotten
D. discuss the matter with the unit head and suggest that he make some mitigating explanation to the subordinate

22. In addition to a report on its activities for the year, the one of the following items which it is MOST appropriate to include in an agency's annual report is   22.____

A. praise for each of the accomplishments of the agency during the year
B. pictures of agency personnel
C. history of the agency
D. descriptions of future activities and plans of the agency

23. Before transferring material from the active to the inactive files, the supervisor of the filing unit always consults the bureau heads directly concerned with the use of this material. This practice by the supervisor is 　23.＿＿＿

    A. *desirable* chiefly because material that is no longer current for some bureaus may still be current for others

    B. *undesirable* chiefly because it can only lead to disagreement among the bureau heads consulted

    C. *desirable* chiefly because it is more economical to store records in transfer files than to keep them in the active files

    D. *undesirable* chiefly because the filing supervisor is expected to make his own decision

24. The determination of essential factors in a specific kind of work and of qualifications of a worker necessary for its competent performance is MOST **accurately defined as** 　24.＿＿＿

    A. job analysis   B. micro-motion study

    C. cost analysis   D. production control

25. In the clinical approach to disciplinary problems, attention is focused on the basic causes of which the overt relations are merely symptomatic rather than on the specific violations which have brought the employee unfavorable notice.
The MOST accurate implication of this quotation is that the clinical approach 　25.＿＿＿

    A. places emphasis on the actual violation rather than on the cause of the violation

    B. attempts to promote greater insight into the underlying factors which have led to the infractions

    C. does not evaluate the justness and utility of applying a specific penalty in a given situation

    D. avoids the necessity for disciplinary action

26. The LEAST accurate of the following statements regarding the conduct of a conference is that 　26.＿＿＿

    A. when there is great disparity in the rank of the participants at a conference, the conference leader should ordinarily refrain from requesting an opinion point blank from a participant of relatively low rank

    B. when the aim of a conference is to obtain the opinion of a group of approxmately the same rank, the rank of the conference leader should ordinarily not be too much higher than that of the participants

    C. in general, the chances that a conference will be fruitful are greatly increased if the conference leader's direct superior is one of the participants

    D. a top administrator invited to present a brief talk sponsoring a series of conferences for line supervisors should generally arrange to leave the conference as soon as appropriate after he has made his speech

27. In preparing a report for release to the general public, the bureau chief should GENERALLY present at the beginning of the report 　27.＿＿＿

    A. a description of the methods used in preparing the report

    B. anticipated criticism of the report and the answer to this criticism

    C. his conclusions and recommendations

    D. a bibliography of the sources used in preparing the report

28. Staff or functional supervision in an organization   28.____

    A. is least justified at the operational level
    B. is contrary to the principle of Unity of Command
    C. is more effective than authoritative supervision
    D. normally does not give the right to take direct disciplinary action

29. Suppose that you are the supervisor of Clerical Unit A in a city agency. Work processed   29.____
in your unit is sent to Clerical Unit B for further processing. One of your subordinates
complains to you that the supervisor of Clerical Unit B has been offering him unwar-
ranted criticism of the method in which his work is performed.
Of the following actions you may take, the MOST appropriate one for you to take
FIRST is to

    A. request the supervisor of Clerical Unit B to meet with you and your subordinate to
       discuss this matter
    B. report this matter to this unit supervisor's immediate superior and request that this
       unsolicited criticism be discontinued
    C. obtain the facts from the subordinate and then discuss the matter with this unit
       supervisor
    D. tell your subordinate to refer the unit supervisor to you the next time he offers any
       criticism

30. This chart presents graphically a comparison of what is done and what is to be done. It is   30.____
so ruled that each division of space represents both an amount of time and the quantity
of work to be done during the particular unit of time. Horizontal lines drawn through these
spaces show the relationship between the quantity of work actually done and that which
is scheduled.
The chart referred to is known generally as a _____ chart.

    A. progress or Gantt   B. job correlation
    C. process or flow of work   D. Simo work simplification

31. The personnel survey is a systematic and reasonably exhaustive analysis and statement   31.____
of the facts and forces in an organization which affect the relations between employees
and management, and between employees and their work, followed by recommendations as to ways of developing better personnel policies and procedures.
On the basis of this statement, it is LEAST accurate to state that one of the purposes
served by a personnel survey is to

    A. appraise operating efficiency through an objective study of methods of production
       and a statistical interpretation of the facts
    B. set forth items and causes of poor morale in an inclusive way and in their proper
       perspective
    C. secure the facts to determine whether there is need of a more progressive person-
       nel policy in an organization where personnel work is as yet undeveloped
    D. evaluate the effectiveness of a personnel policy where a progressive personnel
       policy is already in operation

32. It is generally recognized that there is a relationship between the size of an organiza-   32.____
tion's staff, the number of supervisory levels and the span of control (number of workers
assigned to a supervisor).
The MOST accurate of the following statements regarding the relationship of these
three elements is that

    A. if the size of an organization's staff should remain unchanged and the span of con-
trol should increase, then the number of supervisory levels would tend to increase

    B. if the size of the staff should decrease and the number of levels of supervision
should increase, then the span of control would tend to decrease

    C. if the size of the staff should increase and the number of supervisory levels should
remain unchanged, then the span of control would tend to decrease

    D. if the size of the staff should increase and the span of control should decrease,
then the number of supervisory levels would tend to decrease

Questions 33-35.

DIRECTIONS: Questions 33 to 35 are to answered on the basis of the organization chart
shown below. This chart presents the organizational structure of a division in a
hypothetical agency. Each box designates a position in the organizational
structure of this division. The symbol in each box represents the name of the
individual occupying the position designated by the box. Thus, the name of the
head of this division is represented by the symbol 1A.

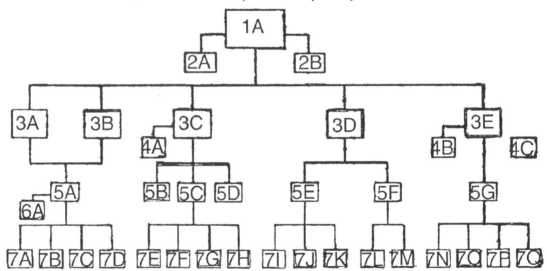

33. The one of the following who heads a subdivision which BEST illustrates in its organiza-   33.____
tional structure the characteristics of the pure line type of organization is

    A. 3B   B. 3C   C. 3D   D. 3E

34. The member of the organization who is MOST LIKELY to receive conflicting orders   34.____
because he is directly accountable to more than one superior is

    A. 5A   B. 4A   C. 5B   D. 4C

35. Assume that 7K and 7P wish to exchange positions. Approval of this exchange must be obtained from each superior in the line of authority extending upward from 7K and from each superior in the line of authority extending upward from 7P. The one of the following who is NOT in a line of authority extending upward from either 7K or 7P is

35._____

    A. 1A   B. 3E   C. 5F   D. 3D

KEY (CORRECT ANSWERS)

1.	B	11.	D	21.	D
2.	B	12.	C	22.	D
3.	D	13.	B	23.	A
4.	C	14.	A/C	24.	A
5.	D	15.	B	25.	B
6.	A	16.	B	26.	C
7.	C	17.	A	27.	C
8.	A	18.	A	28.	D
9.	A	19.	B	29.	C
10.	B	20.	C	30.	A
		31.	A		
		32.	B		
		33.	C		
		34.	A		
		35.	C		

TEST 2

DIRECTIONS: Each question or incomplete statement is followed by several suggested answers or completions. Select the one that BEST answers the question or completes the statement. *PRINT THE LETTER OF THE CORRECT ANSWER IN THE SPACE AT THE RIGHT.*

1. Analysis and simplification of office procedures are functions that should be conducted in all offices and on a continuing basis. These functions may be performed by the line supervisor, by staff methods specialists, or by outside consultants on methods analysis. An appraisal of these three methods of assigning responsibility for improving office procedures reveals that the LEAST accurate of the following statements is that   1.____

    A. outside consultants employed to simplify office procedures frequently bring with them a vast amount of previous experience as well as a fresh viewpoint
    B. line supervisors usually lack the special training which effective procedure analysis work requires
    C. continuity of effort and staff cooperation can better be secured by periodically employed consultants than by a permanent staff of methods analysts
    D. the reason line supervisors fail to keep procedures up to date is that the supervisor is too often overburdened with operating responsibilities

2. A man cannot serve two masters.   2.____
   This statement emphasizes MOST the importance in an organization of

    A. span of control   B. specialization of work
    C. delegation of authority D. unity of command

3. An important aid in good office management is knowledge on the part of subordinates of the significance of their work. The possession of such knowledge by an employee will probably LEAST affect his   3.____

    A. interest in his work
    B. understanding of the relationship between the work of his unit and that of other units
    C. willingness to cooperate with other employees
    D. ability to undertake assignments requiring special skills

4. For mediocre executives who do not have a flair for positive administration, the implanta-tion in subordinates of anxiety about job retention is a safe, if somewhat unimaginative, method of insuring a modicum of efficiency in the working organization.   4.____
   Of the following, the MOST accurate statement according to this quotation is that

    A. implanting anxiety about job retention is a method usually employed by the medio-cre executive to improve the efficiency of his organization
    B. an organization will operate with at least some efficiency if employees realize that unsatisfactory work performance may subject them to dismissal
    C. successful executives with a flair for positive administration relieve their subordi-nates of any concern for their job security
    D. the implantation of anxiety about job security in subordinates should not be used as a method of improving efficiency

120

5. Savings of 20 per cent or more in clerical operating costs can often be achieved by improvement of the physical conditions under which office work is performed.
In general, the MOST valid of the following statements regarding physical conditions is that

    A. conference rooms should have more light than small rooms
    B. the tops of desks should be glossy rather than dull
    C. noise is reflected more by hard-surfaced materials than by soft or porous materials
    D. yellow is a more desirable wall color for offices receiving an abundance of sunlight than for offices receiving little sunlight

5.____

6. To the executive who directs the complex and diverse operations of a large organizational unit, the conference is an important and, at times, indispensable tool of management. The inexperienced executive may, however, ploy the conference for a purpose for which it is ill fitted.
Of the following, the LEAST use of the conference by the executive is to

    A. reconcile conflicting views or interests
    B. develop an understanding by all concerned of a policy already adopted
    C. coordinate an activity involving several line supervisors
    D. perform technical research on a specific project

6.____

7. In planning the layout of office space, the office supervisor should bear in mind that one large room is a more efficient operating unit than the same number of square feet split up into smaller rooms.
Of the following, the LEAST valid basis for the preceding statement is that in the large room

    A. better light and ventilation are possible
    B. flow of work between employees is more direct
    C. supervision and control are more easily maintained
    D. time and motion studies are easier to conduct

7.____

8. The one of the following companies which is BEST known as a manufacturer of filing cabinets and office furniture is

    A. Pitney-Bowes, Inc.   B. Dennison Manufacturing Co.
    C. Wilson-Jones Co.   D. Shaw-Walker Co.

8.____

9. The program used to deliver audio-visual office presentations is known as

    A. PowerPoint   B. Excel   C. CGI   D. Dreamweaver

9.____

10. The principles of scientific office management are MOST FREQUENTLY applied by government office supervisors in

    A. maintaining flexibility in hiring and firing
    B. developing improved pay scales
    C. standardizing clerical practices and procedures
    D. revising organizational structure

10.____

11. The one of the following factors to which the bureau head should attach LEAST impor-   11.____
tance in deciding on the advisability of substituting machine for manual operations in a
given area of office work is the

    A. need for accuracy in the work
    B. relative importance of the work
    C. speed with which the work must be completed
    D. volume of work

12. The clerk displayed a *rudimentary* knowledge of the principles of supervision.   12.____
The word *rudimentary* as used in this sentence means MOST NEARLY

    A. thorough   B. elementary   C. surprising   D. commendable

13. This is an *integral* part of our program.   13.____
The word *integral* as used in this sentence means MOST NEARLY

    A. minor   B. unknown   C. essential   D. well-developed

14. A *contiguous* office is one that is   14.____

    A. spacious   B. rectangular in shape
    C. adjoining   D. crowded

15. This program was *sanctioned* by the department head.   15.____
The word *sanctioned* as used in this sentence means MOST NEARLY

    A. devised   B. approved   C. modified   D. rejected

16. The file clerk performed his work in a *perfunctory* manner.   16.____
The word *perfunctory* as used in this sentence means MOST NEARLY

    A. quiet   B. orderly   C. sullen   D. indifferent

17. He did not *impugn* the reasons given for the change in policy.   17.____
The word *impugn* as used in this sentence means MOST NEARLY

    A. make insinuations against   B. verify in whole or part
    C. volunteer support for   D. overlook or ignore

18. The supervisor was unable to learn the identity of the *culpable* employee.   18.____
The word *culpable* as used in this sentence means MOST NEARLY

    A. inaccurate   B. careless   C. guilty   D. dishonest

19. The announcement was made at a *propitious* time.   19.____
The word *propitious* as used in this sentence means MOST NEARLY

    A. unexpected   B. busy   C. favorable   D. significant

20. He showed no *compunction* in carrying out this order.   20.____
The word *compunction* as used in this sentence means MOST NEARLY

    A. feeling of remorse   B. hesitation or delay
    C. tact or discretion   D. disposition to please

21. He acted in a *fiduciary* capacity.   21._____
The word *fiduciary* as used in this sentence means MOST NEARLY

    A. administrative or executive in nature
    B. quasi-legal in nature
    C. involving confidence or trust
    D. requiring auditing or budgetary ability

22. To *temporize* means MOST NEARLY to   22._____

    A. allay temporarily the fears of
    B. render a temporary service
    C. yield temporarily to prevailing opinion
    D. react temperamentally

23. The new supervisor was *sanguine* about the prospects of success.   23._____
The word *sanguine* as used in this sentence means MOST NEARLY

    A. uncertain   B. confident   C. pessimistic   D. excited

24. The supervisor was asked to *implement* the new policy.   24._____
The word *implement* as used in this sentence means MOST NEARLY

    A. explain   B. revise   C. delay the announcement of
    D. carry into effect

25. The word *intimation* means MOST NEARLY   25._____

    A. friendliness   B. an attempt to frighten
    C. a difficult task   D. an indirect suggestion

26. Mr. Jones has a *penchant* for this type of work.   26._____
The word *penchant* as used in this sentence means MOST NEARLY

    A. record of achievement   B. unexplainable dislike
    C. lack of aptitude   D. strong inclination

27. The speaker's comments were *desultory*.   27._____
The word *desultory* as used in this sentence means MOST NEARLY

    A. inspiring   B. aimless   C. pertinent   D. rude

Questions 28-35.

DIRECTIONS: Questions 28 through 35 are to be answered SOLELY on the basis of the following chart which relates to the Investigation Division of Dept. X. This chart contains four curves which connect the points that show for each year the variations in percentage deviation from normal in the number of investigators, the number of clerical employees, the cost of personnel, and the number of cases processed for the period 2002-2012 inclusive. The year 2002 was designated as the normal year. The personnel of the Investigation Division consists of investigators and clerical employees only.

INVESTIGATION DIVISION, DEPARTMENT X

VARIATIONS IN NUMBER OF CASES PROCESSED, COST OF PERSONNEL.
NUMBER OF CLERICAL EMPLOYEES, AND NUMBER OF INVESTIGATORS
FOR EACH YEAR FROM 2002 to 2012 INCLUSIVE
(In percentages from normal)

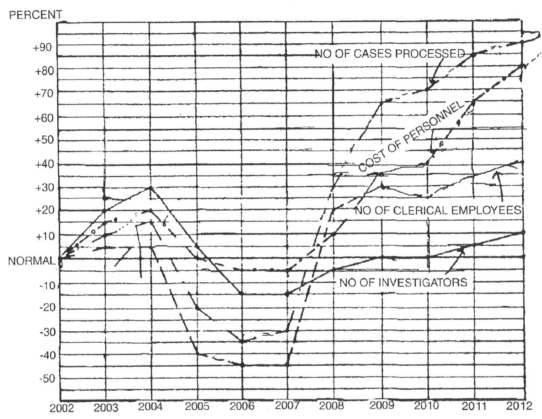

Example: If there were 80 clerical employees in the division in 1992, then the number
of clerical employees in the division in 1999 was 104.

28.   If 1300 cases were processed by the division in 2006, then the number of cases pro-   28._____
cessed in 2002 was

    A.   2000   B.   1755   C.   2145   D.   1650

29.   Of the following, the year in which there was no change in the size of the division's total   29._____
staff from that of the preceding year is

    A.   2005   B.   2006   C.   2009   D.   2011

30.   Of the following, the year in which the size of the division's staff *decreased* MOST   30._____
sharply from that of the preceding year is

    A.   2005   B.   2006   C.   2007   D.   2008

31.   An inspection of the chart discloses that the curve that fluctuates *least* as determined by   31._____
the average deviation from normal, is the curve for the

    A.   number of cases processed   B.   cost of personnel
    C.   number of clerical employees   D.   number of investigators

32. A comparison of 2006 with 2012 reveals an increase in 2006 in the   32.____

    A. cost of personnel for the division
    B. number of cases processed per investigator
    C. number of cases processed per clerical employee
    D. number of clerical employees per investigator

33. If the personnel cost per case processed in 2002 was $12.30, then the personnel cost   33.____
per case processed in 2012 was MOST NEARLY

    A. $9.85   B. $10.95   C. $11.65   D. $13.85

34. Suppose that there was a total of 108 employees in the division in 2002 and a total of   34.____
125 employees in 2010.
On the basis of these figures, it is MOST accurate to state that the number of investigators employed in the division in 2010 was

    A. 40   B. 57   C. 68   D. 85

35. It is predicted that the number of cases processed in 2013 will exceed the number pro-   35.____
cessed in 2002 by exactly the same quantity that the number processed in 2012
exceeded that processed in 2011. It is also predicted that the personnel cost in 2013 will
exceed the personnel cost in 2012 by exactly the same amount that the 2012 personnel
cost exceeded that for 2011. On the basis of these predictions, it is MOST accurate to
state that the personnel cost per case in 2013 will be

    A. ten per cent less than the personnel cost per case in 2012
    B. exactly the same as the personnel cost per case in 2012
    C. twice as much as the personnel cost per case in 2002
    D. exactly the same as the personnel cost per case in 2002

KEY (CORRECT ANSWERS)

1.	C	11.	B	21.	C
2.	D	12.	B	22.	C
3.	D	13.	C	23.	B
4.	B	14.	C	24.	D
5.	C	15.	B	25.	B
6.	D	16.	D	26.	D
7.	D	17.	A	27.	B
8.	D	18.	C	28.	A
9.	A	19.	C	29.	B
10.	C	20.	A	30.	A
		31.	D		
		32.	C		
		33.	C		
		34.	A		
		35.	D		

EXAMINATION SECTION
TEST 1

DIRECTIONS: Each question or incomplete statement is followed by several suggested answers or completions. Select the one that BEST answers the question or completes the statement. *PRINT THE LETTER OF THE CORRECT ANSWER IN THE SPACE AT THE RIGHT.*

1. In discussing with a subordinate the assignment which you are giving him, it is MOST important that you place greatest stress on

   A. the immediate job to be done
   B. what was accomplished in the past
   C. the long-term goals of the organization
   D. what others have accomplished

1.____

2. Personal friendship and intimacy exhibited by the administrative assistant toward his subordinates should ALWAYS be

   A. kept to a bare minimum
   B. free and unrestricted
   C. in accordance with the personal qualities of each individual subordinate
   D. tempered by the need for objectivity

2.____

3. Assume that one of the office assistants under your supervision approaches you and asks if you would give her advice on some problems that she is having with her husband. Of the following, the MOST appropriate action for you to take is to

   A. tell her that she would be making a mistake in discussing it with you
   B. listen briefly to her problem and then suggest how she might get help in solving it
   C. give her whatever advice she needs based on your knowledge or experience in this area
   D. refer her to a lawyer specializing in marital problems

3.____

4. When you return from lunch one day, you find Miss P, one of your subordinates, in your office crying uncontrollably. When she calms down, she tells you that Mr. T, another subordinate, insulted her but she would prefer not to give details because they are very personal.
   Your IMMEDIATE reaction should be to

   A. reprimand Mr. T for his callousness
   B. reprimand the worker in your office for not controlling herself
   C. get as much information as possible about exactly what happened
   D. tell Miss P that she will have to take care of her own affairs

4.____

5. If one of the office assistants under your supervision does not seem to be able to get along well with the other employees, the FIRST step that you should take in such a situation should be to try to find out

   A. more about the background of the office assistant
   B. the reason the office assistant has difficulty in getting along
   C. if another department would be interested in employing the office assistant
   D. the procedures required for dismissal of the office assistant

5.____

6. Suppose that you expect that your department will send two of your subordinates for out-side training on the use of new office equipment while others will be trained on the job. When preparing a yearly budget and schedule for the personnel that you supervise, training costs to be paid for by the department should be

    6._____

    A. excluded and treated separately as a special request when the specific training need arises
    B. estimated and included in the budget and manpower schedules
    C. left out of the schedule since personnel are thoroughly trained before assignment to a position
    D. considered only if training involves time away from the job

7. There is a rumor going around your department that one of the administrative assistants is going to resign.
Since it is not true, the BEST action to take would be to

    7._____

    A. find the person starting the rumor, and advise him that disciplinary action will follow if the rumors do not stop
    B. disregard the rumor since the grapevine is always inaccurate
    C. tell the truth about the situation to those concerned
    D. start another rumor yourself that contradicts this rumor

8. Suppose a student is concerned over the possibility of failing a course and losing matric-ulated status. He comes to you for advice.
The BEST thing for you to do is to

    8._____

    A. tell the student it is not your function to discuss student problems
    B. impress the student with the importance of academic performance and suggest that more study is necessary
    C. send the student to a career counselor for testing
    D. suggest that he see the instructor or appropriate faculty advisor depending on the cause of the problem

9. A member of the faculty had requested that an overhead projector be reserved for a seminar. At the time of the seminar, the projector has not been placed in the room, and you find that one of your office assistants forgot to send the request to the building staff. Of the following possible actions, which one should be taken FIRST?

    9._____

    A. See to it that the projector is moved to the seminar room immediately.
    B. Personally reprimand the subordinate responsible.
    C. Suggest rescheduling the seminar.
    D. Tell the faculty member that the problem was caused by a fault in the machine.

10. Assume that you have to give work assignments to a male office assistant and a female office assistant. It would be BEST to

    10._____

    A. allow the woman to have first choice of assignments
    B. give the female preference in assignments requiring patience
    C. give the male preference in assignments requiring physical action
    D. make assignments to each on the basis of demonstrated ability and interest

11. In the *initial* phase of training a new employee to perform his job, which of the following approaches is MOST desirable?

    A. Have him read the office manual
    B. Tell him to watch the other employees
    C. Give him simple tasks to perform
    D. Have him do exactly what everyone else is doing

11.____

12. Assume that one of the employees under your supervision performs her work adequately, but you feel that she might be more productive if she changed some of her methods.
You should

    A. discuss with her those changes which you think would be helpful
    B. refrain from saying anything since her work is adequate
    C. suggest that she might be helped by talking to a guidance counselor
    D. assign her to another job

12.____

13. One of the office assistants under your supervision complains to you that the report which you assigned her to prepare is monotonous work and unnecessary. The report is a monthly compilation of figures which you submit to your superior.
Of the following, the *best* action to take FIRST is to

    A. ask her why she feels the work is unnecessary
    B. tell her that she is employed to do whatever work is assigned to her
    C. have her do other work at the same time to provide more interest
    D. assign the report to another subordinate

13.____

14. Of the following, the GREATEST advantage of keeping records of the quantity of work produced by the office assistants under your supervision is to

    A. have the statistics available in case they are required
    B. enable you to take appropriate action in case of increase, decrease, or other variation in output
    C. provide a basis for promotion or other personnel action
    D. give you a basis for requesting additional employees

14.____

15. It is not possible to achieve maximum productivity from your subordinates *unless* they are told

    A. what the rewards are for their performance
    B. how they will be punished for failure
    C. what it is they are expected to do
    D. that they must work hard if they are to succeed

15.____

16. Suppose that you observe that one of the assistants on your staff is involved with an extremely belligerent student who is demanding information that is not readily available in your department. One staff member is becoming visibly upset and is apparently about to lose his temper.
Under these circumstances, it would be BEST for you to

16.____

A. leave the room and let the situation work itself out
B. let the assistant lose his temper, then intervene and calm both parties at the same time
C. step in immediately and try to calm the student in order to suggest more expedient ways of getting the information
D. tell the student to come back and discuss the situation when he can do it calmly

17. Suppose you have explained an assignment to a newly appointed clerk and the clerk has demonstrated her ability to do the work. After a short period of time, the clerk tells you that she is afraid of incorrectly completing the assignment.
Of the following, the BEST course of action for you to take is to

   17._____

A. tell her to observe another clerk who is doing the same type of work
B. explain to her the importance of the assignment and tell her not to be nervous
C. assign her another task which is easier to perform
D. try to allay her fears and encourage her to try to do the work

Questions 18-22.

DIRECTIONS: Questions 18 through 22 consist of the names of students who have applied for a certain college program and are to be classified according to the criteria described below.

The following table gives pertinent data for 6 different applicants with regard to:
Grade averages, which are expressed on a scale running from
   0 (low) to 4 (high);
Scores on qualifying test, which run from 200 (low) to 800 (high); Related work experience, which is expressed in number of months; Personal references, which are rated from 1 (low) to 5 (high).

Applicant	Grade Average	Test Score	Work Experience	Reference
Jones	2.2	620	24	3
Perez	3.5	650	0	5
Lowitz	3.2	420	2	4
Uncker	2.1	710	15	2
Farrow	2.8	560	0	3
Shapiro	3.0	560	12	4

An administrative assistant is in charge of the initial screening process for the program. This process requires classifying applicants into the following four groups:

A. SUPERIOR CANDIDATES. Unless the personal reference rating is lower than 3, all applicants with grade averages of 3.0 or higher and test scores of 600 or higher are classified as superior candidates.
B. GOOD CANDIDATES. Unless the personal reference rating is lower than 3, all applicants with one of the following combinations of grade averages and test scores are classified as good candidates: (1) grade average of 2.5 to 2.9 and test score of 600 or higher; (2) grade average of 3.0 or higher and test score of 550 to 599.
C. POSSIBLE CANDIDATES. Applicants with one of the following combinations of qualifications are classified as possible candidates: (1) grade average of 2.5 to 2.9 and test score of 550 to 599 and a personal reference rating of 3 or higher; (2) grade average of 2.0 to 2.4 and test score of 500 or higher and at least 21 months' work experience and a personal reference rating of 3 or higher; (3) a combination

of grade average and test score that would otherwise qualify as *superior* or *good* but a personal reference score lower than 3.

D. REJECTED CANDIDATES. Applicants who do not fall in any of the above groups are to be rejected.

EXAMPLE

Jones' grade average of 2.2 does not meet the standard for either a superior candidate (grade average must be 3.0 or higher) or a good candidate (grade average must be 2.5 to 2.9). Grade average of 2.2 does not qualify Jones as a possible candidate if Jones has a test score of 500 or higher, at least 21 months' work experience, and a personal reference rating of 3 or higher. Since Jones has a test score of 620, 24 months' work experience, and a reference rating of 3, Jones is a possible candidate. The answer is C.

Answer Questions 18 through 22 as explained above, indicating for each whether the applicant should be classified as a

A. superior candidate
C. possible candidate

B. good candidate
D. rejected candidate

18. Perez   18._____

19. Lowitz   19._____

20. Uncker   20._____

21. Farrow   21._____

22. Shapiro   22._____

23. A new training program is being set up for which certain new forms will be needed. You   23._____
have been asked to design these forms.
Of the following, the FIRST step you should take in planning the forms is

   A. finding out the exact purpose for which each form will be used
   B. deciding what size of paper should be used for each form
   C. determining whether multiple copies will be needed for any of the forms
   D. setting up a new filing system to handle the new forms

24. You have been asked to write a report on methods of hiring and training new employees.   24._____
Your report is going to be about ten pages long.
For the convenience of your readers, a brief summary of your findings should

   A. appear at the beginning of your report
   B. be appended to the report as a postscript
   C. be circulated in a separate memo
   D. be inserted in tabular form in the middle of your report

25. Assume that your department is being moved to new and larger quarters, and that you   25._____
have been asked to suggest an office layout for the central clerical office. Of the following, your FIRST step in planning the new layout should ordinarily be to

   A. find out how much money has been budgeted for furniture and equipment
   B. make out work-flow and traffic-flow charts for the clerical operations
   C. measure each piece of furniture and equipment that is presently in use
   D. determine which files should be moved to a storage area or destroyed

KEY (CORRECT ANSWERS)

1.	A	11.	C
2.	D	12.	A
3.	B	13.	A
4.	C	14.	B
5.	B	15.	C
6.	B	16.	C
7.	C	17.	D
8.	D	18.	A
9.	A	19.	D
10.	D	20.	D

21.	C
22.	B
23.	A
24.	A
25.	B

TEST 2

DIRECTIONS: Each question or incomplete statement is followed by several suggested answers or completions. Select the one that BEST answers the question or completes the statement. *PRINT THE LETTER OF THE CORRECT ANSWER IN THE SPACE AT THE RIGHT.*

1. In modern office layouts, screens and dividers are often used instead of walls to set off working groups. Advantages given for this approach have included all of the following EXCEPT

    A. more frequent communication between different working groups
    B. reduction in general noise level
    C. fewer objections from employees who are transferred to different groups
    D. cost savings from increased sharing of office equipment

1.____

2. Of the following, the CHIEF reason for moving less active material from active to inactive files is to

    A. dispose of material that no longer has any use
    B. keep the active files down to a manageable size
    C. make sure that no material over a year old remains in active files
    D. separate temporary records from permanent records

2.____

3. The use of a microfiche system for information storage and retrieval would make MOST sense in an office where

    A. a great number of documents must be kept available for permanent reference
    B. documents are ordinarily kept on file for less than six months
    C. filing is a minor and unimportant part of office work
    D. most of the records on file are working forms on which additional entries are frequently made

3.____

4. The work loads in different offices fluctuate greatly over the course of a year. Ordinarily, the MOST economical way of handling a peak load in a specific office is to

    A. hire temporary help from an outside agency
    B. require regular employees to put in overtime
    C. use employees from other offices that are not busy
    D. buy special equipment for operations that can be automated

4.____

5. A faculty member has given you a long list of student grades to be typed. Since your typed list will be the basis for permanent records, it is essential that it contain no errors. The BEST way of checking this typed list is to

    A. ask the faculty member to glance over the typed version and have him correct any mistakes
    B. have someone read the handwritten list aloud, while you check the typed list as each item is read
    C. read the typed list yourself to see that it makes good sense and that there are no omissions or duplications
    D. make a spot-check by comparing several entries in the typed list against the original entries on the handwritten list

5.____

6. It is necessary to purchase a machine for your department which will be used to make single copies of documents and to make copies of memos that are distributed to as many as 150 people.
Of the following kinds of machines, which one is BEST suited for your department's purposes?
A(n)

   A. laser copier
   C. inkjet printer
   B. fax machine
   D. multipage scanner

6.____

7. Suppose that faculty members have fallen into the habit of asking clerical employees in your department to perform messenger service between your building and other parts of the school. Such demands are becoming increasingly common, and you feel that the two or three man-hours per day involved is too much. Furthermore, these assignments disrupt the work of the department.
Of the following solutions, which one is most likely to result in the GREATEST efficiency?

   A. Hire a full-time messenger whose only job will be to run intra-school errands
   B. Establish a rule that no employees in your department will act as messengers under any circumstances, and that all materials must be sent by ordinary interoffice mail
   C. Notify other departments that from now on they must use their own employees for messenger service to or from your building
   D. Allow the clerical employees to perform messenger service only in cases of urgent need, and have interoffice mail used in all other cases

7.____

8. A new employee is trying to file records for three different students whose names are Robinson, John L., Robinson, John, and Robinson, John Leonard. The employee does not know in what order the records should be filed.
You should

   A. tell the employee to use whatever order seems most convenient
   B. suggest that all the records be put in one folder and arranged chronologically according to date of enrollment
   C. explain that, by the *nothing-before-something* principle, John comes first, John L. second, and John Leonard last
   D. instruct the employee to keep them together but arrange them chronologically according to date of birth

8.____

9. An *out card* or *out guide* should be placed in a file drawer to mark the location of material that

   A. has not yet been received
   B. should be transferred to an inactive file
   C. has been temporarily removed
   D. is no longer needed

9.____

10. Assume that your office does not presently have a formal records-retention program. Your supervisor has suggested that such a program be set up, and has asked you to make a study and submit your recommendations.
The FIRST step in your study should be to

10.____

A. find out how long it has been since the files were last cleaned out
B. take an inventory of the types of materials now in the files
C. learn how much storage space you can obtain for old records
D. decide which files should be thrown out instead of being stored

11. In an organization where a great deal of time and money is spent on information management, it often makes sense to use a *systems analysis* approach in reviewing operations and deciding how they can be carried out more efficiently.
Of the following, the FIRST question that a *systems analysis* should ask about any procedure is

    A. whether the procedure can be handled by automatic data-processing equipment
    B. exactly how the procedure is meshed with other existing procedures used in the organization
    C. how many employees should be hired to carry out the present procedure
    D. what is the end result that the use of the procedure is supposed to achieve

11.____

12. You have been notified that a *work simplification* study is going to be carried out in your department.
The one of the following which is MOST likely to be the purpose of this study is to

    A. increase the productivity of the office by eliminating unnecessary procedures and irrelevant record keeping
    B. produce a new office manual that explains current procedures in a simple and easily understandable way
    C. determine whether there are any procedures so simple that they can be handled by untrained workers
    D. substitute computer processing for all operations that are now performed manually

12.____

13. Suppose that a cost study has been made of various clerical procedures carried out in your college, and that the study shows that the average cost of a dictated business letter is over $5.00 per letter.
Of the following cost factors that go into making up this total cost, the LARGEST *single* factor is certain to be the cost of

    A. stationery and postage   B. office machinery
    C. labor   D. office rental

13.____

14. Which of the following software programs is BEST for collecting and sorting data, creating graphs and preparing spreadsheets?

    A. Microsoft Excel   B. Microsoft Word
    C. Microsoft Powerpoint   D. QuarkXPress

14.____

15. Which of the following software programs is BEST for creating visual presentations containing text, photos and charts?

    A. Microsoft Excel   B. Microsoft Outlook
    C. Microsoft Powerpoint   D. Adobe Photoshop

15.____

16. A supervisor asks you to e-mail a file that has been saved on your computer as a   16.____
photograph. Since you do not remember the file name, you must search by file type.
Which of the following file extensions should you run a search for?

    A. .html   B. .pdf   C. .jpg   D. .doc

17. In records management, the term *vital records* refers generally to papers that   17.____

    A. are essential to life
    B. are needed for an office to continue operating after fire or other disaster
    C. contain statistics about birth and death
    D. can be easily replaced

18. A city agency maintains a complete set of records on its clients on a central computer. A   18.____
branch office finds that it frequently needs access to this data.
A computer output device which could be installed in the branch office to provide the
data is called a

    A. sorter   B. tabulator
    C. card punch   D. terminal

19. A certain employee is paid at the rate of $9.10 per hour, with time-and-a-half for over-   19.____
time. Hours in excess of 40 hours a week count as overtime. During the past week the
employee put in 44 working hours.
The employee's gross wages for the week are MOST NEARLY

    A. $368   B. $396   C. $414   D. $444

20. You are making a report on the number of inside and outside calls handled by a particu-   20.____
lar switchboard. Over a 5-day period, the total number of all inside and outside calls handled by the switchboard was 2,314. The average number of inside calls per day was 274.
You cannot find one day's tally of outside calls, but the total number of outside calls for
the other four days was 776.
Fron this information, how many outside calls must have been reported on the missing
tally?

    A. 168   B. 190   C. 194   D. 274

21. One typist can type 100 address labels in 1 hour. Another typist can type 100 address   21.____
labels in 1 hour and 15 minutes. If there are 450 address labels to be typed and both typists are put to work on the job, how soon can they be expected to finish the work?
In _____ hours.

    A. $2\frac{1}{4}$ B. $2\frac{1}{2}$ C. $4\frac{1}{2}$ D. 5

22. A floor plan has been prepared for a new building, drawn to a scale of $\frac{1}{2}$ inch = 1 foot. A certain area is drawn 1 foot long and $7\frac{1}{2}$ inches wide on the floor plan.
    The actual dimensions of this area in the new building are _____ feet long and _____ feet wide.

    A. 6; $3\frac{1}{4}$ B. 12; $7\frac{1}{2}$ C. 20; 15   D. 24; 15

22._____

23. In recent years a certain college has admitted a number of students with high school grades of C-plus or lower. It has usually turned out that an average of 65% of these students completed their freshman year. Last year 340 such students were admitted. By the end of the year, 102 of these students were no longer in college, but the others completed successfully.
    How many MORE students completed the year than would have been expected, based on the average results of previous years?

    A. 14   B. 17   C. 39   D. 119

23._____

24. The morale of employees is an important factor in the maintenance of job interest. Which of the following is generally LEAST valuable in strengthening morale?

    A. Attempting to take a personal interest in one's subordinates
    B. Encouraging employees to speak openly about their opinions and suggestions
    C. Fostering a feeling of group spirit among the workers
    D. Having all employees work at the same rate

24._____

25. Of the following, the BEST way for a supervisor to determine when *further* on-the-job training in a particular work area is needed is by

    A. asking the employees
    B. evaluating the employees' work performance
    C. determining the ratio of idle time to total work time
    D. classifying the jobs in the work area

25._____

KEY (CORRECT ANSWERS)

1.	B		11.	D
2.	B		12.	A
3.	A		13.	C
4.	C		14.	A
5.	B		15.	C
6.	A		16.	C
7.	D		17.	B
8.	C		18.	D
9.	C		19.	C
10.	B		20.	A

21.	B
22.	D
23.	B
24.	D
25.	B

———

EXAMINATION SECTION
TEST 1

DIRECTIONS: Each question or incomplete statement is followed by several suggested answers or completions. Select the one that BEST answers the question or completes the statement. *PRINT THE LETTER OF THE CORRECT ANSWER IN THE SPACE AT THE RIGHT.*

1. One of the things that can ruin morale in a work group is the failure to exercise judgment in the assignment of overtime work to your subordinates.
   Of the following, the MOST desirable supervisory practice in assigning overtime work is to

   A. *rotate* overtime on a uniform basis among all your subordinates
   B. *assign* overtime to those who are *moonlighting* after regular work hours
   C. *rotate* overtime as much as possible among employees willing to work additional hours
   D. *assign* overtime to those employees who take frequent long weekend vacations

   1._____

2. The consistent delegation of authority by you to experienced and reliable subordinates in your work group is generally considered

   A. *undesirable,* because your authority in the group may be threatened by an unscrupulous subordinate
   B. *undesirable,* because it demonstrates that you cannot handle your own workload
   C. *desirable,* because it shows that you believe that you have been accepted by your subordinates
   D. *desirable,* because the development of subordinates creates opportunities for assuming broader responsibilities yourself

   2._____

3. The MOST effective way for you to deal with a false rumor circulating among your subordinates is to

   A. have a trusted subordinate state a counter-rumor
   B. recommend disciplinary action against the *rumor mongers*
   C. point out to your subordinates that rumors degrade both listener and initiator
   D. furnish your subordinates with sufficient authentic information

   3._____

4. Two of your subordinates tell you about a mistake they made in a report that has already been sent the top management.
   Which of the following questions is *most likely* to elicit the MOST valuable information from your subordinates?

   A. Who is responsible?
   B. How can we explain this to top management?
   C. How did it happen?
   D. Why weren't you more careful?

   4._____

5. Assume that you are responsible for implementing major changes in work flow patterns and personnel assignments in the unit of which you are in charge.
   The *one* of the following actions which is *most likely* to secure the willing cooperation of those persons who will have to change their assignmentsis

   5._____

A. having the top administrators of the agency urge their cooperation at a group meeting
B. issuing very detailed and carefully planned instructions to the affected employees regarding the changes
C. integrating employee participation into the planning of the changes
D. reminding the affected employees that career advancement depends upon compliance with organizational objectives

6. Of the following, the BEST reason for using face-to-face communication *instead of* written communication is that face-to-face communication   6.____

   A. allows for immediate feedback
   B. is more credible
   C. enables greater use of detail and illustration
   D. is more polite

7. Of the following, the *most likely* DISADVANTAGE of giving detailed instructions when assigning a task to a subordinate is that such instructions may   7.____

   A. conflict with the subordinate's ideas of how the task should be done
   B. reduce standardization of work performance
   C. cause confusion in the mind of the subordinate
   D. inhibit the development of new procedures by the subordinate

8. Assume that you are a supervisor of a unit consisting of a number of subordinates and that one subordinate, whose work is otherwise acceptable, keeps on making errors in one particular task assigned to him in rotation. This task consists of routine duties which all your subordinates should be able to perform.
   Of the following, the BEST way for you to handle this situation is to   8.____

   A. do the task yourself when the erring employee is scheduled to perform it and assign this employee other duties
   B. reorganize work assignments so that the task in question is no longer performed in rotation but assigned full-time to your most capable subordinate
   C. find out why this subordinate keeps on making the errors in question and see that he learns how to do the task properly
   D. maintain a well-documented record of such errors and, when the evidence is overwhelming, recommend appropriate disciplinary action

9. In the past, Mr. T, one of your subordinates, had been generally withdrawn and suspicious of others, but he had produced acceptable work. However, Mr. T has lately started to get into arguments with his fellow workers during which he displays intense rage. Friction between this subordinate and the others in your unit is mounting and the unit's work is suffering.
   Of the following, which would be the BEST way for you to handle this situation?   9.____

   A. Rearrange work schedules and assignments so as to give Mr. T no cause for complaint
   B. Instruct the other workers to avoid Mr. T and not to respond to any abuse
   C. Hold a unit meeting and appeal for harmony and submergence of individual differences in the interest of work
   D. Maintain a record of incidents and explore with Mr. T the possibility of seeking professional help

10. You are responsible for seeing to it that your unit is functioning properly in the accom-   10.____
plishment of its budgeted goals.
Which of the following will provide the LEAST information on how well you are accomplishing such goals?

    A. Measurement of employee performance
    B. Identification of alternative goals
    C. Detection of employee errors
    D. Preparation of unit reports

11. Some employees see an agency training program as a threat. Of the following, the *most*   11.____
likely reason for such an employee attitude toward training is that the employee involved
feel that

    A. some trainers are incompetent
    B. training rarely solves real work-a-day problems
    C. training may attempt to change comfortable behavior patterns
    D. training sessions are boring

12. Of the following, the CHIEF characteristic which distinguishes a *good* supervisor from a   12.____
poor supervisor is the *good* supervisor's

    A. ability to favorably impress others
    B. unwillingness to accept monotony or routine
    C. ability to deal constructively with problem situations
    D. strong drive to overcome opposition

13. Of the following, the MAIN disadvantage of on-the-job training is that, *generally,*   13.____

    A. special equipment may be needed
    B. production may be slowed down
    C. the instructor must maintain an individual relationship with the trainee
    D. the on-the-job instructor must be better qualified than the classroom instructor

14. All of the following are *correct* methods for a supervisor to use in connection with   14.____
employee discipline EXCEPT

    A. trying not to be too lenient or too harsh
    B. informing employees of the rules and the penalties for violations of the rules
    C. imposing discipline immediately after the violation is discovered
    D. making sure, when you apply discipline, that the employee understands that you
       do not want to do it

15. Of the following, the MAIN reason for a supervisor to establish standard procedures for   15.____
his unit is to

    A. increase the motivation for his subordinates
    B. make it easier for the subordinates to submit to authority
    C. reduce the number of times that his subordinates have to consult him
    D. reduce the number of mistakes that his subordinates will make

16. Of the following, the BEST reason for using form letters in correspondence is that they are   16._____

    A. concise and businesslike
    B. impersonal in tone
    C. uniform in appearance
    D. economical for large mailings

17. The use of loose-leaf office manuals for the guidance of employees on office policy, organization, and office procedures has won wide acceptance.   17._____
The MAIN advantage of the loose-leaf format is that it

    A. allows speedy reference
    B. facilitates revisions and changes
    C. includes a complete index
    D. presents a professional appearance

18. Office forms sometimes consist of several copies, each of a different color.   18._____
The MAIN reason for using *different* colors is to

    A. make a favorable impression on the users of the form
    B. distinguish each copy from the others
    C. facilitate the preparation of legible carbon copies
    D. reduce cost, since using colored stock permits recycling of paper

19. Which of the following is the BEST justification for obtaining a photocopying machine for the office?   19._____

    A. A photocopying machine can produce an unlimited number of copies at a low fixed cost per copy.
    B. Employees need little training in operating a photocopying machine.
    C. Office costs will be reduced and efficiency increased.
    D. The legibility of a photocopy generally is superior to copy produced by any other office duplicating device.

20. Which one of the following should be the most IMPORTANT overall consideration when preparing a recommendation to automate a large-scale office activity?   20._____
The

    A. number of models of automated equipment available
    B. benefits and costs of automation
    C. fears and resistance of affected employees
    D. experience of offices which have automated similar activities

21. A tickler file is MOST appropriate for filing materials   21._____

    A. chronologically according to date they were received
    B. alphabetically by name
    C. alphabetically by subject
    D. chronologically according to date they should be followed up

22. Which of the following is the BEST reason for decentralizing rather than centralizing the use of duplicating machines?   22.____

    A. Developing and retaining efficient deplicating machine operators
    B. Facilitating supervision of duplicating services
    C. Motivating employees to produce legible duplicated copies
    D. Placing the duplicating machines where they are most convenient and most frequently used

23. Window envelopes are sometimes considered preferable to individually addressed envelopes PRIMARILY because   23.____

    A. window envelopes are available in standard sizes for all purposes
    B. window envelopes are more attractive and official-looking
    C. the use of window envelopes eliminates the risk of inserting a letter in the wrong envelope
    D. the use of window envelopes requires neater typing

24. In planning the layout of a new office, the utilization of space and the arrangement of staff, furnishings and equipment should *usually* be MOST influenced by the   24.____

    A. gross square footage
    B. status differences in the chain of command
    C. framework of informal relationships among employees
    D. activities to be performed

25. When delegating responsibility for an assignment to a subordinate, it is MOST important that you   25.____

    A. retain all authority necessary to complete the assignment
    B. make your self generally available for consultation with the subordinate
    C. inform your superiors that you are no longer responsible for the assignment
    D. decrease the number of subordinates whom you have to supervise

---

KEY (CORRECT ANSWERS)

1.	C	11.	C	21.	D
2.	D	12.	C	22.	D
3.	D	13.	B	23.	C
4.	D	14.	D	24.	D
5.	C	15.	C	25.	B
6.	A	16.	D		
7.	D	17.	B		
8.	C	18.	B		
9.	D	19.	C		
10.	B	20.	B		

TEST 2

DIRECTIONS: Each question or incomplete statement is followed by several suggested answers or completions. Select the one that BEST answers the question or completes the statement. *PRINT THE LETTER OF THE CORRECT ANSWER IN THE SPACE AT THE RIGHT.*

Questions 1-5.

DIRECTIONS: Answer Questions 1 through 5 on the basis of the following passage.

The most effective control mechanism to prevent gross incompetence on the part of public employees is a good personnel program. The personnel officer in the line departments and the central personnel agency should exert positive leadership to raise levels of performance. Although the key factor is the quality of the personnel recruited, staff members other than personnel officers can make important contributions to efficiency. Administrative analysts, now employed in many agencies, make detailed studies of organization and procedures, with the purpose of eliminating delays, waste, and other inefficiencies. Efficiency is, however, more than a question of good organization and procedures; it is also the product of the attitudes and values of the public employees. Personal motivation can provide the will to be efficient. The best management studies will not result in substantial improvement of the performance of those employees who feel no great urge to work up to their abilities.

1. The passage indicates that the *key* factor in preventing gross incompetence of public employees is the

   A. hiring of administrative analysts to assist personnel people
   B. utilization of effective management studies
   C. overlapping of responsibility
   D. quality of the employees hired

1.____

2. According to the above passage, the central personnel agency staff *should*

   A. work more closely with administrative analysts in the line departments than with personnel afficers
   B. make a serious effort to avoid jurisdictional conflicts with personnel officers in line departments
   C. contribute to improving the quality of work of public employees
   D. engage in a comprehensive program to change the public's negative image of public employees

2.____

3. The passage indicates that efficiency in an organization can BEST be brought about by

   A. eliminating ineffective control mechanisms
   B. instituting sound organizational procedures
   C. promoting competent personnel
   D. recruiting people with desire to do good work

3.____

4. According to the passage, the *purpose* of administrative analysis in a public agency is to

   A. prevent injustice to the public employee
   B. promote the efficiency of the agency
   C. protect the interests of the public
   D. ensure the observance of procedural due process

4.____

5. The passage implies that a considerable rise in the quality of work of public employees can be brought about by   5.____

    A. encouraging positive employee attitudes toward work
    B. controlling personnel officers who exceed their powers
    C. creating warm personal associations among public employees in an agency
    D. closing loopholes in personnel organization and procedures

6. Typist *X* can type 20 forms per hour and Typist *I* can type 30 forms per hour. If there are 30 forms to be typed and both typists are put to work on the job, *how soon* should they be expected to finish the work? _____ minutes.   6.____

    A. 32   B. 34   C. 36   D. 38

7. Assume that there were 18 working days in February and that the six clerks in your unit had the following number of absences: 7.____

            Clerk F - 3 absences
            Clerk G - 2 absences
            Clerk H - 8 absences
            Clerk I - 1 absence
            Clerk J - 0 absences
            Clerk K - 5 absences

The average percentage attendance for the six clerks in your unit in February was, *most nearly,*

    A. 80%   B. 82%   C. 84%   D. 86%

8. A certain employee is paid at the rate of $7.50 per hour, with time-and-a-half for overtime. Hours in excess of 40 hours a week count as overtime. During the past week the employee put in 48 working hours.
The employee's gross wages for the week are, *most nearly,*   8.____

    A. $330   B. $350   C. $370   D. $390

9. You are making a report on the number of inside and outside calls handled by a particular switchboard. Over a 15-day period, the total number of all inside and outside calls handled by the switchboard was 5,760. The average number of inside calls per day was 234. You cannot find one day's tally of outside calls, but the total number of outside calls for the other fourteen days was 2,065. From this information, how many *outside calls* must have been reported on the missing tally?   9.____

    A. 175   B. 185   C. 195   D. 205

10. A floor plan has been prepared for a new building, drawn to a scale of 3/4 inch = 1 foot. A certain area is drawn 1 and 1/2 feet long and 6 inches wide on the floor plan. What are the *actual* dimensions of this area in the new building? _____ feet long and _____ feet wide.   10.____

    A. 21; 8   B. 24; 8   C. 27; 9   D. 30; 9

Questions 11 - 15.

DIRECTIONS: In answering Questions 11 through 15, assume that you are in charge of public information for an office which issues reports and answers questions from
other offices and from the public on changes in land use. The charts below
represent comparative land use in four neighborhoods. The area of each
neighborhood is expressed in city blocks. Assume that all city blocks are the
same size.

NEIGHBORHOOD A - 16 CITY BLOCKS

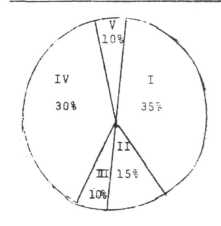

NEIGHBORHOOD B - 24 CITY BLOCKS

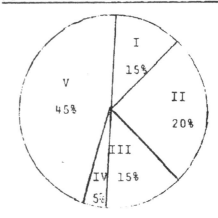

NEIGHBORHOOD C - 20 CITY BLOCKS

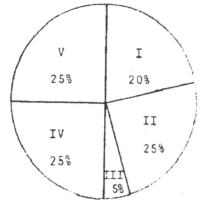

NEIGHBORHOOD D - 12 CITY BLOCKS

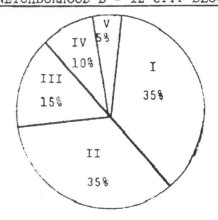

KEY: I- one- and two-family houses   III. Office buildings
       II- Apartment buildings   IV. Rental stores
                    V. Factories and warehouses

11.   In how many of these neighborhoods does residential use (categories I and II together)   11._____
      account for at least 50% of the land use?

      A. One   B. Two   C. Three   D. Four

12.   Which neighborhood has the largest land area occupied by apartment buildings? Neigh-   12._____
      borhood _____ .

      A. A   B. B   C. C   D. D

13. In which neighborhood is the largest percentage of the land devoted to both office build- ings and retail stores? Neighborhood _____ .   13.____

    A. A   B. B   ʳ C. C   D. D

14. What is the difference, to the nearest city block, between the amount of land devoted to retail stores in Neighborhood B and the amount devoted to similar use in Neighborhood C? _____ block(s).   14.____

    A. 1   B. 2   C. 4   D. 6

15. Which one of the following types of buildings occupies the same amount of land area in Neighborhood B as the amount of land area occupied by retail stores in Neighborhood A?   15.____

    A. Factories and warehouses
    B. Office buildings
    C. Retail stores
    D. Apartment buildings

Questions 16 - 20.

DIRECTIONS: Answer Questions 16 through 20 on the basis of the following passage.

    For a period of nearly fifteen years, beginning in the mid-1950's, higher education sustained a phenomenal rate of growth. The factors principally responsible were continuing improvement in the rate of college entrance by high school graduates, a 50-percent increase in the size of the college-age (eighteen to twenty-one) group, and - until about 1967 - a rapid expansion of university research activity supported by the federal government.

    Today, as one looks ahead fifteen years to the year 2020, it is apparent that each of these favorable stimuli will either be abated or turn into a negative factor. The rate of growth of the college-age group has already diminished, and from 2010 to 2015 the size of the college-age group will shrink annually almost as fast as it grew from 1965 to 1970. From 2015 to 2020, this annual decrease will slow down so that by 2020 the age-group will be about the same size as it was in 2019. This substantial net decrease in the size of the college-age group over the next fifteen years will dramatically affect college enrollments since, currently, 83 percent of undergraduates are twenty-one and under, and another 11 percent are twenty-one to twenty-four.

16. Which one of the following factors is NOT mentioned in the above passage as contribut- ing to the high rate of growth of higner education?   16.____

    A. A larger increase in the size of the eighteen to twenty-one age group
    B. The equalization of educational opportunities among socio-economic groups
    C. The federal budget impact on research and development spending in the higher education sector
    D. The increasing rate at which high school graduates enter college

17. Based on the information in the above passage, the size of the college-age group in 2020 will be   17._____

    A. larger than it was in 2019
    B. larger than it was in 2005
    C. smaller than it was in 2015
    D. about the same as it was in 2010

18. According to the above passage, the tremendous rate of growth of higher education started around   18._____

    A. 1950   B. 1955   C. 1960   D. 1965

19. The percentage of undergraduates who are over age 24 is, *most nearly,*   19._____

    A. 6%   B. 8%   C. 11%   D. 17%

20. Which one of the following conclusions can be substantiated by the information given in the above passage?   20._____

    A. The college-age group will be about the same size in 2010 as it was in 1965.
    B. The annual decrease in the size of the college-age group from 2010 to 2015 will be about the same as the annual increase from 1965 to 1970.
    C. The overall decrease in the size of the college-age group from 2010 to 2015 will be followed by an overall increase in its size from 2015 to 2020.
    D. The size of the college-age group will decrease at a fairly constant rate from 1995 to 2010.

21. Because higher status is important to many employees, they will often make an effort to achieve it as an end in itself.   21._____
Of the following, the BEST course of action for the supervisor to take on the basis of the preceding statement is to

    A. attach higher status to that behavior of subordinates which is directed toward reaching the goals of the organization
    B. avoid showing sympathy toward subordinates' wishes for increased wages, improved working conditions, or other benefits
    C. foster interpersonal competitiveness among subordinates so that personal friendliness is replaced by the desire to protect individual status
    D. reprimand subordinates whenever their work is in some way unsatisfactory in order to adjust their status accordingly

22. Assume that a large office in a certain organization operates long hours and is thus on two shifts with a slight overlap. Those employees, including supervisors, who are most productive are given their choice of shifts. The earlier shift is considered preferable by most employees.   22._____
As a result of this method of assignment, which of the following is *most likely* to result?

    A. Most non-supervisory employees will be assigned to the late shift; most supervisors will be assigned to the early shift.
    B. Most supervisors will be assigned to the late shift; most non-supervisory employees will be assigned to the early shift.
    C. The early shift will be more productive than the late shift.
    D. The late shift will be more productive than the early shift.

23. Assume that a supervisor of a unit in which the employees are of avera.ge friendliness tells a newly-hired employee on her first day that her co-workers are very friendly. The other employees hear his remarks to the new employee.
Which of the following is the most *likely* result of this action of the supervisor? The

    A. newly-hired employee will tend to feel less friendly than if the supervisor had said nothing
    B. newly-hired employee will tend to believe that her co-workers are very friendly
    C. other employees will tend to feel less friendly toward one another
    D. other employees will tend to see the newly-hired employee as insincerely friendly

23.____

24. A recent study of employee absenteeism showed that, although unscheduled absence for part of a week is relatively high for young employees, unscheduled absence for a full week is low. However, although full-week unscheduled absence is least frequent for the youngest employees, the frequency of such absence increases as the age of employees increases.
Which of the following statements is the MOST logical explanation for the greater full-week absenteeism among older employees?

    A. *Older* employees are more likely to be males.
    B. *Older* employees are more likely to have more relatively serious illnesses.
    C. *Younger* employees are more likely to take longer vacations.
    D. *Younger* employees are more likely to be newly-hired.

24.____

25. An employee can be motivated to fulfill his needs as he sees them. He is not motivated by what others think he ought to have, but what he himself wants. Which of the following statements follows MOST logically from the foregoing viewpoint?

    A. A person's different traits may be separately classified, but they are all part of one system comprising a whole person.
    B. Every job, however simple, entitles the person who does it to proper respect and recognition of his unique aspirations and abilities.
    C. No matter what equipment and facilities an organization has, they cannot be put to use except by people who have been motivated.
    D. To an observer, a person's need may be unrealistic but they are still controlling.

25.____

KEY (CORRECT ANSWERS)

1.	D	11.	B
2.	C	12.	C
3.	D	13.	A
4.	B	14.	C
5.	A	15.	D
6.	C	16.	B
7.	B	17.	C
8.	D	18.	B
9.	B	19.	A
10.	B	20.	B

21.	A
22.	C
23.	B
24.	B
25.	D

READING COMPREHENSION
UNDERSTANDING AND INTERPRETING WRITTEN MATERIAL
EXAMINATION SECTION
TEST 1

DIRECTIONS: Each question or incomplete statement is followed by several suggested answers or completions. Select the one that BEST answers the question or completes the statement. *PRINT THE LETTER OF THE CORRECT ANSWER IN THE SPACE AT THE RIGHT.*

Questions 1-3.

DIRECTIONS: Questions 1 through 3 are to be answered SOLELY on the basis of the following paragraph.

Every organization needs a systematic method of checking its operations as a means to increase efficiency and promote economy. Many successful private firms have instituted a system of audits or internal inspections to accomplish these ends. Law enforcement organizations, which have an extremely important service to *sell,* should be no less zealous in developing efficiency and economy in their operations. Periodic, organized, and systematic inspections are one means of promoting the achievement of these objectives. The necessity of an organized inspection system is perhaps greatest in those law enforcement groups which have grown to such a size that the principal officer can no longer personally supervise or be cognizant of every action taken. Smooth and effective operation demands that the head of the organization have at hand some tool with which he can study and enforce general policies and procedures and also direct compliance with day-to-day orders, most of which are put into execution outside his sight and hearing. A good inspection system can serve as that tool.

1. The central thought of the above paragraph is that a system of inspections within a police department

    A. is unnecessary for a department in which the principal officer can personally supervise all official actions taken
    B. should be instituted at the first indication that there is any deterioration in job performance by the force
    C. should be decentralized and administered by first-line supervisory officers
    D. is an important aid to the police administrator in the accomplishment of law enforcement objectives

1.____

2. The MOST accurate of the following statements concerning the need for an organized inspection system in a law enforcement organization is: It is

    A. never needed in an organization of small size where the principal officer can give personal supervision
    B. most needed where the size of the organization prevents direct supervision by the principal officer
    C. more needed in law enforcement organizations than in private firms
    D. especially needed in an organization about to embark upon a needed expansion of services

2.____

3. According to the above paragraph, the head of the police organization utilizes the internal inspection system

    A. as a tool which must be constantly re-examined in the light of changing demands for police service
    B. as an administrative technique to increase efficiency and promote economy
    C. by personally visiting those areas of police operation which are outside his sight and hearing
    D. to augment the control of local commanders over detailed field operations

3.____

Questions 4-10.

DIRECTIONS: Questions 4 through 10 are to be answered SOLELY on the basis of the following passage.

Job evaluation and job rating systems are intended to introduce scientific procedures. Any type of approach, when properly used, will give satisfactory results. The Point System, when properly validated by actual use, is more likely to be suitable for general use than the ranking system. In many aspects, the Factor Comparison Plan is a point system tied to money values. Of course, there may be another system that combines the ranking system with the point system, especially during the initial stages of the development of the program. After the program has been in use for some time, the tendency is to drop off the ranking phase and continue the use of the point system.

In the ranking system of rating of jobs, every job within the plant is arranged in some order, either from the one with the simplest qualifications to the one with maximum requirements, or in the reverse order. This system should be preceded by careful job analysis and the writing of accurate job descriptions before the rating process is undertaken. It is possible, of course, to take the jobs as they are found in the business enterprise and use the names as they are without any attempt at standardization, and merely rank them according to the general over-all impression of the raters. Such a procedure is certain to fall short of what may reasonably be expected of job rating. Another procedure that is in reality merely a modification of the simple rating described above is to establish a series of grades or zones and arrange all the jobs in the plant into groups within these grades and zones. The practice in most common use is to arrange all the jobs in the plant according to their requirements by rating them and then to establish the classifications or groups.

The actual ranking of jobs may be done by one individual, several individuals, or a committee. If several individuals are working independently on the task, it will usually be found that, in general, they agree but that their rankings vary in certain details. A conference between the individuals, with each person giving his reasons why he rated one way or another, usually produces agreement. The detailed job descriptions are particularly helpful when there is disagreement among raters as to the rating of certain jobs. It is not only possible but desirable to have workers participate in the construction of the job description and in rating the job.

4. The MAIN theme of this passage is

    A. the elimination of bias in job rating
    B. the rating of jobs by the ranking system

4.____

C. the need for accuracy in allocating points in the point system

D. pitfalls to avoid in selecting key jobs in the Factor Comparison Plan

5. The ranking system of rating jobs consists MAINLY of 5.____

   A. attaching a point value to each ratable factor of each job prior to establishing an equitable pay scale

   B. arranging every job in the organization in descending order and then following this up with a job analysis of the key jobs

   C. preparing accurate job descriptions after a job analysis and then arranging all jobs either in ascending or descending order based on job requirements

   D. arbitrarily establishing a hierarchy of job classes and grades and then fitting each job into a specific class and grade based on the opinions of unit supervisors

6. The above passage states that the system of classifying jobs MOST used in an organization is to 6.____

   A. organize all jobs in the organization in accordance with their requirements and then create categories or clusters of jobs

   B. classify all jobs in the organization according to the titles and rank by which they are currently known in the organization

   C. establish a pre-arranged series of grades or zones and then fit

   D. all jobs into one of the grades or zones

   E. determine the salary currently being paid for each job and then rank the jobs in order according to salary

7. According to the above passage, experience has shown that when a group of raters is assigned to the job evaluation task and each individual rates independently of the others, the raters GENERALLY 7.____

   A. agree with respect to all aspects of their rankings

   B. disagree with respect to all or nearly all aspects of the rankings

   C. disagree on overall ratings, but agree on specific rating factors

   D. agree on overall rankings, but have some variance in some details

8. The above passage states that the use of a detailed job description is of SPECIAL value when 8.____

   A. employees of an organization have participated in the preliminary step involved in actual preparation of the job description

   B. labor representatives are not participating in ranking of the jobs

   C. an individual rater who is unsure of himself is ranking the jobs

   D. a group of raters is having difficulty reaching unanimity with respect to ranking a certain job

9. A comparison of the various rating systems as described in the above passage shows that 9.____

   A. the ranking system is not as appropriate for general use as a properly validated point system

   B. the point system is the same as the Factor Comparison Plan except that it places greater emphasis on money

C.   no system is capable of combining the point system and the Factor Comparison Plan
D.   the point system will be discontinued last when used in combination with the Factor Comparison System

10.   The above passage implies that the PRINCIPAL reason for creating job evaluation and rating systems was to help   10._____

A.   overcome union opposition to existing salary plans
B.   base wage determination on a more objective and orderly foundation
C.   eliminate personal bias on the part of the trained scientific job evaluators
D.   management determine if it was overpricing the various jobs in the organizational hierarchy

Questions 11-13.

DIRECTIONS: Questions 11 through 13 are to be answered SOLELY on the basis of the following paragraph.

The common sense character of the merit system seems so natural to most Americans that many people wonder why it should ever have been inoperative. After all, the American economic system, the most phenomenal the world has ever known, is also founded on a rugged selective process which emphasizes the personal qualities of capacity, industriousness, and productivity. The criteria may not have always been appropriate and competition has not always been fair, but competition there was, and the responsibilities and the rewards — with exceptions, of course — have gone to those who could measure up in terms of intelligence, knowledge, or perseverance. This has been true not only in the economic area, in the money-making process, but also in achievement in the professions and other walks of life.

11.   According to the above paragraph, economic rewards in the United States have   11._____

A.   always been based on appropriate, fair criteria
B.   only recently been based on a competitive system
C.   not gone to people who compete too ruggedly
D.   usually gone to those people with intelligence, knowledge, and perseverance

12.   According to the above passage, a merit system is   12._____

A.   an unfair criterion on which to base rewards
B.   unnatural to anyone who is not American
C.   based only on common sense
D.   based on the same principles as the American economic system

13.   According to the above passage, it is MOST accurate to say that   13._____

A.   the United States has always had a civil service merit system
B.   civil service employees are very rugged
C.   the American economic system has always been based on a merit objective
D.   competition is unique to the American way of life

Questions 14-15.

DIRECTIONS: Questions 14 and 15 are to be answered SOLELY on the basis of the following paragraph.

In-basket tests are often used to assess managerial potential. The exercise consists of a set of papers that would be likely to be found in the in-basket of an administrator or manager at any given time, and requires the individuals participating in the examination to indicate how they would dispose of each item found in the in-basket. In order to handle the in-basket effectively, they must successfully manage their time, refer and assign some work to subordinates, juggle potentially conflicting appointments and meetings, and arrange for follow-up of problems generated by the items in the in-basket. In other words, the in-basket test is attempting to evaluate the participants' abilities to organize their work, set priorities, delegate, control, and make decisions.

14. According to the above paragraph, to succeed in an in-basket test, an administrator must   14.____

    A. be able to read very quickly
    B. have a great deal of technical knowledge
    C. know when to delegate work
    D. arrange a lot of appointments and meetings

15. According to the above paragraph, all of the following abilities are indications of manage-   15.____
    rial potential EXCEPT the ability to

    A. organize and control   B. manage time
    C. write effective reports   D. make appropriate decisions

Questions 16-19.

DIRECTIONS: Questions 16 through 19 are to be answered SOLELY on the basis of the following paragraph.

A personnel researcher has at his disposal various approaches for obtaining information, analyzing it, and arriving at conclusions that have value in predicting and affecting the behavior of people at work. The type of method to be used depends on such factors as the nature of the research problem, the available data, and the attitudes of those people being studied to the various kinds of approaches. While the experimental approach, with its use of control groups, is the most refined type of study, there are others that are often found useful in personnel research. Surveys, in which the researcher obtains facts on a problem from a variety of sources, are employed in research on wages, fringe benefits, and labor relations. Historical studies are used to trace the development of problems in order to understand them better and to isolate possible causative factors. Case studies are generally developed to explore all the details of a particular problem that is representative of other similar problems. A researcher chooses the most appropriate form of study for the problem he is investigating. He should recognize, however, that the experimental method, commonly referred to as the scientific method, if used validly and reliably, gives the most conclusive results.

16. The above paragraph discusses several approaches used to obtain information on par-   16.____
    ticular problems. Which of the following may be MOST reasonably concluded from the
    paragraph?
    A(n)

A. historical study cannot determine causative factors
B. survey is often used in research on fringe benefits
C. case study is usually used to explore a problem that is unique and unrelated to other problems
D. experimental study is used when the scientific approach to a problem fails

17. According to the above paragraph, all of the following are factors that may determine the type of approach a researcher uses EXCEPT

    17.____

    A. the attitudes of people toward being used in control groups
    B. the number of available sources
    C. his desire to isolate possible causative factors
    D. the degree of accuracy he requires

18. The words *scientific method*, as used in the last sentence of the above paragraph, refer to a type of study which, according to the above paragraph

    18.____

    A. uses a variety of sources
    B. traces the development of problems
    C. uses control groups
    D. analyzes the details of a representative problem

19. Which of the following can be MOST reasonably concluded from the above paragraph? In obtaining and analyzing information on a particular problem, a researcher employs the method which is the

    19.____

    A. most accurate
    B. most suitable
    C. least expensive
    D. least time-consuming

Questions 20-25.

DIRECTIONS: Questions 20 through 25 are to be answered SOLELY on the basis of the following passage.

The quality of the voice of a worker is an important factor in conveying to clients and co-workers his attitude and, to some degree, his character. The human voice, when not consciously disguised, may reflect a person's mood, temper, and personality. It has been shown in several experiments that certain character traits can be assessed with better than chance accuracy through listening to the voice of an unknown person who cannot be seen.

Since one of the objectives of the worker is to put clients at ease and to present an encouraging and comfortable atmosphere, a harsh, shrill, or loud voice could have a negative effect. A client who displays emotions of anger or resentment would probably be provoked even further by a caustic tone. In a face-to-face situation, an unpleasant voice may be compensated for, to some degree, by a concerned and kind facial expression. However, when one speaks on the telephone, the expression on one's face cannot be seen by the listener. A supervising clerk who wishes to represent himself effectively to clients should try to eliminate as many faults as possible in striving to develop desirable voice qualities.

20. If a worker uses a sarcastic tone while interviewing a resentful client, the client, according to the above passage, would MOST likely   20.____

    A. avoid the face-to-face situation
    B. be ashamed of his behavior
    C. become more resentful
    D. be provoked to violence

21. According to the passage, experiments comparing voice and character traits have demonstrated that   21.____

    A. prospects for improving an unpleasant voice through training are better than chance
    B. the voice can be altered to project many different psychological characteristics
    C. the quality of the human voice reveals more about the speaker than his words do
    D. the speaker's voice tells the hearer something about the speaker's personality

22. Which of the following, according to the above passage, is a person's voice MOST likely to reveal?   22.____
His

    A. prejudices   B. intelligence
    C. social awareness   D. temperament

23. It may be MOST reasonably concluded from the above passage that an interested and sympathetic expression on the face of a worker   23.____

    A. may induce a client to feel certain he will receive welfare benefits
    B. will eliminate the need for pleasant vocal qualities in the interviewer
    C. may help to make up for an unpleasant voice in the interviewer
    D. is desirable as the interviewer speaks on the telephone to a client

24. Of the following, the MOST reasonable implication of the above paragraph is that a worker should, when speaking to a client, control and use his voice to   24.____

    A. simulate a feeling of interest in the problems of the client
    B. express his emotions directly and adequately
    C. help produce in the client a sense of comfort and security
    D. reflect his own true personality

25. It may be concluded from the above passage that the PARTICULAR reason for a worker to pay special attention to modulating her voice when talking on the phone to a client is that, during a telephone conversation,   25.____

    A. there is a necessity to compensate for the way in which a telephone distorts the voice
    B. the voice of the worker is a reflection of her mood and character
    C. the client can react only on the basis of the voice and words she hears
    D. the client may have difficulty getting a clear under-standing over the telephone

KEY (CORRECT ANSWERS)

1.	D	11.	D
2.	B	12.	D
3.	B	13.	C
4.	B	14.	C
5.	C	15.	C
6.	A	16.	B
7.	D	17.	D
8.	D	18.	C
9.	A	19.	B
10.	B	20.	C

21.	D
22.	D
23.	C
24.	C
25.	C

———

TEST 2

Questions 1-3.

DIRECTIONS: Questions 1 through 3 are to be answered SOLELY on the basis of the following paragraph.

Suppose you are given the job of printing, collating, and stapling 8,000 copies of a ten-page booklet as soon as possible. You have available one photo-offset machine, a collator with an automatic stapler, and the personnel to operate these machines. All will be available for however long the job takes to complete. The photo-offset machine prints 5,000 impressions an hour, and it takes about 15 minutes to set up a plate. The collator, including time for insertion of pages and stapling, can process about 2,000 booklets an hour. (Answers should be based on the assumption that there are no breakdowns or delays.)

1. Assuming that all the printing is finished before the collating is started, if the job is given to you late Monday and your section can begin work the next day and is able to devote seven hours a day, Monday through Friday, to the job until it is finished, what is the BEST estimate of when the job will be finished?

   A. Wednesday afternoon of the same week
   B. Thursday morning of the same week
   C. Friday morning of the same week
   D. Monday morning of the next week

1.____

2. An operator suggests to you that instead of completing all the printing and then beginning collating and stapling, you first print all the pages for 4,000 booklets, so that they can be collated and stapled while the last 4,000 booklets are being printed.
   If you accepted this suggestion, the job would be completed

   A. sooner but would require more man-hours
   B. at the same time using either method
   C. later and would require more man-hours
   D. sooner but there would be more wear and tear on the plates

2.____

3. Assume that you have the same assignment and equipment as described above, but 16,000 copies of the booklet are needed instead of 8,000.
   If you decided to print 8,000 complete booklets, then collate and staple them while you started printing the next 8,000 booklets, which of the following statements would MOST accurately describe the relationship between this new method and your original method of printing all the booklets at one time, and then collating and stapling them?
   The

   A. job would be completed at the same time regardless of the method used
   B. new method would result in the job's being completed 3 1/2 hours earlier
   C. original method would result in the job's being completed an hour later
   D. new method would result in the job's being completed 1 1/2 hours earlier.

3.____

Questions 4-6.

DIRECTIONS: Questions 4 through 6 are to be answered SOLELY on the basis of the following passage.

When using words like company, association, council, committee, and board in place of the full official name, the writer should not capitalize these short forms unless he intends them to invoke the full force of the institution's authority. In legal contracts, in minutes, or in formal correspondence where one is speaking formally and officially on behalf of the company, the term Company is usually capitalized, but in ordinary usage, where it is not essential to load the short form with this significance, capitalization would be excessive. (Example: The company will have many good openings for graduates this June.)

The treatment recommended for short forms of place names is essentially the same as that recommended for short forms of organizational names. In general, we capitalize the full form but not the short form. If Park Avenue is referred to in one sentence, then the *avenue* is sufficient in subsequent references. The same is true with words like building, hotel, station, and airport, which are capitalized when part of a proper name changed (Pan Am Building, Hotel Plaza, Union Station, O'Hare Airport), but are simply lower-cased when replacing these specific names.

4. The above passage states that USUALLY the short forms of names of organizations   4.____

    A. and places should not be capitalized
    B. and places should be capitalized
    C. should not be capitalized, but the short forms of names of places should be capitalized
    D. should be capitalized, but the short forms of names of places should not be capitalized

5. The above passage states that in legal contracts, in minutes, and in formal correspondence, the short forms of names of organizations should   5.____

    A. usually not be capitalized
    B. usually be capitalized
    C. usually not be used
    D. never be used

6. It can be INFERRED from the above passage that decisions regarding when to capitalize certain words   6.____

    A. should be left to the discretion of the writer
    B. should be based on generally accepted rules
    C. depend on the total number of words capitalized
    D. are of minor importance

Questions 7-10.

DIRECTIONS: Questions 7 through 10 are to be answered SOLELY on the basis of the following passage.

Use of the systems and procedures approach to office management is revolutionizing the supervision of office work. This approach views an enterprise as an entity which seeks to fulfill definite objectives. Systems and procedures help to organize repetitive work into a routine, thus reducing the amount of decision making required for its accomplishment. As a result, employees are guided in their efforts and perform only necessary work. Supervisors are relieved of any details of execution and are free to attend to more important work. Establishing work guides which require that identical tasks be performed the same way each time permits standardization of forms, machine operations, work methods, and controls. This approach also reduces the probability of errors. Any error committed is usually discovered quickly because the incorrect work does not meet the requirement of the work guides. Errors are also reduced through work specialization, which allows each employee to become thoroughly proficient in a particular type of work. Such proficiency also tends to improve the morale of the employees.

7. The above passage states that the accuracy of an employee's work is INCREASED by 7._____

    A. using the work specialization approach
    B. employing a probability sample
    C. requiring him to shift at one time into different types of tasks
    D. having his supervisor check each detail of work execution

8. Of the following, which one BEST expresses the main theme of the above passage? The 8._____

    A. advantages and disadvantages of the systems and procedures approach to office management
    B. effectiveness of the systems and procedures approach to office management in developing skills
    C. systems and procedures approach to office management as it relates to office costs
    D. advantages of the systems and procedures approach to office management for supervisors and office workers

9. Work guides are LEAST likely to be used when 9._____

    A. standardized forms are used
    B. a particular office task is distinct and different from all others
    C. identical tasks are to be performed in identical ways
    D. similar work methods are expected from each employee

10. According to the above passage, when an employee makes a work error, it USUALLY 10._____

    A. is quickly corrected by the supervisor
    B. necessitates a change in the work guides
    C. can be detected quickly if work guides are in use
    D. increases the probability of further errors by that employee

Questions 11-12.

DIRECTIONS: Questions 11 and 12 are to be answered SOLELY on the basis of the following passage.

The coordination of the many activities of a large public agency is absolutely essential. Coordination, as an administrative principle, must be distinguished from and is independent of cooperation. Coordination can be of either the horizontal or the vertical type. In large organizations, the objectives of vertical coordination are achieved by the transmission of orders and statements of policy down through the various levels of authority. It is an accepted generalization that the more authoritarian the organization, the more easily may vertical coordination be accomplished. Horizontal coordination is arrived at through staff work, administrative management, and conferences of administrators of equal rank. It is obvious that of the two types of coordination, the vertical kind is more important, for at best horizontal coordination only supplements the coordination effected up and down the line.

11. According to the above passage, the ease with which vertical coordination is achieved in a large agency depends upon

11.____

    A. the extent to which control is firmly exercised from above
    B. the objectives that have been established for the agency
    C. the importance attached by employees to the orders and statements of policy transmitted through the agency
    D. the cooperation obtained at the various levels of authority

12. According to the above passage,

12.____

    A. vertical coordination is dependent for its success upon horizontal coordination
    B. one type of coordination may work in opposition to the other
    C. similar methods may be used to achieve both types of coordination
    D. horizontal coordination is at most an addition to vertical coordination

Questions 13-17.

DIRECTIONS: Questions 13 through 17 are to be answered SOLELY on the basis of the following situation.

Assume that you are a newly appointed supervisor in the same unit in which you have been acting as a provisional for some time. You have in your unit the following workers:

WORKER I - He has always been an efficient worker. In a number of his cases, the clients have recently begun to complain that they cannot manage on the departmental budget.

WORKER II - He has been under selective supervision for some time as an experienced, competent worker. He now begins to be late for his supervisory conferences and to stress how much work he has to do.

WORKER III - He has been making considerable improvement in his ability to handle the details of his job. He now tells you, during an individual conference, that he does not need such close supervision and that he wants to operate more independently. He says that Worker II is always available when he needs a little information or help but, in general, he can manage very well by himself.

WORKER IV - He brings you a complex case for decision as to eligibility. Discussion of the case brings out the fact that he has failed to consider all the available resources adequately but has stressed the family's needs to include every extra item in the budget. This is the third case of a similar nature that this worker has brought to you recently. This worker and Worker I work in adjacent territory and are rather friendly.

In the following questions, select the option that describes the method of dealing with these workers that illustrates BEST supervisory practice.

13. With respect to supervision of Worker I, the assistant supervisor should   13.____

    A. discuss with the worker, in an individual conference, any problems that he may be having due to the increase in the cost of living

    B. plan a group conference for the unit around budgeting, as both Workers I and IV seem to be having budgetary difficulties

    C. discuss with Workers I and IV together the meaning of money as acceptance or rejection to the clients

    D. discuss with Worker I the budgetary data in each case in relation to each client's situation

14. With respect to supervision of Worker II, the supervisor should   14.____

    A. move slowly with this worker and give him time to learn that the supervisor's official appointment has not changed his attitudes or methods of supervision

    B. discuss the worker's change of attitude and ask him to analyze the reasons for his change in behavior

    C. take time to show the worker how he is avoiding his responsibility in the supervisor-worker relationship and that he is resisting supervision

    D. hold an evaluatory conference with the worker and show him how he is taking over responsibilities that are not his by providing supervision for Worker III

15. With respect to supervision of Worker III, the supervisor should discuss with this worker   15.____

    A. why he would rather have supervision from Worker II than from the supervisor

    B. the necessity for further improvement before he can go on selective supervision

    C. an analysis of the improvement that has been made and the extent to which the worker is able to handle the total job for which he is responsible

    D. the responsibility of the supervisor to see that clients receive adequate service

16. With respect to supervision of Worker IV, the supervisor should   16.____

    A. show the worker that resources figures are incomplete but that even if they were complete, the family would probably be eligible for assistance

    B. ask the worker why he is so protective of these families since there are three cases so similar

    C. discuss with the worker all three cases at the same time so that the worker may see his own role in the three situations

    D. discuss with the worker the reasons for departmental policies and procedures around budgeting

17. With respect to supervision of Workers I and IV, since these two workers are friends and would seem to be influencing each other, the supervisor should   17.____

    A. hold a joint conference with them both, pointing out how they should clear with the supervisor and not make their own rules together

    B. handle the problems of each separately in individual conferences

    C. separate them by transferring one to another territory or another unit

    D. take up the problem of workers asking help of each other rather than from the supervisor in a group meeting

Questions 18-20.

DIRECTIONS: Questions 18 through 20 are to be answered SOLELY on the basis of the following passage.

One of the key supervisory problems in a large municipal recreation department is that many leaders are assigned to isolated playgrounds or small centers, where it is difficult to observe their work regularly. Often their facilities are extremely limited. In such settings, as well as in larger recreation centers, where many recreation leaders tend to have other jobs as well, there tends to be a low level of morale and incentive. Still, it is the supervisor's task to help recreation personnel to develop pride in their work and to maintain a high level of performance. With isolated leaders, the supervisor may give advice or assistance. Leaders may be assigned to different tasks or settings during the year to maximize their productivity and provide new challenges. When it is clear that leaders are not willing to make a real effort to contribute to the department, the possibility of penalties must be considered, within the scope of departmental policy and the union contract. However, the supervisor should be constructive, encourage and assist workers to take a greater interest in their work, be innovative, and try to raise morale and to improve performance in positive ways.

18. The one of the following that would be the MOST appropriate title for the above passage is   18.____

    A. SMALL COMMUNITY CENTERS - PRO AND CON
    B. PLANNING BETTER RECREATION PROGRAMS
    C. THE SUPERVISOR'S TASK IN UPGRADING PERSONNEL PERFORMANCE
    D. THE SUPERVISOR AND THE MUNICIPAL UNION - RIGHTS AND OBLIGATIONS

19. The above passage makes clear that recreation leadership performance in ALL recreation playgrounds and centers throughout a large city is   19.____

    A. generally above average, with good morale on the part of most recreation leaders
    B. beyond description since no one has ever observed or evaluated recreation leaders
    C. a key test of the personnel department's effort to develop more effective hiring standards
    D. of mixed quality, with many recreation leaders having poor morale and a low level of achievement

20. According to the above passage, the supervisor's role is to   20.____

    A. use disciplinary action as his major tool in upgrading performance
    B. tolerate the lack of effort of individual employees since they are assigned to isolated playgrounds or small centers
    C. employ encouragement, advice, and, when appropriate, disciplinary action to improve performance
    D. inform the county supervisor whenever malfeasance or idleness is detected

Questions 21-25.

DIRECTIONS: Questions 21 through 25 are to be answered SOLELY on the basis of the following passage.

EMPLOYEE LEAVE REGULATIONS

Peter Smith, as a full-time permanent city employee under the Career and Salary Plan, earns an *annual leave allowance*. This consists of a certain number of days off a year with pay and may be used for vacation, personal business, and for observing religious holidays. As a newly appointed employee, during his first 8 years of city service, he will earn an annual leave allowance of 20 days off a year (an average of 1 2/3 days off a month). After he has finished 8 full years of working for the city, he will begin earning an additional 5 days off a year. His *annual leave allowance*, therefore, will then be 25 days a year and will remain at this amount for seven full years. He will begin earning an additional two days off a year after he has completed a total of 15 years of city employment. Therefore, in his sixteenth year of working for the city, Mr. Smith will be earning 27 days off a year as his *annual leave allowance* (an average of 2 1/4 days off a month).

A sick leave allowance of one day a month is also given to Mr. Smith, but it can be used only in cases of actual illness. When Mr. Smith returns to work after *using sick leave allowance*, he must have a doctor's note if the absence is for a total of more than 3 days, but he may also be required to show a doctor's note for absences of 1, 2, or 3 days.

21. According to the above passage, Mr. Smith's *annual leave allowance* consists of a certain number of days off a year which he

    A. does not get paid for
    B. gets paid for at time and a half
    C. may use for personal business
    D. may not use for observing religious holidays

21.____

22. According to the above passage, after Mr. Smith has been working for the city for 9 years, his *annual leave allowance* will be _____ days a year.

    A. 20   B. 25   C. 27   D. 37

22.____

23. According to the above passage, Mr. Smith will begin earning an average of 2 days off a month as his *annual leave allowance* after he has worked for the city for full years.

    A. 7   B. 8   C. 15   D. 17

23.____

24. According to the above passage, Mr. Smith is given a *sick leave allowance* of

    A. 1 day every 2 months   B. 1 day per month
    C. 1 2/3 days per month   D. 2 1/4 days a month

24.____

25. According to the above passage, when he uses *sick leave allowance*, Mr. Smith may be required to show a doctor's note

    A. even if his absence is for only 1 day
    B. only if his absence is for more than 2 days
    C. only if his absence is for more than 3 days
    D. only if his absence is for 3 days or more

25.____

KEY (CORRECT ANSWERS)

1.	C		11.	A
2.	C		12.	D
3.	D		13.	D
4.	A		14.	A
5.	B		15.	C
6.	B		16.	C
7.	A		17.	B
8.	D		18.	C
9.	B		19.	D
10.	C		20.	C

21.	C
22.	B
23.	C
24.	B
25.	A

TEST 3

Questions 1-6.

DIRECTIONS: Questions 1 through 6 are to be answered SOLELY on the basis of the following passage.

A folder is made of a sheet of heavy paper (manila, kraft, pressboard, or red rope stock) that has been folded once so that the back is about one-half inch higher than the front. Folders are larger than the papers they contain in order to protect them. Two standard folder sizes are *letter size* for papers that are 8 1/2" x 11" and *legal cap* for papers that are 8 1/2" x 13".

Folders are cut across the top in two ways: so that the back is straight (straight-cut) or so that the back has a tab that projects above the top of the folder. Such tabs bear captions that identify the contents of each folder. Tabs vary in width and position. The tabs of a set of folders that are *one-half cut* are half the width of the folder and have only two positions.

One-third cut folders have three positions, each tab occupying a third of the width of the folder. Another standard tabbing is *one-fifth cut*, which has five positions. There are also folders with *two-fifths cut*, with the tabs in the third and fourth or fourth and fifth positions.

1. Of the following, the BEST title for the above passage is   1.____

    A. FILING FOLDERS   B. STANDARD FOLDER SIZES
    C. THE USES OF THE FOLDER   D. THE USE OF TABS

2. According to the above passage, one of the standard folder sizes is called   2.____

    A. Kraft cut   B. legal cap
    C. one-half cut   D. straight-cut

3. According to the above passage, tabs are GENERALLY placed along the _____ of the   3.____
    folder.

    A. back   B. front
    C. left side   D. right side

4. According to the above passage, a tab is GENERALLY used to   4.____

    A. distinguish between standard folder sizes
    B. identify the contents of a folder
    C. increase the size of the folder
    D. protect the papers within the folder

5. According to the above passage, a folder that is two-fifths cut has _____ tabs.   5.____

    A. no   B. two   C. three   D. five

6. According to the above passage, one reason for making folders larger than the papers   6.____
    they contain is that

    A. only a certain size folder can be made from heavy paper
    B. they will protect the papers
    C. they will aid in setting up a tab system
    D. the back of the folder must be higher than the front

Questions 7-15.

DIRECTIONS: Questions 7 through 15 are to be answered SOLELY on the basis of the following passage.

The City University of New York traces its origins to 1847, when the Free Academy, which later became City College, was founded as the first tuition-free municipal college. City and Hunter Colleges were placed under the direction of the Board of Higher Education in 1926, and Brooklyn and Queens Colleges were subsequently added to the system of municipal colleges. In 1955, Staten Island Community College, the first of the two-year colleges sponsored by the Board of Higher Education under the program of the State University of New York, joined the system.

In 1961, the four senior colleges and three community colleges then under the jurisdiction of the Board of Higher Education became the City University of New York, and a University Graduate Division was organized to offer programs leading to the Ph.D. Since then, the university has undergone even more rapid growth. Today, it consists of nine senior colleges, an upper division college which admits students at the junior level, eight community colleges, a graduate division, and an affiliated medical center.

In the summer of 1969, the Board of Higher Education resolved that the time had come to commit the resources of the university to meeting an urgent social need—unrestricted access to higher education for all youths of the City. Determined to prevent the waste of human potential represented by the thousands of high school graduates whose limited educational opportunities left them unable to meet existing admission standards, the Board moved to adopt a policy of Open Admissions. It was their judgment that the best way of determining whether a potential student can benefit from college work is to admit him to college, provide him with the learning assistance he needs, and then evaluate his performance.

Beginning with the class of June 1970, every New York City resident who received a high school diploma from a public or private high school was guaranteed a place in one of the colleges of City University.

7. Of the following, the BEST title for the above passage is   7._____

    A. A BRIEF HISTORY OF THE CITY UNIVERSITY
    B. HIGH SCHOOLS AND THE CITY UNIVERSITY
    C. THE COMPONENTS OF THE UNIVERSITY
    D. TUITION-FREE COLLEGES

8. According to the above passage, which one of the following colleges of the City University was ORIGINALLY called the Free Academy?   8._____

    A. Brooklyn College   B. City College
    C. Hunter College   D. Queens College

9. According to the above passage, the system of municipal colleges became the City University of New York in   9._____

    A. 1926   B. 1955   C. 1961   D. 1969

10. According to the above passage, Staten Island Community College came under the juris-   10.____
diction of the Board of Higher Education

    A. 6 years after a Graduate Division was organized
    B. 8 years before the adoption of the Open Admissions Policy
    C. 29 years after Brooklyn and Queens Colleges
    D. 29 years after City and Hunter Colleges

11. According to the above passage, the Staten Island Community College is   11.____

    A. a graduate division center
    B. a senior college
    C. a two-year college
    D. an upper division college

12. According to the above passage, the TOTAL number of colleges, divisions, and affiliated   12.____
branches of the City University is

    A. 18   B. 19   C. 20   D. 21

13. According to the above passage, the Open Admissions Policy is designed to determine   13.____
whether a potential student will benefit from college by PRIMARILY

    A. discouraging competition for placement in the City University among high school
       students
    B. evaluating his performance after entry into college
    C. lowering admission standards
    D. providing learning assistance before entry into college

14. According to the above passage, the FIRST class to be affected by the Open Admissions   14.____
Policy was the

    A. high school class which graduated in January 1970
    B. City University class which graduated in June 1970
    C. high school class when graduated in June 1970
    D. City University class which graduated in June 1970

15. According to the above passage, one of the reasons that the Board of Higher Education   15.____
initiated the policy of Open Admissions was to

    A. enable high school graduates with a background of limited educational opportuni-
       ties to enter college
    B. expand the growth of the City University so as to increase the number and variety
       of degrees offered
    C. provide a social resource to the qualified youth of the City
    D. revise admission standards to meet the needs of the City

Questions 16-18.

DIRECTIONS: Questions 16 through 18 are to be answered SOLELY on the basis of the following passage.

Hereafter, all probationary students interested in transferring to community college
career programs (associate degrees) from liberal arts programs in senior colleges (bachelor

degrees) will be eligible for such transfers if they have completed no more than three semesters.

For students with averages of 1.5 or above, transfer will be automatic. Those with 1.0 to 1.5 averages can transfer provisionally and will be required to make substantial progress during the first semester in the career program. Once transfer has taken place, only those courses in which passing grades were received will be computed in the community college grade-point average.

No request for transfer will be accepted from probationary students wishing to enter the liberal arts programs at the community college.

16. According to this passage, the one of the following which is the BEST statement concerning the transfer of probationary students is that a probationary student   16.____

    A.   may transfer to a career program at the end of one semester
    B.   must complete three semester hours before he is eligible for transfer
    C.   is not eligible to transfer to a career program
    D.   is eligible to transfer to a liberal arts program

17. Which of the following is the BEST statement of academic evaluation for transfer purposes in the case of probationary students?   17.____

    A.   No probationary student with an average under 1.5 may transfer.
    B.   A probationary student with an average of 1.3 may not transfer.
    C.   A probationary student with an average of 1.6 may transfer.
    D.   A probationary student with an average of .8 may transfer on a provisional basis.

18. It is MOST likely that, of the following, the next degree sought by one who already holds the Associate in Science degree would be a(n)   18.____

    A.   Assistantship in Science degree
    B.   Associate in Applied Science degree
    C.   Bachelor of Science degree
    D.   Doctor of Philosophy degree

Questions 19-20.

DIRECTIONS: Questions 19 and 20 are to be answered SOLELY on the basis of the following passage.

Auto: Auto travel requires prior approval by the President and/or appropriate Dean and must be indicated in the *Request for Travel Authorization* form. Employees authorized to use personal autos on official College business will be reimbursed at the rate of 28¢ per mile for the first 500 miles driven and 18¢ per mile for mileage driven in excess of 500 miles. The Comptroller's Office may limit the amount of reimbursement to the expenditure that would have been made if a less expensive mode of transportation (railroad, airplane, bus, etc.) had been utilized. If this occurs, the traveler will have to pick up the excess expenditure as a personal expense.

Tolls, Parking Fees, and Parking Meter Fees are not reimbursable and may not be claimed.

19. Suppose that Professor T. gives the office assistant the following memorandum:
Used car for official trip to Albany, New York, and return. Distance from New York to
Albany is 148 miles. Tolls were $3.50 each way. Parking garage cost $3.00.
When preparing the Travel Expense Voucher for Professor T., the figure which should
be claimed for transportation is

   A. $120.88   B. $113.88   C. $82.88   D. $51.44

19.____

20. Suppose that Professor V. gives the office assistant the following memorandum:
Used car for official trip to Pittsburgh, Pennsylvania, and return.
Distance from New York to Pittsburgh is 350 miles. Tolls were $3.30, $11.40 going, and
$3.30, $2.00 returning.
When preparing the Travel Expense Voucher for Professor V., the figure which should
be claimed for transportation is

   A. $225.40   B. $176.00   C. $127.40   D. $98.00

20.____

Questions 21-25.

DIRECTIONS: Questions 21 through 25 are to be answered SOLELY on the basis of the following passage.

For a period of nearly fifteen years, beginning in the mid-1950's, higher education sustained a phenomenal rate of growth. The factors principally responsible were continuing
improvement in the rate of college entrance by high school graduates, a 50 percent increase
in the size of the college-age (eighteen to twenty-one) group, and – until about 1967 – a rapid
expansion of university research activity supported by the Federal government.

Today, as one looks ahead to the year 2010, it is apparent that each of these favorable
stimuli will either be abated or turn into a negative factor. The rate of growth of the college-
age group has already diminished; and from 2000 to 2005, the size of the college-age group
has shrunk annually almost as fast as it grew from 1965 to 1970. From 2005 to 2010, this
annual decrease will slow down so that by 2010 the age group will be about the same size as
it was in 2009. This substantial net decrease in the size of the college-age group (from 1995
to 2010) will dramatically affect college enrollments since, currently, 83 percent of undergraduates are twenty-one and under, and another 11 percent are twenty-two to twenty-four.

21. Which one of the following factors is NOT mentioned in the above passage as contributing to the high rate of growth of higher education?

   A. A large increase in the size of the eighteen to twenty-one age group
   B. The equalization of educational opportunities among socio-economic groups
   C. The Federal budget impact on research and development spending in the higher
       education sector
   D. The increasing rate at which high school graduates enter college

21.____

22. Based on the information in the above passage, the size of the college-age group in
2010 will be

   A. larger than it was in 2009
   B. larger than it was in 1995
   C. smaller than it was in 2005
   D. about the same as it was in 2000

22.____

23. According to the above passage, the tremendous rate of growth of higher education started around   23.____

    A. 1950   B. 1955   C. 1960   D. 1965

24. The percentage of undergraduates who are over age 24 is MOST NEARLY   24.____

    A. 6%   B. 8%   C. 11%   D. 17%

25. Which one of the following conclusions can be substantiated by the information given in the above passage?   25.____

    A. The college-age group was about the same size in 2000 as it was in 1965.
    B. The annual decrease in the size of the college-age group from 2000 to 2005 is about the same as the annual increase from 1965 to 1970.
    C. The overall decrease in the size of the college-age group from 2000 to 2005 will be followed by an overall increase in its size from 2005 to 2010.
    D. The size of the college-age group is decreasing at a fairly constant rate from 1995 to 2010.

KEY (CORRECT ANSWERS)

1.	A		11.	C
2.	B		12.	C
3.	A		13.	B
4.	B		14.	C
5.	B		15.	A
6.	B		16.	A
7.	A		17.	C
8.	B		18.	C
9.	C		19.	C
10.	D		20.	B

21.	B
22.	C
23.	B
24.	A
25.	B

REPORT WRITING
EXAMINATION SECTION
TEST 1

DIRECTIONS: Each question or incomplete statement is followed by several suggested answers or completions. Select the one that BEST answers the question or completes the statement. *PRINT THE LETTER OF THE CORRECT ANSWER IN THE SPACE AT THE RIGHT.*

Questions 1-4.

DIRECTIONS: Answer Questions 1 through 4 on the basis of the following report which was prepared by a supervisor for inclusion in his agency's annual report.

Line
#
1   On Oct. 13, I was assigned to study the salaries paid
2   to clerical employees in various titles by the city and by
3   private industry in the area.
4   In order to get the data I needed, I called Mr. Johnson at
5   the Bureau of the Budget and the payroll officers at X Corp.—
6   a brokerage house, Y Co.—an insurance company, and Z Inc.—
7   a publishing firm. None of them was available and I had to call
8   all of them again the next day.
9   When I finally got the information I needed, I drew up a
10 chart, which is attached. Note that not all of the companies I
11 contacted employed people at all the different levels used in the
12 city service.
13 The conclusions I draw from analyzing this information is
14 as follows: The city's entry-level salary is about average for
15 the region; middle-level salaries are generally higher in the
16 city government than in private industry; but salaries at the
17 highest levels in private industry are better than city em-
18 ployees' pay.

1. Which of the following criticisms about the style in which this report is written is *most valid?*

    A. It is too informal.   B. It is too concise.
    C. It is too choppy.   D. The syntax is too complex.

1.____

2. Judging from the statements made in the report, the method followed by this employee in performing his research was

    A. *good;* he contacted a representative sample of businesses in the area
    B. *poor;* he should have drawn more definite conclusions
    C. *good;* he was persistent in collecting information
    D. *poor;* he did not make a thorough study

2.____

3. One sentence in this report contains a grammatical error. This sentence *begins* on line number

    3.____

    A. 4   B. 7   C. 10   D. 13

4. The type of information given in this report which should be presented in footnotes or in an appendix, is the

    4.____

    A. purpose of the study
    B. specifics about the businesses contacted
    C. reference to the chart
    D. conclusions drawn by the author

5. The use of a graph to show statistical data in a report is *superior* to a table because it

    5.____

    A. features approximations
    B. emphasizes facts and relationships more dramatically
    C. C. presents data more accurately
    D. is easily understood by the average reader

6. Of the following, the degree of formality required of a written report in tone is *most likely* to depend on the

    6.____

    A. subject matter of the report
    B. frequency of its occurrence
    C. amount of time available for its preparation
    D. audience for whom the report is intended

7. Of the following, a distinguishing characteristic of a written report intended for the head of your agency as compared to a report prepared for a lower-echelon staff member, is that the report for the agency head should *usually* include

    7.____

    A. considerably more detail, especially statistical data
    B. the essential details in an abbreviated form
    C. all available source material
    D. an annotated bibliography

8. Assume that you are asked to write a lengthy report for use by the administrator of your agency, the subject of which is "The Impact of Proposed New Data Processing Operations on Line Personnel" in your agency. You decide that the *most appropriate* type of report for you to prepare is an analytical report, including recommendations. The MAIN reason for your decision is that

    8.____

    A. the subject of the report is extremely complex
    B. large sums of money are involved
    C. the report is being prepared for the administrator
    D. you intend to include charts and graphs

9. Assume that you are preparing a report based on a survey dealing with the attitudes of employees in Division X regarding proposed new changes in compensating employees for working overtime. Three per cent of the respondents to the survey voluntarily offer an unfavorable opinion on the method of assigning overtime work, a question not specifically asked of the employees.
   On the basis of this information, the *most appropriate* and *significant* of the following comments for you to make in the report with regard to employees' attitudes on assigning overtime work, is that

   A. an insignificant percentage of employees dislike the method of assigning overtime work
   B. three per cent of the employees in Division X dislike the method of assigning overtime work
   C. three per cent of the sample selected for the survey voiced an unfavorable opinion on the method of assigning overtime work
   D. some employees voluntarily voiced negative feelings about the method of assigning overtime work, making it impossible to determine the extent of this attitude

9.____

10. A supervisor should be able to prepare a report that is well-written and unambiguous. Of the following sentences that might appear in a report, select the one which communicates *most clearly* the intent of its author.

    A. When your subordinates speak to a group of people, they should be well-informed.
    B. When he asked him to leave, SanMan King told him that he would refuse the request.
    C. Because he is a good worker, Foreman Jefferson assigned Assistant Foreman D'Agostino to replace him.
    D. Each of us is responsible for the actions of our subordinates.

10.____

11. In some reports, especially longer ones, a list of the resources (books, papers, magazines, etc.) used to prepare it is included. This list is called the

    A. accreditation   B. bibliography
    C. summary   D. glossary

11.____

12. Reports are usually divided into several sections, some of which are more necessary than others.
    Of the following, the section which is ABSOLUTELY necessary to include in a report is

    A. a table of contents   B. the body
    C. an index   D. a bibliography

12.____

13. Suppose you are writing a report on an interview you have just completed with a particularly hostile applicant. Which of the following BEST describes what you should include in this report?

    A. What you think caused the applicant's hostile attitude during the interview
    B. Specific examples of the applicant's hostile remarks and behavior
    C. The relevant information uncovered during the interview
    D. A recommendation that the applicant's request be denied because of his hostility

13.____

14. When including recommendations in a report to your supervisor, which of the following is MOST important for you to do?

    A. Provide several alternative courses of action for each recommendation
    B. First present the supporting evidence, then the recommendations
    C. First present the recommendations, then the supporting evidence
    D. Make sure the recommendations arise logically out of the information in the report

14.____

15. It is often necessary that the writer of a report present facts and sufficient arguments to gain acceptance of the points, conclusions, or recommendations set forth in the report. Of the following, the LEAST advisable step to take in organizing a report, when such argumentation is the important factor, is a(n)

    A. elaborate expression of personal belief
    B. businesslike discussion of the problem as a whole
    C. orderly arrangement of convincing data
    D. reasonable explanation of the primary issues

15.____

16. In some types of reports, visual aids add interest, meaning, and support. They also provide an essential means of effectively communicating the message of the report. Of the following, the selection of the suitable visual aids to use with a report is LEAST dependent on the

    A. nature and scope of the report
    B. way in which the aid is to be used
    C. aids used in other reports
    D. prospective readers of the report

16.____

17. Visual aids used in a report may be placed either in the text material or in the appendix. Deciding where to put a chart, table, or any such aid *should* depend on the

    A. title of the report   B. purpose of the visual aid
    C. title of the visual aid   D. length of the report

17.____

18. A report is often revised several times before final preparation and distribution in an effort to make certain the report meets the needs of the situation for which it is designed. Which of the following is the BEST way for the author to be sure that a report covers the areas he intended?

    A. Obtain a co-worker's opinion
    B. Compare it with a content checklist
    C. Test it on a subordinate
    D. Check his bibliography

18.____

19. In which of the following situations is an oral report preferable to a written report? When a(n)

    A. recommendation is being made for a future plan of action
    B. department head requests immediate information
    C. long standing policy change is made
    D. analysis of complicated statistical data is involved

19.____

20. When an applicant is approved, the supervisor must fill in standard forms with certain information.
The GREATEST advantage of using standard forms in this situation rather than having the supervisor write the report as he sees fit, is that

    A. the report can be acted on quickly
    B. the report can be written without directions from a supervisor
    C. needed information is less likely to be left out of the report
    D. information that is written up this way is more likely to be verified

20.____

21. Assume that it is part of your job to prepare a monthly report for your unit head that eventually goes to the director. The report contains information on the number of applicants you have interviewed that have been approved and the number of applicants you have interviewed that have been turned down.
Errors on such reports are serious because

    A. you are expected to be able to prove how many applicants you have interviewed each month
    B. accurate statistics are needed for effective management of the department
    C. they may not be discovered before the report is transmitted to the director
    D. they may result in loss to the applicants left out of the report

21.____

22. The frequency with which job reports are submitted should depend MAINLY on

    A. how comprehensive the report has to be
    B. the amount of information in the report
    C. the availability of an experienced man to write the report
    D. the importance of changes in the information included in the report

22.____

23. The CHIEF purpose in preparing an outline for a report is *usually* to insure that

    A. the report will be grammatically correct
    B. every point will be given equal emphasis
    C. principal and secondary points will be properly integrated
    D. the language of the report will be of the same level and include the same technical terms

23.____

24. The MAIN reason for requiring written job reports is to

    A. avoid the necessity of oral orders
    B. develop better methods of doing the work
    C. provide a permanent record of what was done
    D. increase the amount of work that can be done

24.____

25. Assume you are recommending in a report to your supervisor that a radical change in a standard maintenance procedure should be adopted.
Of the following, the MOST important information to be included in this report is

    A. a list of the reasons for making this change
    B. the names of others who favor the change
    C. a complete description of the present procedure
    D. amount of training time needed for the new procedure

25.____

KEY (CORRECT ANSWERS)

1.	A		11.	B
2.	D		12.	B
3.	D		13.	C
4.	B		14.	D
5.	B		15.	A
6.	D		16.	C
7.	B		17.	B
8.	A		18.	B
9.	D		19.	B
10.	D		20.	C

21.	B
22.	D
23.	C
24.	C
25.	A

TEST 2

DIRECTIONS: Each question or incomplete statement is followed by several suggested answers or completions. Select the one that BEST answers the question or completes the statement. *PRINT THE LETTER OF THE CORRECT ANSWER IN THE SPACE AT THE RIGHT.*

1. It is often necessary that the writer of a report present facts and sufficient arguments to gain acceptance of the points, conclusions, or recommendations set forth in the report. Of the following, the LEAST advisable step to take in organizing a report, when such argumentation is the important factor, is a(n)

    A. elaborate expression of personal belief
    B. businesslike discussion of the problem as a whole
    C. orderly arrangement of convincing data
    D. reasonable explanation of the primary issues

1.____

2. Of the following, the factor which is generally considered to be LEAST characteristic of a good control report is that it

    A. stresses performance that adheres to standard rather than emphasizing the exception
    B. supplies information intended to serve as the basis for corrective action
    C. provides feedback for the planning process
    D. includes data that reflect trends as well as current status

2.____

3. An administrative assistant has been asked by his superior to write a concise, factual report with objective conclusions and recommendations based on facts assembled by other researchers.
Of the following factors, the administrative assistant should give LEAST consideratio to

    A. the educational level of the person or persons for whom the report is being prepared
    B. the use to be made of the report
    C. the complexity of the problem
    D. his own feelings about the importance of the problem

3.____

4. When making a written report, it is often recommended that the findings or conclusions be presented near the beginning of the report.
Of the following, the MOST important reason for doing this is that it

    A. facilitates organizing the material clearly
    B. assures that all the topics will be covered
    C. avoids unnecessary repetition of ideas
    D. prepares the reader for the facts that will follow

4.____

5. You have been asked to write a report on methods of hiring and training new employees. Your report is going to be about ten pages long.
For the convenience of your readers, a brief summary of your findings *should*

    A. appear at the beginning of your report
    B. be appended to the report as a postscript
    C. be circulated in a separate memo
    D. be inserted in tabular form in the middle of your report

5.____

6. In preparing a report, the MAIN reason for writing an outline is *usually* to   6._____

    A. help organize thoughts in a logical sequence
    B. provide a guide for the typing of the report
    C. allow the ultimate user to review the report in advance
    D. ensure that the report is being prepared on schedule

7. The one of the following which is *most appropriate* as a reason for including footnotes in   7._____
a report is to

    A. correct capitalization   B. delete passages
    C. improve punctuation   D. cite references

8. A completed formal report may contain all of the following EXCEPT   8._____

    A. a synopsis   B. a preface
    C. marginal notes   D. bibliographical references

9. Of the following, the MAIN use of proofreaders' marks is to   9._____

    A. explain corrections to be made
    B. indicate that a manuscript has been read and approved
    C. let the reader know who proofread the report
    D. indicate the format of the report

10. Informative, readable and concise reports have been found to observe the following   10._____
rules:
    Rule I.   Keep the report short and easy to understand.
    Rule II.   Vary the length of sentences.
    Rule III.   Vary the style of sentences so that, for example, they are not all just sub
                ject-verb, subject-verb.
Consider this hospital laboratory report: The experiment was started in January. The
apparatus was put together in six weeks. At that time the synthesizing process was
begun. The synthetic chemicals were separated. Then they were used in tests on
patients.
Which one of the following choices MOST accurately classifies the above rules into
those which are *violated* by this report and those which are *not*?

    A. II is violated, but I and III are not.
    B. III is violated, but I and II are not.
    C. II and III are violated, but I is not.
    D. I, II, and III are violated.

Questions 11-13.

DIRECTIONS: Questions 11 through 13 are based on the following example of a report. The
                report consists of eight numbered sentences, some of which are not consis-
                tent with the principles of good report writing.

(1) I interviewed Mrs. Loretta Crawford in Room 424 of County Hospital. (2) She had collapsed on the street and been brought into emergency. (3) She is an attractive woman with many friends judging by the cards she had received. (4) She did not know what her husband's last job had been, or what their present income was. (5) The first thing that Mrs. Crawford said was that she had never worked and that her husband was presently unemployed. (6) She did not know if they had any medical coverage or if they could pay the bill. (7) She said that her husband could not be reached by telephone but that he would be in to see her that afternoon. (8) I left word at the nursing station to be called when he arrived.

11. A good report should be arranged in logical order. Which of the following sentences from the report does NOT appear in its proper sequence in the report? Sentence   11.____

   A. 1   B. 4   C. 7   D. 8

12. Only material that is relevant to the main thought of a report should be included. Which of the following sentences from the report contains material which is LEAST relevant to this report? Sentence   12.____

   A. 3   B. 4   C. 6   D. 8

13. Reports should include all essential information.   13.____
   Of the following, the MOST important fact that is *missing* from this report is:

   A. Who was involved in the interview
   B. What was discovered at the interview
   C. When the interview took place
   D. Where the interview took place

Questions 14-15.

DIRECTIONS: Each of Questions 14 and 15 consists of four numbered sentences which constitute a paragraph in a report. They are not in the right order. Choose the numbered arrangement appearing after letter A, B, C, or D which is MOST logical and which BEST expresses the thought of the paragraph.

14.   I.   Congress made the commitment explicit in the Housing Act of 1949, establishing   14.____
           as a national goal the realization of a decent home and suitable environment for
           every American family.
       II. The result has been that the goal of decent home and suitable environment is
           still as far distant as ever for the disadvantaged urban family.
       III. In spite of this action by Congress, federal housing programs have continued to
           be fragmented and grossly under-funded.
       IV. The passage of the National Housing Act signaled a new federal commitment to
           provide housing for the nation's citizens.

   A. I, IV, III, II   B. IV, I, III, II
   C. IV, I, III, II   D. II, IV, I, III

15.   I.   The greater expense does not necessarily involve "exploitation," but it is often perceived as exploitative and unfair by those who are aware of the price differences
involved, but unaware of operating costs.
     II.   Ghetto residents believe they are "exploited" by local merchants, and evidence
substantiates some of these beliefs.
    III.   However, stores in low-income areas were more likely to be small independents,
which could not achieve the economies available to supermarket chains and
were, therefore, more likely to charge higher prices, and the customers were
more likely to buy smaller-sized packages which are more expensive per unit of
measure.
    IV.   A study conducted in one city showed that distinctly higher prices were charged
for goods sold in ghetto stores than in other areas.

     A.   IV, II, I, III   B.   IV, I, III, II
     C.   II, IV, III, I   D.   II, III, IV, I

16.   In organizing data to be presented in a formal report, the FIRST of the following steps
should be

     A.   determining the conclusions to be drawn
     B.   establishing the time sequence of the data
     C.   sorting and arranging like data into groups
     D.   evaluating how consistently the data support the recommendations

17.   All reports should be prepared with *at least* one copy so that

     A.   there is one copy for your file
     B.   there is a copy for your supervisor
     C.   the report can be sent to more than one person
     D.   the person getting the report can forward a copy to someone else

18.   Before turning in a report of an investigation he has made, a supervisor discovers some
additional information he did not include in this report.
Whether he rewrites this report to include this additional information should PRIMA-
RILY depend on the

     A.   importance of the report itself
     B.   number of people who will eventually review this report
     C.   established policy covering the subject matter of the report
     D.   bearing this new information has on the conclusions of the report

KEY (CORRECT ANSWERS)

1.	A	11.	B
2.	A	12.	A
3.	D	13.	C
4.	D	14.	B
5.	A	15.	C
6.	A	16.	C
7.	D	17.	A
8.	C	18.	D
9.	A		
10.	C		

PREPARING WRITTEN MATERIALS

EXAMINATION SECTION
TEST 1

DIRECTIONS: Each question or incomplete statement is followed by several suggested answers or completions. Select the one that BEST answers the question or completes the statement. *PRINT THE LETTER OF THE CORRECT ANSWER IN THE SPACE AT THE RIGHT.*

Questions 1-21.

DIRECTIONS: In each of the following sentences, which were taken from students' transcripts, there may be an error. Indicate the appropriate correction in the space at the right. If the sentence is correct as is, indicate this choice. Unnecessary changes will be considered incorrect.

1.   In that building there seemed to be representatives of Teachers College, the Veterans Bureau, and the Businessmen's Association.   1.____

    A.   Teacher's College   B.   Veterans' Bureau
    C.   Businessmens Association   D.   Correct as is

2.   In his travels, he visited St. Paul, San Francisco, Springfield, Ohio, and Washington, D.C.   2.____

    A.   Ohio and   B.   Saint Paul
    C.   Washington, D.C.   D.   Correct as is

3.   As a result of their purchasing a controlling interest in the syndicate, it was well-known that the Bureau of Labor Statistics' calculations would be unimportant.   3.____

    A.   of them purchasing   B.   well known
    C.   Statistics   D.   Correct as is

4.   Walter Scott, Jr.'s, attempt to emulate his father's success was doomed to failure.   4.____

    A.   Junior's,   B.   Scott's, Jr.
    C.   Scott, Jr.'s attempt   D.   Correct as is

5.   About B.C. 250 the Romans invaded Great Britain, and remains of their highly developed civilization can still be seen.   5.____

    A.   250 B.C.   B.   Britain and
    C.   highly-developed   D.   Correct as is

6.   The two boss's sons visited the children's department.   6.____

    A.   bosses   B.   bosses'
    C.   childrens'   D.   Correct as is

7.   Miss Amex not only approved the report, but also decided that it needed no revision.   7.____

    A.   report; but   B.   report but
    C.   report. But   D.   Correct as is

8. Here's brain food in a jiffy—economical, too!   8.____

    A. economical too!   B. 'brain food'
    C. jiffy-economical   D. Correct as is

9. She said, "He likes the "Gatsby Look" very much."   9.____

    A. said "He   B. "he
    C. 'Gatsby Look'   D. Correct as is

10. We anticipate that we will be able to visit them briefly in Los Angeles on Wednesday after 10.____
a five-day visit.

    A. Wednes-   B. 5 day
    C. five day   D. Correct as is

11. She passed all her tests, and, she now has a good position.   11.____

    A. tests, and she   B. past
    C. tests;   D. Correct as is

12. The billing clerk said, "I will send the bill today"; however, that was a week ago, and it 12.____
hasn't arrived yet!

    A. today;"   B. today,"
    C. ago and   D. Correct as is

13. "She types at more-than-average speed," Miss Smith said, "but I feel that it is a result of 13.____
marvelous concentration and self control on her part."

    A. more than average   B. "But
    C. self-control   D. Correct as is

14. The state of Alaska, the largest state in the union, is also the northernmost state. 14.____

    A. Union   B. Northernmost State
    C. State of Alaska   D. Correct as is

15. The memoirs of Ex-President Nixon, according to figures, sold more copies than <u>Six Cri-</u> 15.____
<u>ses</u>, the book he wrote in the 60's.

    A. Six Crises   B. ex-President
    C. 60s   D. Correct as is

16. "There are three principal elements, determining the hazard of buildings: the contents 16.____
hazard, the fire resistance of the structure, and the character of the interior finish," concluded the speaker.
The one of the following statements that is MOST acceptable is that, in the above passage,

    A. the comma following the word *elements* is incorrect
    B. the colon following the word *buildings* is incorrect
    C. the comma following the word *finish* is incorrect
    D. there is no error in the punctuation of the sentence

17. He spoke on his favorite topic, "Why We Will Win." (How could I stop him?) 17.____

    A. Win".   B. him?).
    C. him)?   D. Correct as is

18. "All any insurance policy is, is a contract for services," said my insurance agent, Mr. Newton.   18.____

    A. Insurance Policy   B. Insurance Agent
    C. policy is is a   D. Correct as is

19. Inasmuch as the price list has now been up dated, we should send it to the printer.   19.____

    A. In as much   B. updated
    C. pricelist   D. Correct as is

20. We feel that "Our know-how" is responsible for the improvement in technical developments.   20.____

    A. "our   B. know how
    C. that,   D. Correct as is

21. Did Cortez conquer the Incas? the Aztecs? the South American Indians?   21.____

    A. Incas, the Aztecs, the South American Indians?
    B. Incas; the Aztecs; the South American Indians?
    C. south American Indians?
    D. Correct as is

22. Which one of the following forms for the typed name of the dictator in the closing lines of a letter is generally MOST acceptable in the United States?   22.____

    A. (Dr.) James F. Farley
    B. Dr. James F. Farley
    C. Mr. James F. Farley, Ph.D.
    D. James F. Farley

23. The plural of   23.____

    A. turkey is turkies
    B. cargo is cargoes
    C. bankruptcy is bankruptcys
    D. son-in-law is son-in-laws

24. The abbreviation *viz.* means MOST NEARLY   24.____

    A. namely   B. for example
    C. the following   D. see

25. In the sentence, *A man in a light-gray suit waited thirty-five minutes in the ante-room for the all-important document,* the word IMPROPERLY hyphenated is   25.____

    A. light-gray   B. thirty-five
    C. ante-room   D. all-important

KEY (CORRECT ANSWERS)

1.	D		11.	A
2.	C		12.	D
3.	B		13.	D
4.	D		14.	A
5.	A		15.	B
6.	B		16.	A
7.	B		17.	D
8.	D		18.	D
9.	C		19.	B
10.	C		20.	A

21.	D
22.	D
23.	B
24.	A
25.	C

TEST 2

DIRECTIONS: Each question or incomplete statement is followed by several suggested answers or completions. Select the one that BEST answers the question or completes the statement. *PRINT THE LETTER OF THE CORRECT ANSWER IN THE SPACE AT THE RIGHT.*

Questions 1-10.

DIRECTIONS: In each of the following groups of four sentences, one sentence contains an error in sentence structure, grammar, usage, diction, or punctuation. Indicate the INCORRECT sentence.

1.   A.   The lecture finished, the audience began asking questions.   1._____
      B.   Any man who could accomplish that task the world would regard as a hero.
      C.   Our respect and admiration are mutual.
      D.   George did like his mother told him, despite the importunities of his playmates.

2.   A.   I cannot but help admiring you for your dedication to your job.   2._____
      B.   Because they had insisted upon showing us films of their travels, we have lost many friends whom we once cherished.
      C.   I am constrained to admit that your remarks made me feel bad.
      D.   My brother having been notified of his acceptance by the university of his choice, my father immediately made plans for a vacation.

3.   A.   In no other country is freedom of speech and assembly so jealously guarded.   3._____
      B.   Being a beatnik, he felt that it would be a betrayal of his cause to wear shoes and socks at the same time.
      C.   Riding over the Brooklyn Bridge gave us an opportunity to see the Manhattan skyline.
      D.   In 1961, flaunting SEATO, the North Vietnamese crossed the line of demarcation.

4.   A.   I have enjoyed the study of the Spanish language not only because of its beauty   4._____
            and the opportunity it offers to understand the Hispanic culture but also to make
            use of it in the business associations I have in South America.
      B.   The opinions he expressed were decidedly different from those he had held in his youth.
      C.   Had he actually studied, he certainly would have passed.
      D.   A supervisor should be patient, tactful, and firm.

5.   A.   At this point we were faced with only three alternatives: to push on, to remain   5._____
            where we were, or to return to the village.
      B.   We had no choice but to forgive so venial a sin.
      C.   In their new picture, the Warners are flouting tradition.
      D.   Photographs taken revealed that 2.5 square miles had been burned.

6. A. He asked whether he might write to his friends.   6._____
   B. There are many problems which must be solved before we can be assured of world peace.
   C. Each person with whom I talked expressed his opinion freely.
   D. Holding on to my saddle with all my strength the horse galloped down the road at a terrifying pace.

7. A. After graduating high school, he obtained a position as a runner in Wall Street.   7._____
   B. Last night, in a radio address, the President urged us to subscribe to the Red Cross.
   C. In the evening, light spring rain cooled the streets.
   D. "Un-American" is a word which has been used even by those whose sympathies may well have been pro-Nazi.

8. A. It is hard to conceive of their not doing good work.   8._____
   B. Who won - you or I?
   C. He having read the speech caused much comment.
   D. Their finishing the work proves that it can be done.

9. A. Our course of study should not be different now than it was five years ago.   9._____
   B. I cannot deny myself the pleasure of publicly thanking the mayor for his actions.
   C. The article on "Morale" has appeared in the Times Literary Supplement.
   D. He died of tuberculosis contracted during service with the Allied Forces.

10. A. If it wasn't for a lucky accident, he would still be an office-clerk.   10._____
    B. It is evident that teachers need help.
    C. Rolls of postage stamps may be bought at stationery stores.
    D. Addressing machines are used by firms that publish magazines.

11. The one of the following sentences which contains NO error in usage is: 11._____

    A. After the robbers left, the proprietor stood tied in his chair for about two hours before help arrived.
    B. In the cellar I found the watchmans' hat and coat.
    C. The persons living in adjacent apartments stated that they had heard no unusual noises.
    D. Neither a knife or any firearms were found in the room.

12. The one of the following sentences which contains NO error in usage is: 12._____

    A. The policeman lay a firm hand on the suspect's shoulder.
    B. It is true that neither strength nor agility are the most important requirement for a good patrolman.
    C. Good citizens constantly strive to do more than merely comply the restraints imposed by society.
    D. Twenty years is considered a severe sentence for a felony.

13. Select the sentence containing an adverbial objective.   13._____

    A. Concepts can only acquire content when they are connected, however indirectly, with sensible experience.
    B. The cloth was several shades too light to match the skirt which she had discarded.

C. The Gargantuan Hall of Commons became a tri-daily horror to Kurt, because two youths discerned that he had a beard and courageously told the world about it.
D. Brooding morbidly over the event, Elsie found herself incapable of engaging in normal activity.

14. Select the sentence containing a verb in the subjunctive mood.   14.____

    A. Had he known of the new experiments with penicillin dust for the cure of colds, he might have been tempted to try them in his own office.
    B. I should be very much honored by your visit.
    C. Though he has one of the highest intelligence quotients in his group, he seems far below the average in actual achievement.
    D. Long had I known that he would be the man finally selected for such signal honors.

15. Select the sentence containing one (or more) passive perfect participle(s).   15.____

    A. Having been apprised of the consequences of his refusal to answer, the witness finally revealed the source of his information.
    B. To have been placed in such an uncomfortable position was perhaps unfair to a journalist of his reputation.
    C. When deprived of special immunity he had, of course, no alternative but to speak.
    D. Having been obdurate until now, he was reluctant to surrender under this final pressure exerted upon him.

16. Select the sentence containing a predicate nominative.   16.____

    A. His dying wish, which he expressed almost with his last breath, was to see that justice was done toward his estranged wife.
    B. So long as we continue to elect our officials in truly democratic fashion, we shall have the power to preserve our liberties.
    C. We could do nothing, at this juncture, but walk the five miles back to camp.
    D. There was the spaniel, wet and cold and miserable, waiting silently at the door.

17. Select the sentence containing exactly TWO adverbs.   17.____

    A. The gentlemen advanced with exasperating deliberateness, while his lonely partner waited.
    B. If you are well, will you come early?
    C. I think you have guessed right, though you were rather slow, I must say.
    D. The last hundred years have seen more change than a thousand years of the Roman Empire, than a hundred thousand years of the stone age.

Questions 18-24.

DIRECTIONS: Select the choice describing the error in the sentence.

18. If us seniors do not support school functions, who will?   18.____

    A. Unnecessary shift in tense
    B. Incomplete sentence
    C. Improper case of pronoun
    D. Lack of parallelism

19. The principal has issued regulations which, in my opinion, I think are too harsh.   19.____

  A. Incorrect punctuation   B. Faulty sentence structure
  C. Misspelling   D. Redundant expression

20. The freshmens' and sophomores' performances equaled those of the juniors and   20.____
  seniors.

  A. Ambiguous reference
  B. Incorrect placement of punctuation
  C. Misspelling of past tense
  D. Incomplete comparison

21. Each of them, Anne and her, is an outstanding pianist; I can't tell you which one is best.   21.____

  A. Lack of agreement
  B. Improper degree of comparison
  C. Incorrect case of pronoun
  D. Run-on sentence

22. She wears clothes that are more expensive than my other friends.   22.____

  A. Misuse of *than*   B. Incorrect relative pronoun
  C. Shift in tense   D. Faulty comparison

23. At the very end of the story it implies that the children's father died tragically.   23.____

  A. Misuse of *implies*   B. Indefinite use of pronoun
  C. Incorrect spelling   D. Incorrect possessive

24. At the end of the game both of us, John and me, couldn't scarcely walk because we were   24.____
  so tired.

  A. Incorrect punctuation
  B. Run-on sentence
  C. Incorrect case of pronoun
  D. Double negative

Questions 25-30.

DIRECTIONS: Questions 25 through 30 consist of a sentence lacking certain needed punctu-
            ation. Pick as your answer the description of punctuation which will COR-
            RECTLY complete the sentence.

25. If you take the time to keep up your daily correspondence you will no doubt be most effi-   25.____
  cient.

  A. Comma only after *doubt*
  B. Comma only after *correspondence*
  C. Commas after *correspondence, will,* and *be*
  D. Commas after *if, correspondence,* and *will*

26. Because he did not send the application soon enough he did not receive the up to date   26.____
    copy of the book.

    A. Commas after *application* and *enough*, and quotation marks before *up* and after
       date
    B. Commas after *application* and *enough*, and hyphens between *to* and *date*
    C. Comma after *enough*, and hyphens between *up* and *to* and between *to* and *date*
    D. Comma after *application*, and quotation marks before *up* and after *date*

27. The coordinator requested from the department the following items a letter each week   27.____
    summarizing progress personal forms and completed applications for tests.

    A. Commas after *items* and *completed*
    B. Semi-colon after *items* and *progress*, comma after *forms*
    C. Colon after *items*, commas after *progress* and *forms*
    D. Colon after *items*, commas after *forms* and *applications*

28. The supervisor asked Who will attend the conference next month.   28.____

    A. Comma after *asked*, period after *month*
    B. Period after *asked*, question mark after *month*
    C. Comma after *asked*, quotation marks before *Who*, quotation marks after *month*,
       and question mark after the quotation marks
    D. Comma after *asked*, quotation marks before *Who*, question mark after *month*, and
       quotation marks after the question mark

29. When the statistics are collected, we will forward the results to you as soon as possible.   29.____

    A. Comma after *you*
    B. Commas after *forward* and *you*
    C. Commas after *collected, results,* and *you*
    D. Comma after *collected*

30. The ecology of our environment is concerned with mans pollution of the atmosphere.   30.____

    A. Comma after *ecology*
    B. Apostrophe after *n* and before *s* in *mans*
    C. Commas after *ecology* and *environment*
    D. Apostrophe after *s* in *mans*

KEY (CORRECT ANSWERS)

1.	D	16.	A
2.	A	17.	C
3.	D	18.	C
4.	A	19.	D
5.	B	20.	B
6.	D	21.	B
7.	A	22.	D
8.	C	23.	B
9.	A	24.	D
10.	A	25.	B
11.	C	26.	C
12.	D	27.	C
13.	B	28.	D
14.	A	29.	D
15.	A	30.	B

TEST 3

DIRECTIONS: Each question or incorrect statement is followed by several suggested answers or completions. Select the one that BEST answers the question or completes the statement. *PRINT THE LETTER OF THE CORRECT ANSWER IN THE SPACE AT THE RIGHT.*

Questions 1-6.

DIRECTIONS: From the four choices offered in Questions 1 through 6, select the one which is INCORRECT.

1. A. Before we try to extricate ourselves from this struggle in which we are now engaged in, we must be sure that we are not severing ties of honor and duty.   1.____
      B. Besides being an outstanding student, he is also a leader in school government and a trophy-winner in school sports.
      C. If the framers of the Constitution were to return to life for a day, their opinion of our amendments would be interesting.
      D. Since there are three m's in the word, it is frequently misspelled.

2. A. It was a college with an excellance beyond question.   2.____
      B. The coach will accompany the winners, whomever they may be.
      C. The dean, together with some other faculty members, is planning a conference.
      D. The jury are arguing among themselves.

3. A. This box is less nearly square than that one.   3.____
      B. Wagner is many persons' choice as the world's greatest composer.
      C. The habits of Copperheads are different from Diamond Backs.
      D. The teacher maintains that the child was insolent.

4. A. There was a time when the Far North was unknown territory. Now American soldiers manning radar stations there wave to Boeing jet planes zooming by overhead.   4.____
      B. Exodus, the psalms, and Deuteronomy are all books of the Old Testament.
      C. Linda identified her china dishes by marking their bottoms with india ink.
      D. Harry S. Truman, former president of the United States, served as a captain in the American army during World War I.

5. A. The sequel of their marriage was a divorce.   5.____
      B. We bought our car secondhand.
      C. His whereabouts is unknown.
      D. Jones offered to use his own car, providing the company would pay for gasoline, oil, and repairs.

6. A. I read Golding's "Lord of the Flies".   6.____
      B. The orator at the civil rights rally thrilled the audience when he said, "I quote Robert Burns's line, 'A man's a man for a' that."
      C. The phrase "producer to consumer" is commonly used by market analysts.
      D. The lawyer shouted, "Is not this evidence illegal?"

Questions 7-9.

DIRECTIONS: In answering Questions 7 through 9, mark the letter A if faulty because of incorrect grammar, mark the letter B if faulty because of incorrect punctuation, mark the letter C if correct.

7.   Mr. Brown our accountant, will audit the accounts next week.   7.____

8.   Give the assignment to whomever is able to do it most efficiently.   8.____

9.   The supervisor expected either your or I to file these reports.   9.____

Questions 10-14.

DIRECTIONS: In each of the following groups of four sentences, one sentence contains an error in sentence structure, grammar, usage, diction, or punctuation. Indicate the INCORRECT sentence.

10.   A.   The agent asked, "Did you say, 'Never again?"   10.____
      B.   Kindly let me know whether you can visit us on the 17th.
      C.   "I cannot accept that!" he exploded. "Please show me something else."
      D.   Ed, will you please lend me your grass shears for an hour or so.

11.   A.   Recalcitrant though he may have been, Alexander was wilfully destructive. 11.____
      B.   Everybody should look out for himself.
      C.   John is one of those students who usually spends most of his time in the princi-
           pal's office.
      D.   She seems to feel that what is theirs is hers.

12.   A.   Be he ever so much in the wrong, I'll support the man while deploring his actions. 12.____
      B.   The schools' lack of interest in consumer education is shortsighted.
      C.   I think that Fitzgerald's finest stanza is one which includes the reference to
           youth's "sweet-scented manuscript."
      D.   I never would agree to Anderson having full control of the company's policies.

13.   A.   We had to walk about five miles before finding a gas station.   13.____
      B.   The willful sending of a false alarm has, and may, result in homicide.
      C.   Please bring that book to me at once!
      D.   Neither my sister nor I am interested in bowling.

14.   A.   He is one of the very few football players who doesn't wear a helmet with a face 14.____
           guard.
      B.   But three volunteers appeared at the recruiting office.
      C.   Such consideration as you can give us will be appreciated.
      D.   When I left them, the group were disagreeing about the proposed legislation.

Question 15.

DIRECTIONS: Question 15 contains two sentences concerning criminal law. The sentences could contain errors in English grammar or usage. A sentence does not contain an error simply because it could be written in a different manner. In answering this question, choose answer
- A. if only sentence I is correct
- B. if only sentence II is correct .
- C. if both sentences are correct
- D. if neither sentence is correct

15. I. The use of fire or explosives to destroy tangible property is proscribed by the criminal mischief provisions of the Revised Penal Law.   15.____
     II. The defendant's taking of a taxicab for the immediate purpose of affecting his escape did not constitute grand larceny.

KEY (CORRECT ANSWERS)

1.	A		6.	A
2.	B		7.	B
3.	C		8.	A
4.	B		9.	A
5.	D		10.	A

11.	C
12.	D
13.	B
14.	A
15.	A

PRINCIPLES AND PRACTICES OF ADMINISTRATION, SUPERVISION & MANAGEMENT

TABLE OF CONTENTS

PRINCIPLES AND PRACTICES OF
ADMINISTRATION, SUPERVISION & MANAGEMENT

Most people are inclined to think of administration as something that only a few persons are responsible for in a large organization. Perhaps this is true if you are thinking of Administration with a capital *A*, but administration with a lower case a is a responsibility of supervisors at all levels each working day.

All of us feel we are pretty good supervisors and that we do a good job of administering the workings of our agency. By and large, this is true, but every so often it is good to check up on ourselves. Checklists appear from time to time in various publications which psychologists say, tell whether or not a person will make a good wife, husband, doctor, lawyer, or supervisor.

The following questions are an excellent checklist to test yourself as a supervisor and administrator.

Remember, Administration gives direction and points the way but administration carries the ideas to fruition. Each is dependent on the other for its success. Remember, too, that no unit is too small for these departmental functions to be carried out. These statements apply equally as well to the Chief Librarian as to the Department Head with but one or two persons to supervise.

GENERAL ADMINISTRATION - General Responsibilities of Supervisors

    1.   Have I prepared written statements of functions, activities, and duties for my organizational unit?

    2.   Have I prepared procedural guides for operating activities?

    3.   Have I established clearly in writing, lines of authority and responsibility for my organizational unit?

    4.   Do I make recommendations for improvements in organization, policies, administrative and operating routines and procedures, including simplification of work and elimination of non-essential operations?

    5.   Have I designated and trained an understudy to function in my absence?

    6.   Do I supervise and train personnel within the unit to effectively perform their assignments?

    7.   Do I assign personnel and distribute work on such a basis as to carry out the organizational unit's assignment or mission in the most effective and efficient manner?

    8.   Have I established administrative controls by:

        a.   Fixing responsibility and accountability on all supervisors under my direction for the proper performance of their functions and duties.

b. Preparing and submitting periodic work load and progress reports covering the operations of the unit to my immediate superior.

c. Analysis and evaluation of such reports received from subordinate units.

d. Submission of significant developments and problems arising within the organizational unit to my immediate superior.

e. Conducting conferences, inspections, etc., as to the status and efficiency of unit operations.

9. Do I maintain an adequate and competent working force?

10. Have I fostered good employee-department relations, seeing that established rules, regulations, and instructions are being carried out properly?

11. Do I collaborate and consult with other organizational units performing related functions to insure harmonious and efficient working relationships?

12. Do I maintain liaison through prescribed channels with city departments and other governmental agencies concerned with the activities of the unit?

13. Do I maintain contact with and keep abreast of the latest developments and techniques of administration (professional societies, groups, periodicals, etc.) as to their applicability to the activities of the unit?

14. Do I communicate with superiors and subordinates through prescribed organizational channels?

15. Do I notify superiors and subordinates in instances where bypassing is necessary as soon thereafter as practicable?

16. Do I keep my superior informed of significant developments and problems?

SEVEN BASIC FUNCTIONS OF THE SUPERVISOR

1. PLANNING
This means working out goals and means to obtain goals. What needs to be done, who will do it, how, when, and where it is to be done.

SEVEN STEPS IN PLANNING

1. Define job or problem clearly.
2. Consider priority of job.
3. Consider time-limit - starting and completing.
4. Consider minimum distraction to, or interference with, other activities.
5. Consider and provide for contingencies - possible emergencies.
6. Break job down into components.
7. Consider the 5 W's and H:

WHY	...	is it necessary to do the job? (Is the purpose clearly defined?)
WHAT	...	needs to be done to accomplish the defined purpose?
	...	is needed to do the job? (money, materials, etc.)
WHO	...	is needed to do the job?
	...	will have responsibilities?
WHERE	...	is the work to be done?
WHEN	...	is the job to begin and end? (schedules, etc.)
HOW	...	is the job to be done? (methods, controls, records, etc.)

2. ORGANIZING

This means dividing up the work, establishing clear lines of responsibility and authority and coordinating efforts to get the job done.

3. STAFFING

The whole personnel function of bringing in and training staff, getting the right man and fitting him to the right job - the job to which he is best suited.

In the normal situation, the supervisor's responsibility regarding staffing normally includes providing accurate job descriptions, that is, duties of the jobs, requirements, education and experience, skills, physical, etc.; assigning the work for maximum use of skills; and proper utilization of the probationary period to weed out unsatisfactory employees.

4. DIRECTING

Providing the necessary leadership to the group supervised. Important work gets done to the supervisor's satisfaction.

5. COORDINATING

The all-important duty of inter-relating the various parts of the work.

The supervisor is also responsible for controlling the coordinated activities. This means measuring performance according to a time schedule and setting quotas to see that the goals previously set are being reached. Reports from workers should be analyzed, evaluated, and made part of all future plans.

6. REPORTING

This means proper and effective communication to your superiors, subordinates, and your peers (in definition of the job of the supervisor). Reports should be read and information contained therein should be used not be filed away and forgotten. Reports should be written in such a way that the desired action recommended by the report is forthcoming.

7. BUDGETING

This means controlling current costs and forecasting future costs. This forecast is based on past experience, future plans and programs, as well as current costs.

You will note that these seven functions can fall under three topics:

Planning	)	
Organizing	)	Make a Plan
Staffing	)	
Directing	)	Get things done
Controlling	)	

```
Reporting    )
Budgeting    )    Watch it work
```

PLANNING TO MEET MANAGEMENT GOALS

I. <u>WHAT IS PLANNING?</u>
   A. Thinking a job through before new work is done to determine the best way to do it
   B. A method of doing something
   C. Ways and means for achieving set goals
   D. A means of enabling a supervisor to deliver with a minimum of effort, all details involved in coordinating his work

II. <u>WHO SHOULD MAKE PLANS?</u>
   Everybody!
   All levels of supervision must plan work. (Top management, heads of divisions or bureaus, first line supervisors, and individual employees.) The higher the level, the more planning required.

III. <u>WHAT ARE THE RESULTS OF POOR PLANNING?</u>
   A. Failure to meet deadline
   B. Low employee morale
   C. Lack of job coordination
   D. Overtime is frequently necessary
   E. Excessive cost, waste of material and manhours

IV. <u>PRINCIPLES OF PLANNING</u>
   A. Getting a clear picture of your objectives. What exactly are you trying to accomplish?
   B. Plan the whole job, then the parts, in proper sequence.
   C. Delegate the planning of details to those responsible for executing them.
   D. Make your plan flexible.
   E. Coordinate your plan with the plans of others so that the work may be processed with a minimum of delay.
   F. Sell your plan before you execute it.
   G. Sell your plan to your superior, subordinate, in order to gain maximum participation and coordination.
   H. Your plan should take precedence. Use knowledge and skills that others have brought to a similar job.
   I. Your plan should take account of future contingencies; allow for future expansion.
   J. Plans should include minor details. Leave nothing to chance that can be anticipated.
   K. Your plan should be simple and provide standards and controls. Establish quality and quantity standards and set a standard method of doing the job. The controls will indicate whether the job is proceeding according to plan.
   L. Consider possible bottlenecks, breakdowns, or other difficulties that are likely to arise.

V. Q. WHAT ARE THE *YARDSTICKS* BY WHICH PLANNING SHOULD BE MEASURED?
   A. Any plan should:
     - Clearly state a definite course of action to be followed and goal to be achieved, with consideration for emergencies.
     - Be realistic and practical.

- State what's to be done, when it's to be done, where, how, and by whom.
- Establish the most efficient sequence of operating steps so that more is accomplished in less time, with the least effort, and with the best quality results.
- Assure meeting deliveries without delays.
- Establish the standard by which performance is to be judged.

Q. WHAT KINDS OF PLANS DOES EFFECTIVE SUPERVISION REQUIRE?
A. Plans should cover such factors as:
- Manpower - right number of properly trained employees on the job.
- Materials - adequate supply of the right materials and supplies.
- Machines - full utilization of machines and equipment, with proper maintenance.
- Methods - most efficient handling of operations.
- Deliveries - making deliveries on time.
- Tools - sufficient well-conditioned tools
- Layout - most effective use of space.
- Reports - maintaining proper records and reports.
- Supervision - planning work for employees and organizing supervisor's own time.

I. MANAGEMENT

Question: *What do we mean by management?*

Answer: *Getting work done through others.*

Management could also be defined as planning, directing, and controlling the operations of a bureau or division so that all factors will function properly and all persons cooperate efficiently for a common objective.

II. MANAGEMENT PRINCIPLES

1. There should be a hierarchy - wherein authority and responsibility run upward and downward through several levels - with a broad base at the bottom and a single head at the top.

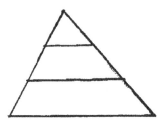

2. Each and every unit or person in the organization should be answerable ultimately to the manager at the apex. In other words, *The buck stops here!*

3. Every necessary function involved in the bureau's objectives is assigned to a unit in that bureau.
4. Responsibilities assigned to a unit are specifically clear-cut and understood.

5. Consistent methods of organizational structure should be applied at each level of the organization.

6. Each member of the bureau from top to bottom knows:
   to whom he reports
   who reports to him.

7. No member of one bureau reports to more than one supervisor.
   No dual functions

8. Responsibility for a function is matched by authority necessary to perform that function.
   Weight of authority

9. Individuals or units reporting to a supervisor do not exceed the number which can be feasibly and effectively coordinated and directed.
   Concept of *span of control*

10. Channels of command (management) are not violated by staff units, although there should be staff services to facilitate and coordinate management functions.

11. Authority and responsibility should be decentralized to units and individuals who are responsible for the actual performance of operations.
    Welfare - down to Welfare Centers
    Hospitals - down to local hospitals

12. Management should exercise control through attention to policy problems of exceptional importance, rather than through review of routine actions of subordinates.

13. Organizations should never be permitted to grow so elaborate as to hinder work accomplishments.
    Empire building

II. ORGANIZATION STRUCTURE
Types of Organizations.
The purest form is a leader and a few followers, such as:

```
                    ┌─────────────┐
                    │  Supervisor │
                    └─────────────┘
 ┌──────────┐  ┌──────────┐  ┌──────────┐  ┌──────────┐
 │  Worker  │  │  Worker  │  │  Worker  │  │  Worker  │
 └──────────┘  └──────────┘  └──────────┘  └──────────┘
```

(Refer to organization chart) from supervisor to workers.

The line of authority is direct, The workers know exactly where they stand in relation to their boss, to whom they report for instructions and direction.

Unfortunately, in our present complex society, few organizations are similar to this example of a pure line organization. In this era of specialization, other people are often needed in the simplest of organizations. These specialists are known as staff. The sole purpose for their existence (staff) is to assist, advise, suggest, help or counsel line organizations. Staff has no authority to direct line people - nor do they give them direct instructions.

```
                        ┌─────────────┐
                        │ SUPERVISOR  │
                        └─────────────┘
                               │
    ──────────────────────────┴────────────────────────────
    ┌───────────┐   ┌────────────┐   ┌────────────┐   ┌─────────┐
    │ Personnel │   │ Accounting │   │ Inspection │   │ Legal   │
    └───────────┘   └────────────┘   └────────────┘   └─────────┘
    ┌───────────┐   ┌────────────┐   ┌────────────┐   ┌─────────┐
    │  Worker   │   │   Worker   │   │   Worker   │   │ Worker  │
    └───────────┘   └────────────┘   └────────────┘   └─────────┘
```

Line Functions	Staff Functions
1. Directs	1. Advises
2. Orders	2. Persuades and sells
3. Responsibility for carrying out activities from beginning to end	3. Staff studies, reports, recommends but does not carry out
4. Follows chain of command	4. May advise across department lines
5. Is identified with what it does	5. May find its ideas identified with others
6. Decides when and how to use staff advice	6. Has to persuade line to want its advice
7. Line executes	7. Staff - Conducts studies and research. Provides advice and instructions in technical matters. Serves as technical specialist to render specific services

Types and Functions of Organization Charts.
An organization chart is a picture of the arrangement and inter-relationship of the subdivisions of an organization.

1. Types of Charts:
    a. Structural - basic relationships only
    b. Functional - includes functions or duties
    c. Personnel - positions, salaries, status, etc.
    d. Process Chart - work performed
    e. Gantt Chart - actual performance against planned
    f. Flow Chart - flow and distribution of work

2. Functions of Charts:
    a. Assist in management planning and control
    b. Indicate duplication of functions
    c. Indicate incorrect stressing of functions
    d. Indicate neglect of important functions
    e. Correct unclear authority
    f. Establish proper span of control

3. Limitations of Charts:
    a. Seldom maintained on current basis

b. Chart is oversimplified
c. Human factors cannot adequately be charted

4. Organization Charts should be:
   a. Simple
   b. Symmetrical
   c. Indicate authority
   d. Line and staff relationship differentiated
   e. Chart should be dated and bear signature of approving officer
   f. Chart should be displayed, not hidden

ORGANIZATION

There are four basic principles of organization:

1. Unity of command
2. Span of control
3. Uniformity of assignment
4. Assignment of responsibility and delegation of authority

Unity of Command
Unity of command means that each person in the organization should receive orders from one, and only one, supervisor. When a person has to take orders from two or more people, (a) the orders may be in conflict and the employee is upset because he does not know which he should obey, or, (b) different orders may reach him at the same time and he does not know which he should carry out first.

Equally as bad as having two bosses is the situation where the supervisor is by-passed. Let us suppose you are a supervisor whose boss by-passes you (deals directly with people reporting to you). To the worker, it is the same as having two bosses; but to you, the supervisor, it is equally serious. By-passing on the part of your boss will undermine your authority, and the people under you will begin looking to your boss for decisions and even for routine orders.

You can prevent by-passing by telling the people you supervise that if anyone tries to give them orders, they should direct that person to you.

Span of Control
Span of control on a given level involves:

a. The number of people being supervised
b. The distance
c. The time involved in supervising the people. (One supervisor cannot supervise too many workers effectively.)

Span of control means that a supervisor has the right number (not too many and not too few) of subordinates that he can supervise well.

Uniformity of Assignment
In assigning work, you as the supervisor should assign to each person jobs that are similar in nature. An employee who is assigned too many different types of jobs will waste time in

going from one kind of work to another. It takes time for him to get to top production in one kind of task and, before he does so, he has to start on another.

When you assign work to people, remember that:

a. Job duties should be definite. Make it clear from the beginning <u>what</u> they are to do, <u>how</u> they are to do it, and <u>why</u> they are to do it. Let them know how much they are expected to do and how well they are expected to do it.

b. Check your assignments to be certain that there are no workers with too many unrelated duties, and that no two people have been given overlapping responsibilities. Your aim should be to have every task assigned to a specific person with the work fairly distributed and with each person doing his part.

<u>Assignment of Responsibility and Delegation of Authority</u>
A supervisor cannot delegate his final responsibility for the work of his department. The experienced supervisor knows that he gets his work done through people. He can't do it all himself. So he must assign the work and the responsibility for the work to his employees. Then they must be given the authority to carry out their responsibilities.

By assigning responsibility and delegating authority to carry out the responsibility, the supervisor builds in his workers initiative, resourcefulness, enthusiasm, and interest in their work. He is treating them as responsible adults. They can find satisfaction in their work, and they will respect the supervisor and be loyal to the supervisor.

PRINCIPLES OF ORGANIZATION

1. <u>Definition</u>
Organization is the method of dividing up the work to provide the best channels for coordinated effort to get the agency's mission accomplished.

2. <u>Purpose of Organization</u>
a. To enable each employee within the organization to clearly know his responsibilities and relationships to his fellow employees and to organizational units.
b. To avoid conflicts of authority and overlapping of jurisdiction.
c. To ensure teamwork.

3. <u>Basic Considerations in Organizational Planning</u>
a. The basic plans and objectives of the agency should be determined, and the organizational structure should be adapted to carry out effectively such plans and objectives.
b. The organization should be built around the major functions of the agency and not individuals or groups of individuals.
c. The organization should be sufficiently flexible to meet new and changing conditions which may be brought about from within or outside the department.
d. The organizational structure should be as simple as possible and the number of organizational units kept at a minimum.
e. The number of levels of authority should be kept at a minimum. Each additional management level lengthens the chain of authority and responsibility and increases the time for instructions to be distributed to operating levels and for decisions to be obtained from higher authority.

f. The form of organization should permit each executive to exercise maximum initiative within the limits of delegated authority.

4. Bases for Organization
   a. Purpose (Examples: education, police, sanitation)
   b. Process (Examples: accounting, legal, purchasing)
   c. Clientele (Examples: welfare, parks, veteran)
   d. Geographic (Examples: borough offices, precincts, libraries)

5. Assignments of Functions
   a. Every function of the agency should be assigned to a specific organizational unit. Under normal circumstances, no single function should be assigned to more than one organizational unit.
   b. There should be no overlapping, duplication, or conflict between organizational elements.
   c. Line functions should be separated from staff functions, and proper emphasis should be placed on staff activities.
   d. Functions which are closely related or similar should normally be assigned to a single organizational unit.
   e. Functions should be properly distributed to promote balance, and to avoid overemphasis of less important functions and underemphasis of more essential functions.

6. Delegation of Authority and Responsibility
   a. Responsibilities assigned to a specific individual or organizational unit should carry corresponding authority, and all statements of authority or limitations thereof should be as specific as possible.
   b. Authority and responsibility for action should be decentralized to organizational units and individuals responsible for actual performance to the greatest extent possible, without relaxing necessary control over policy or the standardization of procedures. Delegation of authority will be consistent with decentralization of responsibility but such delegation will not divest an executive in higher authority of his overall responsibility.
   c. The heads of organizational units should concern themselves with important matters and should delegate to the maximum extent details and routines performed in the ordinary course of business.
   d. All responsibilities, authorities, and relationships should be stated in simple language to avoid misinterpretation.
   e. Each individual or organizational unit charged with a specific responsibility will be held responsible for results.

7. Employee Relationships
   a. The employees reporting to one executive should not exceed the number which can be effectively directed and coordinated. The number will depend largely upon the scope and extent of the responsibilities of the subordinates.
   b. No person should report to more than one supervisor. Every supervisor should know who reports to him, and every employee should know to whom he reports. Channels of authority and responsibility should not be violated by staff units.
   c. Relationships between organizational units within the agency and with outside organizations and associations should be clearly stated and thoroughly understood to avoid misunderstanding.

DELEGATING

1. <u>What is Delegating?</u>
    Delegating is assigning a job to an employee, giving him the authority to get that job done, and giving him the responsibility for seeing to it that the job is done.

    a. <u>What to Delegate</u>
        (1) Routine details
        (2) Jobs which may be necessary and take a lot of time, but do not have to be done by the supervisor personally (preparing reports, attending meetings, etc.)
        (3) Routine decision-making (making decisions which do not require the supervisor's personal attention)

    b. <u>What Not to Delegate</u>
        (1) Job details which are *executive functions* (setting goals, organizing employees into a good team, analyzing results so as to plan for the future)
        (2) Disciplinary power (handling grievances, preparing service ratings, reprimands, etc.)
        (3) Decision-making which involves large numbers of employees or other bureaus and departments
        (4) Final and complete responsibility for the job done by the unit being supervised

    c. <u>Why Delegate?</u>
        (1) To strengthen the organization by developing a greater number of skilled employees
        (2) To improve the employee's performance by giving him the chance to learn more about the job, handle some responsibility, and become more interested in getting the job done
        (3) To improve a supervisor's performance by relieving him of routine jobs and giving him more time for *executive functions* (planning, organizing, controlling, etc.) which cannot be delegated

2. <u>To Whom to Delegate</u>
    People with abilities not being used. Selection should be based on ability, not on favoritism.

REPORTS

<u>Definition</u>
    A report is an orderly presentation of factual information directed to a specific reader for a specific purpose.

<u>Purpose</u>
    The general purpose of a report is to bring to the reader useful and factual information about a condition or a problem. Some specific purposes of a report may be:

1. To enable the reader to appraise the efficiency or effectiveness of a person or an operation
2. To provide a basis for establishing standards
3. To reflect the results of expenditures of time, effort, and money
4. To provide a basis for developing or altering programs

Types
1. Information Report - Contains facts arranged in sequence
2. Summary (Examination) Report - Contains facts plus an analysis or discussion of the significance of the facts. Analysis may give advantages and disadvantages or give qualitative and quantitative comparisons
3. Recommendation Report - Contains facts, analysis, and conclusion logically drawn from the facts and analysis, plus a recommendation based upon the facts, analysis, and conclusions

Factors to Consider Before Writing Report

1. Why write the report - The purpose of the report should be clearly defined.
2. Who will read the report - What level of language should be used? Will the reader understand professional or technical language?
3. What should be said - What does the reader need or want to know about the subject?
4. How should it be said - Should the subject be presented tactfully? Convincingly? In a stimulating manner?

Preparatory Steps

1. Assemble the facts - Find out who, why, what, where, when, and how.
2. Organize the facts - Eliminate unnecessary information.
3. Prepare an outline - Check for orderliness, logical sequence.
4. Prepare a draft - Check for correctness, clearness, completeness, conciseness, and tone.
5. Prepare it in final form - Check for grammar, punctuation, appearance.

Outline For a Recommendation Report
    Is the report:

1. Correct in information, grammar, and tone?
2. Clear?
3. Complete?
4. Concise?
5. Timely?
6. Worth its cost?

Will the report accomplish its purpose?

MANAGEMENT CONTROLS

1. Control
    What is control? What is controlled? Who controls?

    The essence of control is action which adjusts operations to predetermined standards, and its basis is information in the hands of managers. Control is checking to determine whether plans are being observed and suitable progress toward stated objectives is being made, and action is taken, if necessary, to correct deviations.

We have a ready-made model for this concept of control in the automatic systems which are widely used for process control in the chemical and petroleum industries. A process control system works this way. Suppose, for example, it is desired to maintain a constant rate of flow of oil through a pipe at a predetermined or set-point value. A signal, whose strength represents the rate of flow, can be produced in a measuring device and transmitted to a control mechanism. The control mechanism, when it detects any deviation of the actual from the set-point signal, will reposition the value regulating flow rate.

2. <u>Basis For Control</u>
A process control mechanism thus acts to adjust operations to predetermined standards and does so on the basis of information it receives. In a parallel way, information reaching a manager gives him the opportunity for corrective action and is his basis for control. He cannot exercise control without such information, and he cannot do a complete job of managing without controlling.

3. <u>Policy</u>
What is policy?

Policy is simply a statement of an organization's intention to act in certain ways when specified types of circumstances arise. It represents a general decision, predetermined and expressed as a principle or rule, establishing a normal pattern of conduct for dealing with given types of business events - usually recurrent. A statement is therefore useful in economizing the time of managers and in assisting them to discharge their responsibilities equitably and consistently.

Policy is not a means of control, but policy does generate the need for control.

Adherence to policies is not guaranteed nor can it be taken on faith. It has to be verified. Without verification, there is no basis for control. Policy and procedures, although closely related and interdependent to a certain extent, are not synonymous. A policy may be adopted, for example, to maintain a materials inventory not to exceed one million dollars. A procedure for inventory control would interpret that policy and convert it into methods for keeping within that limit, with consideration, too, of possible but foreseeable expedient deviation.

4. <u>Procedure</u>
What is procedure?

A procedure specifically prescribes:

    a. What work is to be performed by the various participants
    b. Who are the respective participants
    c. When and where the various steps in the different processes are to be performed
    d. The sequence of operations that will insure uniform handling of recurring transactions
    e. The *paper* that is involved, its origin, transition, and disposition

Necessary appurtenances to a procedure are:

    a. Detailed organizational chart

b. Flow charts

c. Exhibits of forms, all presented in close proximity to the text of the procedure

5. Basis of Control - Information in the Hands of Managers

If the basis of control is information in the hands of managers, then reporting is elevated to a level of very considerable importance.

Types of reporting may include:

a. Special reports and routine reports
b. Written, oral, and graphic reports
c. Staff meetings
d. Conferences
e. Television screens
f. Non-receipt of information, as where management is by exception
g. Any other means whereby information is transmitted to a manager as a basis for control action

FRAMEWORK OF MANAGEMENT

Elements

1. Policy - It has to be verified, controlled.

2. Organization - is part of the giving of an assignment. The organizational chart gives to each individual in his title, a first approximation of the nature of his assignment and orients him as being accountable to a certain individual. Organization is not in a true sense a means of control. Control is checking to ascertain whether the assignment is executed as intended and acting on the basis of that information.

3. Budgets - perform three functions:

a. They present the objectives, plans, and programs of the organization in financial terms.
b. They report the progress of actual performance against these predetermined objectives, plans, and programs.
c. Like organizational charts, delegations of authority, procedures and job descriptions, they define the assignments which have flowed from the Chief Executive. Budgets are a means of control in the respect that they report progress of actual performance against the program. They provide information which enables managers to take action directed toward bringing actual results into conformity with the program.

4. Internal Check - provides in practice for the principle that the same person should not have responsibility for all phases of a transaction. This makes it clearly an aspect of organization rather than of control. Internal Check is static, or built-in.

5. Plans, Programs, Objectives

People must know what they are trying to do. Objectives fulfill this need. Without them, people may work industriously and yet, working aimlessly, accomplish little.

Plans and Programs complement Objectives, since they propose how and according to what time schedule the objectives are to be reached.

6. Delegations of Authority

Among the ways we have for supplementing the titles and lines of authority of an organizational chart are delegations of authority. Delegations of authority clarify the extent of authority of individuals and in that way serve to define assignments. That they are not means of control is apparent from the very fact that wherever there has been a delegation of authority, the need for control increases. This could hardly be expected to happen if delegations of authority were themselves means of control.

Manager's Responsibility

Control becomes necessary whenever a manager delegates authority to a subordinate because he cannot delegate and then simply sit back and forget all about it. A manager's accountability to his own superior has not diminished one whit as a result of delegating part of his authority to a subordinate. The manager must exercise control over actions taken under the authority so delegated. That means checking serves as a basis for possible corrective action.

Objectives, plans, programs, organizational charts, and other elements of the managerial system are not fruitfully regarded as either controls or means of control. They are pre-established standards or models of performance to which operations are adjusted by the exercise of management control. These standards or models of performance are dynamic in character for they are constantly altered, modified, or revised. Policies, organizational set-up, procedures, delegations, etc. are constantly altered but, like objectives and plans, they remain in force until they are either abandoned or revised. All of the elements (or standards or models of performance), objectives, plans and prpgrams, policies, organization, etc. can be regarded as a *framework of management*.

Control Techniques

Examples of control techniques:
1. Compare against established standards
2. Compare with a similar operation
3. Compare with past operations
4. Compare with predictions of accomplishment

Where Forecasts Fit

Control is after-the-fact while forecasts are before. Forecasts and projections are important for setting objectives and formulating plans.

Information for aiming and planning does not have to before-the-fact. It may be an after-the-fact analysis proving that a certain policy has been impolitic in its effect on the relation of the company or department with customer, employee, taxpayer, or stockholder; or that a certain plan is no longer practical, or that a certain procedure is unworkable.

The prescription here certainly would not be in control (in these cases, control would simply bring operations into conformity with obsolete standards) but the establishment of new standards, a new policy, a new plan, and a new procedure to be controlled too.

Information is, of course, the basis for all communication in addition to furnishing evidence to management of the need for reconstructing the framework of management.

PROBLEM SOLVING

The accepted concept in modern management for problem solving is the utilization of the following steps:

1. Identify the problem
2. Gather data
3. List possible solutions
4. Test possible solutions
5. Select the best solution
6. Put the solution into actual practice

Occasions might arise where you would have to apply the second step of gathering data before completing the first step.

You might also find that it will be necessary to work on several steps at the same time.

1. Identify the Problem

Your first step is to define as precisely as possible the problem to be solved. While this may sound easy, it is often the most difficult part of the process.

It has been said of problem solving that you are halfway to the solution when you can write out a clear statement of the problem itself.

Our job now is to get below the surface manifestations of the trouble and pinpoint the problem. This is usually accomplished by a logical analysis, by going from the general to the particular; from the obvious to the not-so-obvious cause.
Let us say that production is behind schedule. WHY? Absenteeism is high. Now, is absenteeism the basic problem to be tackled, or is it merely a symptom of low morale among the workforce? Under these circumstances, you may decide that production is not the problem; the problem is *employee morale.*

In trying to define the problem, remember there is seldom one simple reason why production is lagging, or reports are late, etc.

Analysis usually leads to the discovery that an apparent problem is really made up of several subproblems which must be attacked separately.

Another way is to limit the problem, and thereby ease the task of finding a solution, and concentrate on the elements which are within the scope of your control.

When you have gone this far, write out a tentative statement of the problem to be solved.

2. Gather Data

In the second step, you must set out to collect all the information that might have a bearing on the problem. Do not settle for an assumption when reasonable fact and figures are available.

If you merely go through the motions of problem-solving, you will probably shortcut the information-gathering step. Therefore, do not stack the evidence by confining your research to your own preconceived ideas.

As you collect facts, organize them in some form that helps you make sense of them and spot possible relationships between them. For example: Plotting cost per unit figures on a graph can be more meaningful than a long column of figures.

Evaluate each item as you go along. Is the source material: absolutely reliable, probably reliable, or not to be trusted.

One of the best methods for gathering data is to go out and look the situation over carefully. Talk to the people on the job who are most affected by this problem.

Always keep in mind that a primary source is usually better than a secondary source of information.

3. List Possible Solutions

This is the creative thinking step of problem solving. This is a good time to bring into play whatever techniques of group dynamics the agency or bureau might have developed for a joint attack on problems.

Now the important thing for you to do is: Keep an open mind. Let your imagination roam freely over the facts you have collected. Jot down every possible solution that occurs to you. Resist the temptation to evaluate various proposals as you go along. List seemingly absurd ideas along with more plausible ones. The more possibilities you list during this step, the less risk you will run of settling for merely a workable, rather than the best, solution.

Keep studying the data as long as there seems to be any chance of deriving additional - ideas, solutions, explanations, or patterns from it.

4. Test Possible Solutions

Now you begin to evaluate the possible solutions. Take pains to be objective. Up to this point, you have suspended judgment but you might be tempted to select a solution you secretly favored all along and proclaim it as the best of the lot.

The secret of objectivity in this phase is to test the possible solutions separately, measuring each against a common yardstick. To make this yardstick try to enumerate as many specific criteria as you can think of. Criteria are best phrased as questions which you ask of each possible solution. They can be drawn from these general categories:

Suitability - Will this solution do the job?
Will it solve the problem completely or partially?

Is it a permanent or a stopgap solution?

Feasibility - Will this plan work in actual practice?
Can we afford this approach?
How much will it cost?

Acceptability - Will the boss go along with the changes required in the plan?
Are we trying to drive a tack with a sledge hammer?

5. <u>Select the Best Solution</u>

This is the area of executive decision.

Occasionally, one clearly superior solution will stand out at the conclusion of the testing process. But often it is not that simple. You may find that no one solution has come through all the tests with flying colors.

You may also find that a proposal, which flunked miserably on one of the essential tests, racked up a very high score on others.

The best solution frequently will turn out to be a combination.

Try to arrange a marriage that will bring together the strong points of one possible solution with the particular virtues of another. The more skill and imagination that you apply, the greater is the likelihood that you will come out with a solution that is not merely adequate and workable, but is the best possible under the circumstances.

6. <u>Put the Solution Into Actual Practice</u>
As every executive knows, a plan which works perfectly on paper may develop all sorts of bugs when put into actual practice.

Problem-solving does not stop with selecting the solution which looks best in theory. The next step is to put the chosen solution into action and watch the results. The results may point towards modifications.

If the problem disappears when you put your solution into effect, you know you have the right solution.

If it does not disappear, even after you have adjusted your plan to cover unforeseen difficulties that turned up in practice, work your way back through the problem-solving solutions.

Would one of them have worked better?
Did you overlook some vital piece of data which would have given you a different slant on the whole situation? Did you apply all necessary criteria in testing solutions? If no light dawns after this much rechecking, it is a pretty good bet that you defined the problem incorrectly in the first place.

You came up with the wrong solution because you tackled the wrong problem.

Thus, step six may become step one of a new problem-solving cycle.

COMMUNICATION

1. <u>What is Communication?</u>
We communicate through writing, speaking, action or inaction. In speaking to people face-to-face, there is opportunity to judge reactions and to adjust the message. This makes the supervisory chain one of the most, and in many instances the most, important channels of communication.

In an organization, communication means keeping employees informed about the organization's objectives, policies, problems, and progress. Communication is the free interchange of information, ideas, and desirable attitudes between and among employees and between employees and management.

2. <u>Why is Communication Needed?</u>
   a. People have certain social needs
   b. Good communication is essential in meeting those social needs
   c. While people have similar basic needs, at the same time they differ from each other
   d. Communication must be adapted to these individual differences

An employee cannot do his best work unless he knows why he is doing it. If he has the feeling that he is being kept in the dark about what is going on, his enthusiasm and productivity suffer.

Effective communication is needed in an organization so that employees will understand what the organization is trying to accomplish; and how the work of one unit contributes to or affects the work of other units in the organization and other organizations.

3. <u>How is Communication Achieved?</u>
Communication flows downward, upward, sideways.

   a. Communication may come from top management down to employees. This is <u>downward communication</u>.

   Some means of downward communication are:
   (1) Training (orientation, job instruction, supervision, public relations, etc.)
   (2) Conferences
   (3) Staff meetings
   (4) Policy statements
   (5) Bulletins
   (6) Newsletters
   (7) Memoranda
   (8) Circulation of important letters

   In downward communication, it is important that employees be informed in advance of changes that will affect them.

   b. Communications should also be developed so that the ideas, suggestions, and knowledge of employees will flow <u>upward</u> to top management.

Some means of upward communication are:
(1) Personal discussion conferences
(2) Committees
(3) Memoranda
(4) Employees suggestion program
(5) Questionnaires to be filled in giving comments and suggestions about proposed actions that will affect field operations

Upward communication requires that management be willing to listen, to accept, and to make changes when good ideas are present. Upward communication succeeds when there is no fear of punishment for speaking out or lack of interest at the top. Employees will share their knowledge and ideas with management when interest is shown and recognition is given.

   c. The *advantages* of downward communication:
     (1) It enables the passing down of orders, policies, and plans necessary to the continued operation of the station.
     (2) By making information available, it diminishes the fears and suspicions which result from misinformation and misunderstanding.
     (3) It fosters the pride people want to have in their work when they are told of good work.
     (4) It improves the morale and stature of the individual to be *in the know.*
     (5) It helps employees to understand, accept, and cooperate with changes when they know about them in advance.

   d. The *advantages* of upward communication:
     (1) It enables the passing upward of information, attitudes, and feelings.
     (2) It makes it easier to find out how ready people are to receive downward communication.
     (3) It reveals the degree to which the downward communication is understood and accepted.
     (4) It helps to satisfy the basic *social* needs.
     (5) It stimulates employees to participate in the operation of their organization.
     (6) It encourages employees to contribute ideas for improving the efficiency and economy of operations.
     (7) It helps to solve problem situations before they reach the explosion point.

4. <u>Why Does Communication Fail</u>?
   a. The technical difficulties of conveying information clearly
   b. The emotional content of communication which prevents complete transmission
   c. The fact that there is a difference between what management needs to say, what it wants to say, and what it does say
   d. The fact that there is a difference between what employees would like to say, what they think is profitable or safe to say, and what they do say

5. <u>How to Improve Communication.</u>
As a supervisor, you are a key figure in communication. To improve as a communicator, you should:
   a. <u>Know</u> - Knowing your subordinates will help you to recognize and work with individual differences.

b. <u>Like</u> - If you like those who work for you and those for whom you work, this will foster the kind of friendly, warm, work atmosphere that will facilitate communication.

c. <u>Trust</u> - Showing a sincere desire to communicate will help to develop the mutual trust and confidence which are essential to the free flow of communication.

d. <u>Tell</u> - Tell your subordinates and superiors *what's doing.* Tell your subordinates *why* as well as *how.*

e. <u>Listen</u> - By listening, you help others to talk and you create good listeners. Don't forget that listening implies action.

f. <u>Stimulate</u> - Communication has to be stimulated and encouraged. Be receptive to ideas and suggestions and motivate your people so that each member of the team identifies himself with the job at hand.

g. <u>Consult</u> - The most effective way of consulting is to let your people participate, insofar as possible, in developing determinations which affect them or their work.

6. <u>How to Determine Whether You are Getting Across.</u>
   a. Check to see that communication is received and understood
   b. Judge this understanding by actions rather than words
   c. Adapt or vary communication, when necessary
   d. Remember that good communication cannot cure all problems

7. <u>The Key Attitude.</u>
Try to see things from the other person's point of view. By doing this, you help to develop the permissive atmosphere and the shared confidence and understanding which are essential to effective two-way communication.

Communication is a two-way process.
   a. The basic purpose of any communication is to get action.
   b. The only way to get action is through acceptance.
   c. In order to get acceptance, communication must be humanly satisfying as well as technically efficient.

HOW ORDERS AND INSTRUCTIONS SHOULD BE GIVEN

<u>Characteristics of Good Orders and Instructions</u>

1. <u>Clear</u>
Orders should be definite as to
   - <u>What</u> is to be done
   - <u>Who</u> is to do it
   - <u>When</u> it is to be done
   - <u>Where</u> it is to be done
   - <u>How</u> it is to be done

2. <u>Concise</u>
Avoid wordiness. Orders should be brief and to the point.

3. <u>Timely</u>
Instructions and orders should be sent out at the proper time and not too long in advance of expected performance.

4. Possibility of Performance
    Orders should be feasible:
    a. Investigate before giving orders
    b. Consult those who are to carry out instructions before formulating and issuing them

5. Properly Directed
    Give the orders to the people concerned. Do not send orders to people who are not concerned. People who continually receive instructions that are not applicable to them get in the habit of neglecting instructions generally.

6. Reviewed Before Issuance
    Orders should be reviewed before issuance:
    a. Test them by putting yourself in the position of the recipient
    b. If they involve new procedures, have the persons who are to do the work review them for suggestions

7. Reviewed After Issuance
    Persons who receive orders should be allowed to raise questions and to point out unforeseen consequences of orders.

8. Coordinated
    Orders should be coordinated so that work runs smoothly.

9. Courteous
    Make a request rather than a demand. There is no need to continually call attention to the fact that you are the boss.

10. Recognizable as an Order
    Be sure that the order is recognizable as such.

11. Complete
    Be sure recipient has knowledge and experience sufficient to carry out order. Give illustrations and examples.

A DEPARTMENTAL PERSONNEL OFFICE IS RESPONSIBLE FOR THE FOLLOWING FUNCTIONS

1. Policy
2. Personnel Programs
3. Recruitment and Placement
4. Position Classification
5. Salary and Wage Administration
6. Employee Performance Standards and Evaluation
7. Employee Relations
8. Disciplinary Actions and Separations
9. Health and Safety
10. Staff Training and Development
11. Personnel Records, Procedures, and Reports
12. Employee Services
13. Personnel Research

SUPERVISION

<u>Leadership</u>

All leadership is based essentially on authority. This comes from two sources: it is received from higher management or it is earned by the supervisor through his methods of supervision. Although effective leadership has always depended upon the leader's using his authority in such a way as to appeal successfully to the motives of the people supervised, the conditions for making this appeal are continually changing. The key to today's problem of leadership is flexibility and resourcefulness on the part of the leader in meeting changes in conditions as they occur.

Three basic approaches to leadership are generally recognized:

1. <u>The Authoritarian Approach</u>
    a. The methods and techniques used in this approach emphasize the *I* in leadership and depend primarily on the formal authority of the leader. This authority is sometimes exercised in a hardboiled manner and sometimes in a benevolent manner, but in either case the dominating role of the leader is reflected in the thinking, planning, and decisions of the group.
    b. Group results are to a large degree dependent on close supervision by the leader. Usually, the individuals in the group will not show a high degree of initiative or acceptance of responsibility and their capacity to grow and develop probably will not be fully utilized. The group may react with resentment or submission, depending upon the manner and skill of the leader in using his authority
    c. This approach develops as a natural outgrowth of the authority that goes with the leader's job and his feeling of sole responsibility for getting the job done. It is relatively easy to use and does not require much resourcefulness.
    d. The use of this approach is effective in times of emergencies, in meeting close deadlines as a final resort, in settling some issues, in disciplinary matters, and with dependent individuals and groups.

2. <u>The Laissez-Faire or *Let 'em Alone* Approach</u>
    a. This approach generally is characterized by an avoidance of leadership responsibility by the leader. The activities of the group depend largely on the choice of its members rather than the leader.
    b. Group results probably will be poor. Generally, there will be disagreements over petty things, bickering, and confusion. Except for a few aggressive people, individuals will not show much initiative and growth and development will be retarded. There may be a tendency for informal leaders to take over leadership of the group.
    c. This approach frequently results from the leader's dislike of responsibility, from his lack of confidence, from failure of other methods to work, from disappointment or criticism. It is usually the easiest of the three to use and requires both understanding and resourcefulness on the part of the leader.
    d. This approach is occasionally useful and effective, particularly in forcing dependent individuals or groups to rely on themselves, to give someone a chance to save face by clearing his own difficulties, or when action should be delayed temporarily for good cause.

3. The Democratic Approach
   a. The methods and techniques used in this approach emphasize the *we* in leadership and build up the responsibility of the group to attain its objectives. Reliance is placed largely on the earned authority of the leader.
   b. Group results are likely to be good because most of the job motives of the people will be satisfied. Cooperation and teamwork, initiative, acceptance of responsibility, and the individual's capacity for growth probably will show a high degree of development.
   c. This approach grows out of a desire or necessity of the leader to find ways to appeal effectively to the motivation of his group. It is the best approach to build up inside the person a strong desire to cooperate and apply himself to the job.
      It is the most difficult to develop, and requires both understanding and resourcefulness on the part of the leader.
   d. The value of this approach increases over a long period where sustained efficiency and development of people are important. It may not be fully effective in all situations, however, particularly when there is not sufficient time to use it properly or where quick decisions must be made.

All three approaches are used by most leaders and have a place in supervising people. The extent of their use varies with individual leaders, with some using one approach predominantly. The leader who uses these three approaches, and varies their use with time and circumstance, is probably the most effective. Leadership which is used predominantly with a democratic approach requires more resourcefulness on the part of the leader but offers the greatest possibilities in terms of teamwork and cooperation.

The one best way of developing democratic leadership is to provide a real sense of participation on the part of the group, since this satisfies most of the chief job motives. Although there are many ways of providing participation, consulting as frequently as possible with individuals and groups on things that affect them seems to offer the most in building cooperation and responsibility. Consultation takes different forms, but it is most constructive when people feel they are actually helping in finding the answers to the problems on the job.

There are some requirements of leaders in respect to human relations which should be considered in their selection and development. Generally, the leader should be interested in working with other people, emotionally stable, self-confident, and sensitive to the reactions of others. In addition, his viewpoint should be one of getting the job done through people who work cooperatively in response to his leadership. He should have a knowledge of individual and group behavior, but, most important of all, he should work to combine all of these requirements into a definite, practical skill in leadership.

Nine Points of Contrast Between *Boss* and *Leader*

1. The boss drives his men; the leader coaches them.
2. The boss depends on authority; the leader on good will.
3. The boss inspires fear; the leader inspires enthusiasm.
4. The boss says J; the leader says *We*.
5. The boss says *Get here on time;* the leader gets there ahead of time.
6. The boss fixes the blame for the breakdown; the leader fixes the breakdown.
7. The boss knows how it is done; the leader shows how.
8. The boss makes work a drudgery; the leader makes work a game.
9. The boss says *Go*; the leader says *Let's go.*

EMPLOYEE MORALE

Employee morale is the way employees feel about each other, the organization or unit in which they work, and the work they perform.

<u>Some Ways to Develop and Maintain Good Employee Morale</u>

1. Give adequate credit and praise when due.
2. Recognize importance of all jobs and equalize load with proper assignments, always giving consideration to personality differences and abilities.
3. Welcome suggestions and do not have an *all-wise* attitude. Request employees' assistance in solving problems and use assistants when conducting group meetings on certain subjects.
4. Properly assign responsibilities and give adequate authority for fulfillment of such assignments.
5. Keep employees informed about matters that affect them.
6. Criticize and reprimand employees privately.
7. Be accessible and willing to listen.
8. Be fair.
9. Be alert to detect training possibilities so that you will not miss an opportunity to help each employee do a better job, and if possible with less effort on his part.
10. Set a good example.
11. Apply the golden rule.

<u>Some Indicators of Good Morale</u>
1. Good quality of work
2. Good quantity
3. Good attitude of employees
4. Good discipline
5. Teamwork
6. Good attendance
7. Employee participation

MOTIVATION

<u>Drives</u>

A *drive,* stated simply, is a desire or force which causes a person to do or say certain things. These are some of the most usual drives and some of their identifying characteristics recognizable in people motivated by such drives:

1. <u>Security</u> (desire to provide for the future)
   Always on time for work
   Works for the same employer for many years
   Never takes unnecessary chances Seldom resists doing what he is told

2. <u>Recognition</u> (desire to be rewarded for accomplishment)
   Likes to be asked for his opinion
   Becomes very disturbed when he makes a mistake
   Does things to attract attention

Likes to see his name in print

3. <u>Position</u> (desire to hold certain status in relation to others)
Boasts about important people he knows
Wants to be known as a key man
Likes titles
Demands respect
Belongs to clubs, for prestige

4. <u>Accomplishment</u> (desire to get things done)
Complains when things are held up
Likes to do things that have tangible results
Never lies down on the job
Is proud of turning out good work

5. <u>Companionship</u> (desire to associate with other people)
Likes to work with others
Tells stories and jokes
Indulges in horseplay
Finds excuses to talk to others on the job

6. <u>Possession</u> (desire to collect and hoard objects)
Likes to collect things
Puts his name on things belonging to him
Insists on the same work location

Supervisors may find that identifying the drives of employees is a helpful step toward motivating them to self-improvement and better job performance. For example: An employee's job performance is below average. His supervisor, having previously determined that the employee is motivated by a drive for security, suggests that taking training courses will help the employee to improve, advance, and earn more money. Since earning more money can be a step toward greater security, the employee's drive for security would motivate him to take the training suggested by the supervisor. In essence, this is the process of charting an employee's future course by using his motivating drives to positive advantage.

EMPLOYEE PARTICIPATION

<u>What is Participation?</u>

Employee participation is the employee's giving freely of his time, skill and knowledge to an extent which cannot be obtained by demand.

<u>Why is it Important?</u>

The supervisor's responsibility is to get the job done through people. A good supervisor gets the job done through people who work willingly and well. The participation of employees is important because:
1. Employees develop a greater sense of responsibility when they share in working out operating plans and goals.
2. Participation provides greater opportunity and stimulation for employees to learn, and to develop their ability.

3. Participation sometimes provides better solutions to problems because such solutions may combine the experience and knowledge of interested employees who want the solutions to work.
4. An employee or group may offer a solution which the supervisor might hesitate to make for fear of demanding too much.
5. Since the group wants to make the solution work, they exert *pressure* in a constructive way on each other.
6. Participation usually results in reducing the need for close supervision.

How May Supervisors Obtain It?

Participation is encouraged when employees feel that they share some responsibility for the work and that their ideas are sincerely wanted and valued. Some ways of obtaining employee participation are:

1. Conduct orientation programs for new employees to inform them about the organization and their rights and responsibilities as employees.
2. Explain the aims and objectives of the agency. On a continuing basis, be sure that the employees know what these aims and objectives are.
3. Share job successes and responsibilities and give credit for success.
4. Consult with employees, both as individuals and in groups, about things that affect them.
5. Encourage suggestions for job improvements. Help employees to develop good suggestions. The suggestions can bring them recognition. The city's suggestion program offers additional encouragement through cash awards.

The supervisor who encourages employee participation is not surrendering his authority. He must still make decisions and initiate action, and he must continue to be ultimately responsible for the work of those he supervises. But, through employee participation, he is helping his group to develop greater ability and a sense of responsibility while getting the job done faster and better.

STEPS IN HANDLING A GRIEVANCE

1. Get the facts
   a. Listen sympathetically.
   b. Let him talk himself out.
   c. Get his story straight.
   d. Get his point of view.
   e. Don't argue with him.
   f. Give him plenty of time.
   g. Conduct the interview privately.
   h. Don't try to shift the blame or pass the buck.

2. Consider the facts
   a. Consider the employee's viewpoint.
   b. How will the decision affect similar cases.
   c. Consider each decision as a possible precedent.
   d. Avoid snap judgments - don't jump to conclusions.

3. <u>Make or get a decision</u>
    a. Frame an effective counter-proposal.
    b. Make sure it is fair to all.
    c. Have confidence in your judgment.
    d. Be sure you can substantiate your decision.

4. <u>Notify the employee of your decision</u>
    Be sure he is told; try to convince him that the decision is fair and just.

5. <u>Take action when needed and if within your authority</u>
    Otherwise, tell employee that the matter will be called to the attention of the proper person or that nothing can be done, and why it cannot.

6. <u>Follow through</u> to see that the desired result is achieved.

7. <u>Record key facts</u> concerning the complaint and the action taken.

8. <u>Leave the way open to him to appeal your decision</u> to a higher authority.

9. <u>Report all grievances to your superior</u>, whether they are appealed or not.

DISCIPLINE

Discipline is training that develops self-control, orderly conduct, and efficiency.

To discipline does not necessarily mean to punish.

To discipline does mean to train, to regulate, and to govern conduct.

<u>The Disciplinary Interview</u>

Most employees sincerely want to do what is expected of them. In other words, they are self-disciplined. Some employees, however, fail to observe established rules and standards, and disciplinary action by the supervisor is required.

The primary purpose of disciplinary action is to improve conduct without creating dissatisfaction, bitterness, or resentment in the process.

Constructive disciplinary action is more concerned with causes and explanations of breaches of conduct than with punishment. The disciplinary interview is held to get at the causes of apparent misbehavior and to motivate better performance in the future.

It is important that the interview be kept on as impersonal a basis as possible. If the supervisor lets the interview descend to the plane of an argument, it loses its effectiveness.

<u>Planning the Interview</u>

Get all pertinent facts concerning the situation so that you can talk in specific terms to the employee.

Review the employee's record, appraisal ratings, etc.

Consider what you know about the temperament of the employee. Consider your attitude toward the employee. Remember that the primary requisite of disciplinary action is fairness.

Don't enter upon the interview when angry.

Schedule the interview for a place which is private and out of hearing of others.

<u>Conducting the Interview</u>

1. Make an effort to establish accord.

2. Question the employee about the apparent breach of discipline. Be sure that the question is not so worded as to be itself an accusation.

3. Give the employee a chance to tell his side of the story. Give him ample opportunity to talk.

4. Use understanding-listening except where it is necessary to ask a question or to point out some details of which the employee may not be aware. If the employee misrepresents facts, make a plain, accurate statement of the facts, but don't argue and don't engage in personal controversy.

5. Listen and try to understand the reasons for the employee's (mis)conduct. First of all, don't assume that there has been a breach of discipline. Evaluate the employee's reasons for his conduct in the light of his opinions and feelings concerning the consistency and reasonableness of the standards which he was expected to follow. Has the supervisor done his part in explaining the reasons for the rules? Was the employee's behavior unintentional or deliberate? Does he think he had real reasons for his actions? What new facts is he telling? Do the facts justify his actions? What causes, other than those mentioned, could have stimulated the behavior?

6. After listening to the employee's version of the situation, and if censure of his actions is warranted, the supervisor should proceed with whatever criticism is justified. Emphasis should be placed on future improvement rather than exclusively on the employee's failure to measure up to expected standards of job conduct.

7. Fit the criticism to the individual. With one employee, a word of correction may be all that is required.

8. Attempt to distinguish between unintentional error and deliberate misbehavior. An error due to ignorance requires training and not censure.

9. Administer criticism in a controlled, even tone of voice, never in anger. Make it clear that you are acting as an agent of the department. In general, criticism should refer to the job or the employee's actions and not to the person. Criticism of the employee's work is not an attack on the individual.

10. Be sure the interview does not destroy the employee's self-confidence. Mention his good qualities and assure him that you feel confident that he can improve his performance.

11. Wherever possible, before the employee leaves the interview, satisfy him that the incident is closed, that nothing more will be said on the subject unless the offense is repeated.

Made in the USA
Middletown, DE
20 May 2024

54592832R00144